Crank It Up!

Keith Aleshire

NRP
NEW RIDERS PUBLISHING

New Riders Publishing, Carmel, Indiana

Crank It UP!

By Keith Aleshire

Published by:
New Riders Publishing
11711 N. College Ave., Suite 140
Carmel, IN 46032 USA

Copyright © 1993 by New Riders Publishing

Printed in the United States of America 1 2 3 4 5 6 7 8 9 0

Library of Congress Cataloging-in-Publication Data

Aleshire, Keith. 1963-
  Crank It Up! / Keith Aleshire.
          p.   cm.
  Includes index.
  ISBN 1-56205-173-3 : $16.95
  1. Microcomputers. 2. Computer software. 3. Computer sound processing.   I. Title.
  QA76.5.A3684   1993
  006.5—dc20   93-8194
                                                              CIP

Crank It Up!

About the Author

Keith R. Aleshire has worked for various high-tech firms, including Minnesota state government's central computer center, Northgate Computer Systems Inc., Digi International, and LaserMaster Corp. He has been a senior producer and columnist for Prodigy Services Co. and writes for several computer and technology magazines. In 1992, PRODIGY's service's Computer Club, which he produced, received the Computer Press Association's award for "Best Online Computer Publication." He is a Phi Beta Kappa graduate from the University of Minnesota School of Journalism and is president of Computer Consumer Services Inc., an Eden Prairie, Minnesota, consulting and documentation company.

Dedication

This book is dedicated to my grandmother, Mary Elizabeth Aleshire (1904-1993), who died during the writing of this book. She may have preferred a washboard to Windows, but both are practical tools for their generation.

This book also is dedicated to my wife, Pauline Aleshire, for propping me up when I stumbled during this work. (I hope I can return the favor, dear.)

Acknowledgments

Thanks to Brad Craig of Advanced Gravis, Catherine Panos of CH Products, Cameryne Roberts of Koss, Andrew Clarke of ATI Technologies, Inc., Anne Vinton of Media Vision, Kelly Pittman of Creative Labs, Sharon Prentice of Orchid Technology, Inc., Margo of Bose Corp., Nichole of PersonaTechnologies, Kelly of Roland Corp., Gabe of Covox, Barbara of Walt Disney Computer Software, Inc., Denise of Cardinal Technologies, Inc., Ann of Digispeech, Inc., Serge of Logitech, and Jeff of Turtle Beach Systems.

Thanks also to the following vendors: Logitech, for the use of ThunderBOARD; Media Vision, for the use of Soundman 16 and Pro AudioSpectrum 16.

A special thanks to Jeff Wilson and Al Pickard of Digital Audio Labs in Plymouth, Minnesota, for their technical advice and support.

Also, thanks to Rob Tidrow and Rob Lawson of New Riders Publishing, for helping with this book as much as they could prior to my impending house purchase and move. And thanks to Stacey Beheler, also of New Riders Publishing, for doing much of the ground work of contacting many of the sound card vendors.

Trademark Acknowledgments

Warning and Disclaimer

Contents at a Glance

Crank It Up! Contents xix

Introduction

Some revolutions aren't sudden or dramatic. Instead, they sneak up on you. Consider, for example, the way multimedia and sound cards have crept into business and home computing. Phrases like *business audio* or *digital audio* have become the banner of many industry stories.

Initially, you may have dismissed multimedia as a pie-in-the-sky prospect, a buzzword in search of a technology. (That's okay; so did I.) Since then, you may have been quietly won over by an intriguing ad, a favorable word about a product, or the gift of a sound card-compatible game.

Today's sound cards provide CD- or near-CD quality sound for under $300. The sound revolution is on... and it's affordable. The utilities bundled with sound cards start your enjoyment and efficiency immediately. Whether using a talking appointment calendar or adding a verbal Post-It note to an important business document, you soon can put the impact of sound to work for you.

Danger in Paradise

Despite the promising possibilities of a sound card, some dangers do exist. Foremost, sound specifications can be deceiving. If you ask about sound quality, you may hear gobbledygook about signal filters, sampling rates, line level output, and more.

Although I've provided charts and tables for this book, take them with a grain of salt. On paper, one product may seem superior to another. You can't listen to paper; audition a sound card or speaker before you buy. In the end, sound quality can't be measured by engineering specs.

What's in This for Me?

Crank It Up! is divided into seven sections:

The first section covers sound card basics. Chapter 1, "A Sound Footing," describes the possible uses for a sound card. Next, you're exposed to basic sound terminology in Chapter 2, "Sound Terms."

The second section helps you select a sound card and its accessories. Chapter 3, "Do You Have What It Takes?," describes the requirements for a sound card. The recent MPC Level 2 specifications have raised the standards for what is considered a multimedia system, of which a sound card is key. Chapter 4, "Sound à la Card," describes the various sound cards, from external audio ports to internal models. Chapter 5, "Options Are Extra," describes the several accessories you may need to purchase, such as a joystick or speakers.

The third section describes how to install the sound card itself. Chapter 6, "Presto Sound," instructs you how to safely open your computer and install the sound card. In Chapter 7, "Where's That Speaker?," you learn how to attach to your

sound card such accessories as speakers, joysticks, MIDIs, your stereo system, and other external sound devices.

The fourth section of *Crank It Up!* focuses on installing and customizing your sound card's software. Chapter 8, "Giving Your Card Its Voice," tells you how to install the DOS drivers for your sound card. Chapter 9, "Interrupts, Addresses, and Other Hazards," explains how to avoid hardware conflicts that may make both you and your sound card sputter.

The fifth section focuses on using your sound card. In Chapter 10, "Games with a Rumble and a Roar!," you learn how to optimize your sound card for game playing. Chapter 11, "Recording Studio on a Disk," shows you how to use the free DOS utilities included with your sound card to help you record, edit, and play sound files. Chapter 12, "Pane-less Windows Sound," illustrates how you can use Windows' object linking and embedding (OLE) to become more efficient. We also explore the Windows utilities available to you for digital audio recording and playback. Chapter 13, "Making the Most of MIDI," explores the music-making capabilities of sound cards and the utilities that make it possible. Chapter 14, "Lights, Camera... Sound!," discusses multimedia, of which sound cards are but a building block. Finally, Chapter 15, "Sound Investments," discusses some additional software you can purchase to add to your library of digitized audio and music files.

The sixth section of *Crank It Up!* consists of two appendixes. Appendix A, "The Crank It Up! Disk," shows you how to install your bonus disk that comes with this book. You also find in this appendix a brief synopsis of the bonus disk's contents. Appendix B, "Noisy Vendors," is a vendors list arranged in various hardware categories and by product name. Suggested retail prices for products as well as the names and addresses of manufacturers are included.

The final section is a sound card glossary that will put your feet on a *sound footing* as you immerse yourself in this new technology!

Happy Hearing!

I hope you enjoy exploring the world of sound cards through this book. What VGA video cards did for game playing and presentations, sound cards will do for multimedia and Microsoft Windows. The future will be heard, not seen.

Best wishes,

Keith Aleshire

P.S. Don't forget to buy good speakers!

Special Text Used in This Book

Throughout *Crank It Up!*, you will find examples of special text. These characters, lines, and passages have been given special treatment so that you can instantly recognize their significance and so that you can find them for future reference.

♪ *Shortcut keys* are normally found in the text where appropriate. In most applications, for example, Shift-Ins is the shortcut key for the Paste command.

♪ *Key combinations* appear in the following formats:

Key1-Key2: When you see a hyphen (-) between key names, you should hold down the first key while pressing the second key. Then release both keys.

Key1,Key2: When a comma (,) appears between key names, you should press and release the first key and then press and release the second key.

♪ *Hotkeys* are used in some menu choices. These on-screen, underlined letters of menu names, file names, and option names enable you to access the item by pressing the indicated letter. For example, the File menu may be displayed on-screen as <u>F</u>ile. The underlined letter is the letter you can type to choose that option.

In this book, such letters, or hotkeys, are displayed in bold, underlined type: <u>**F**</u>ile. If there are two or more hotkeys that can be pressed one after the other, you may see them displayed as follows: select <u>**E**</u>dit,<u>**I**</u>nsert,<u>**N**</u>ew <u>**O**</u>bject, and then select Sound Recorder to call up Windows' Sound Recorder.

♪ *New terms* appear in *italics*.

♪ *Information you type as input* appears in a `special boldface`.

♪ *Text generated as program output* appears in a `special typeface`.

Notes, Tips, and Warnings

Crank It Up! features two distinct types of sidebars that are set aside by icons: *Sound Checks* and *Listen Ups*. Sound Checks are notes of interest and appear as follows:

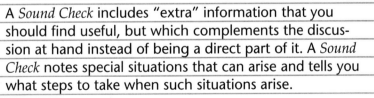

Sound Check

A *Sound Check* includes "extra" information that you should find useful, but which complements the discussion at hand instead of being a direct part of it. A *Sound Check* notes special situations that can arise and tells you what steps to take when such situations arise.

Listen Ups are either tips or warnings and appear as follows:

Listen Up!

Some *Listen Ups* provide you with quick instructions for getting the most from your system. A *Listen Up* might tell you how to speed up a procedure or how to perform one of many time-saving and system-enhancing techniques.

Other *Listen Ups* tell you when a procedure may be dangerous—that is, when you run the risk of losing data, locking up your system, or even damaging your hardware. These *Listen Ups* generally tell you how to avoid such losses or describe the steps you can take to remedy them.

New Riders Publishing

The staff of New Riders Publishing is committed to bringing you the very best in computer reference material. Each New Riders book is the result of months of work by authors and staff, who research and refine the information contained within its covers.

As part of this commitment to you, the NRP reader, New Riders invites your input. Please let us know if you enjoy this book, if you have trouble with the information and examples presented, or if you have a suggestion for the next edition.

Please note, however, that the New Riders staff cannot serve as a technical resource for sound card-related questions, including software-related problems. Refer to the documentation that accompanies your hardware/application package for help with

specific problems.

If you have a question or comment about any New Riders book, please write to NRP at the following address. We will respond to as many readers as we can. Your name, address, or phone number will never become part of a mailing list or be used for any other purpose than to help us continue to bring you the best books possible.

New Riders Publishing
Attn: Associate Publisher
11711 N. College Avenue
Carmel, IN 46032

If you prefer, you can FAX New Riders Publishing at the following number:

(317) 571-3484

We welcome your electronic mail to our CompuServe ID:

70031,2231

Thank you for selecting *Crank It Up!*

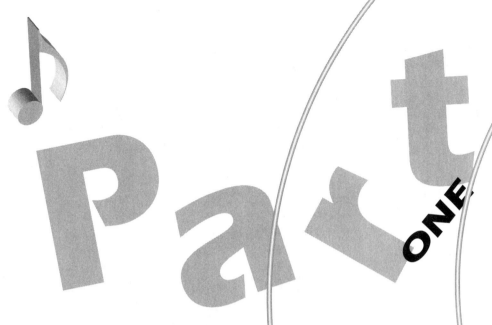

Sound Card Basics

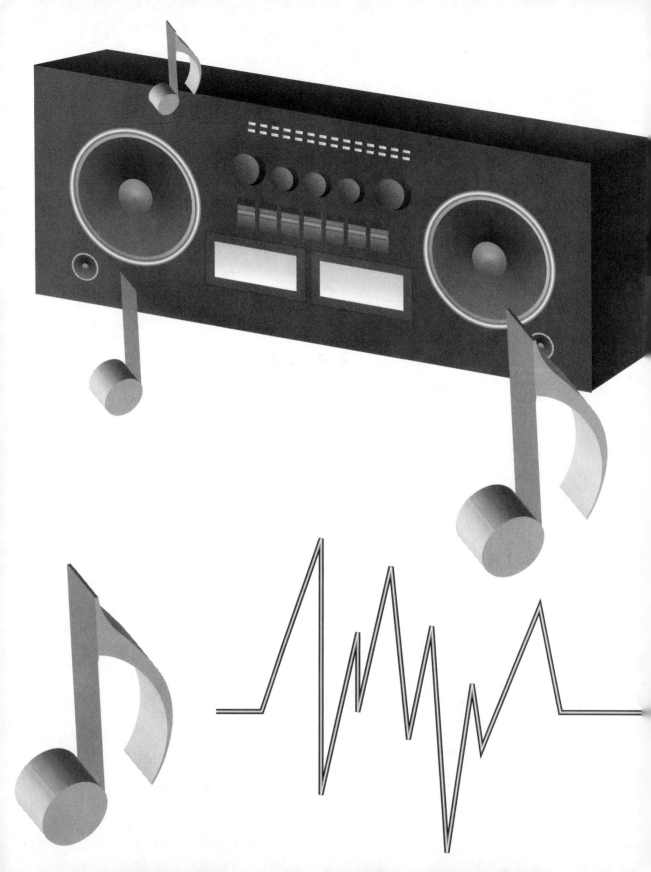

A Sound Footing

If a PC falls in a forest, does it make any sound? Not if it lacks a sound card.

Since we were small children, we have made and have heard sounds. One infant's scream might be an expression of frustration, "Hey Mom, feed me...NOW!" or it might be the delighted self-observation, "Hey, the cat's on the table, and it's eating the butter."

Sound can be a powerful medium. Hearing is second only to vision as a sensory channel. Through sounds, we express ourselves, our ambitions, our thoughts, and our desires. Long before television, the radio painted verbal pictures in the minds of its listeners. Today, radio provides music and news and, with the help of sound effects, markets products—even ideas—very effectively.

Today, you can add a sound card onto your computer system, which allows you to record and play back your own voice and music. With it, the personal computer truly becomes personal.

Chapter 1

In this chapter, you learn about:

♪ The importance of sound

♪ The basic sound-card system

♪ The many uses of sound cards, including game playing, multimedia, and proofreading text and numbers

Seeking a Voice

In today's society, the desktop computer has become an extension of ourselves. With it, we have been able to write books and poetry, compose drawings, prioritize our life's goals, and more. Yet the PC has lacked a voice. Although the Apple Macintosh and Commodore Amiga have long had standardized, high-quality sound, most PCs include an anemic two-inch speaker. Worse yet, this speaker is hidden inside and muffled by the computer's plastic case.

Sound Check

How do I define a PC? A *PC*, short for personal computer, refers to a computer that conforms to the PC standard, originally developed by IBM Corp and subsequently governed by Intel, Microsoft, and major PC vendors collectively. About 100 million PCs are in use today.

Then the sound revolution came. PC owners can now buy sound cards (see fig. 1.1) that give their software the capability to speak and sing. By buying a Sound Blaster Pro, Pro AudioSpectrum 16, Microsoft Sound System, or any of several other sound-card models and makes, a PC can inherit a voice.

Figure 1.1:
Sound cards like these will add a new dimension to your PC environment.

Sound Check

Market researcher Dataquest Inc. predicts the sound-card market will grow from 1.8 million units shipped in 1992 to 4.9 million units in 1994.

At first, sound cards were used only for games. Nothing can add more excitement to a tank game than hearing the impact of shells on your vehicle's Kevlar armor. In flight simulation games, you can hear your jet's engines scream before takeoff. In combat, the whoosh of surface-to-air missiles is heard as they dislodge from your wing and lock onto their targets (see fig. 1.2).

Figure 1.2:
"Rebel Assault" from LucasArts incorporates sound to fully approximate real combat.

Sound Check

The first sound cards for the PC were the AdLib Music Synthesizer Card ($195) and the Roland MT-32 Sound Module ($500). The AdLib card was introduced in August 1987 with little fanfare. It provided music and sound effects to computer games. Taito of America released one of the very first games to support this novel card. In the summer of 1989, Game Blaster was introduced by Creative Labs. Game Blaster could play 12 stereo instruments at the same time compared to AdLib's 11 monaural (mono) instruments. However, Game Blaster used AM, not FM, synthesis. Even in stereo, Game Blaster didn't sound that good. The question many buyers faced was: Why spend $100 for a card that adds sound to a $50 game? More importantly, no sound standards existed at the time so your sound card might have been useless with other games.

A few months after the debut of Game Blaster, Creative Labs announced the Sound Blaster sound card, which originally sold for $239.95. Sound Blaster was compatible with the AdLib sound card and Creative Labs' own Game Blaster card. It included a built-in microphone jack and a *musical instrument digital interface* (MIDI) for connecting to a musical synthesizer. (I'll discuss MIDI exclusively in a later chapter.) Finally, the sound card was finding uses besides games.

Sound Basics

What's required to add a sound card to your PC? First, you need a *sound card*—an expansion card you insert inside your PC. Some sound cards may work in older PC/XT computers (which have eight-bit slots). Other cards require the 16-bit slots found in 286 (PC/AT), 386, and 486 PCs.

The next important component is a pair of external speakers that let you enjoy the new stereo sound. In some cases, you may spend more for the speakers than the sound card.

Listen Up!

To test the sound waters, I once bought a Media Vision ThunderBOARD sound card. This sound card cost only $95. I figured this modest investment would allow me to tinker with the sound revolution. When I purchased speakers from a stereo superstore, however, I was shocked—$150 for a pair of bookshelf speakers! (The AC adapter was extra.) Yet, I didn't want to forego quality speakers to enjoy my purchase. My $95 sound card had now drained me of over $250.

With a sound card and a set of speakers, you have the basics for playing with sound on your PC. Of course, you don't have to stop there but can add a joystick for playing games, a microphone for recording sounds to your hard disk, an electronic synthesizer for composing music, and a CD-ROM drive for accessing large amounts of audio and visual information. I'll talk about these options in future chapters.

The Call for Standards Is Mute

Unfortunately, sound cards have had no standards. Like other aspects of the computer industry, the standard is developed by the market leader. For example, Hayes-compatible modems use the escape codes used by Hayes Microcomputer Products, Inc. to connect two computers. (Hayes now collects royalties from many modem manufacturers who use their codes.)

Over the last few years, sound-card manufacturers have fought for dominance. Today, a sound card may claim to be "AdLib-compatible" or "Sound Blaster-compatible." Until the PC's anemic speaker is bolstered with a built-in sound chip, adding a sound card hardly constitutes a standard.

What Can You Do with a Sound Card?

Despite the lack of standards, the following examples demonstrate what a sound card can do for you.:

♪ Add stereo sound to entertainment (game) software

♪ Form the backbone for multimedia

♪ Add sound effects to business presentations and training software

♪ Make your own music

♪ Make your screen saver talk

♪ Add voice notes to Windows files

♪ Add your own sound effects to Windows

♪ Give your PC voice commands

♪ Allow your computer to talk back

♪ Play your audio CDs from DOS and within Windows

Whoosh! Play Games

The sound card originally was designed to play games. In fact, many sound cards include *joystick ports*, connectors for adding a joystick. Typically, you tell your game software that you have a sound card to avoid using the PC's own speaker, such as when using Nighthawk F-117A Stealth Fighter from Microprose (see fig. 1.3).

```
Select Sound Driver:

1) IBM Sound
2) Ad Lib Sound Board
3) Roland Sound Board
4) No Sound
```

Figure 1.3:
In many games, you select which sound card you have.

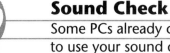

Sound Check
Some PCs already come with joystick ports. If you decide to use your sound card's joystick port, you'll need to disable the joystick port that came with your PC. Otherwise, disable the joystick port on your sound card and use the one you already own.

continues

continued

Does it matter which joystick port you use for your games? Not really. The sound card is already busy handling your sound and other functions, so it may be overworked if it also handles your joystick. Similarly, the joystick port that came with your PC is also probably overworked. (Often, the joystick port, serial port, parallel printer port, and disk controller are all part of the same expansion card.) When a joystick is overworked, you may find yourself suddenly upside down or otherwise unable to control your game's vehicle. A separate game card, such as CH Products' Gamecard III, provides a higher-quality joystick port. In fact, such cards include connections for two joysticks so you can fly with a friend.

After your sound card is chosen, your games will take on human qualities. For example, the CD-ROM game Sherlock Holmes, the Consulting Detective, from Icom Simulations uses recorded human voices and film clips. In this game, you navigate through London, attempting to solve three different mysteries. Each new location brings up a 30- to 90-second film clip of real actors, including Holmes and Dr. Watson. The characters in Sherlock Holmes get their dialogue from the digitized voices of real actors.

Similarly, games, such as Monkey Island from LucasFilm Games, are using beautiful musical scores. In Monkey Island, you become the character Guybrush Threepwood, roaming the Caribbean to become a pirate. To fit the tropical scenes, Monkey Island's musical score includes reggae music.

Messin' with Multimedia

A sound card is a prerequisite if you want to turn your PC into a *multimedia PC* (MPC).

What is multimedia? The phrase multimedia embraces a gamut of PC technologies. Basically, *multimedia* means the capability to merge voice, images, data, and video on a computer at the same time. Multimedia applications range from talking encyclopedias (see fig. 1.4) to databases of stored video clips.

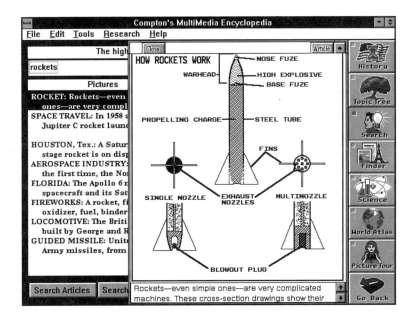

Figure 1.4:

An example of a multimedia encyclopedia.

An organization called the *Multimedia PC (MPC) Marketing Council* has been formed to generate "standards" for multimedia. This group of hardware and software manufacturers already boasts Tandy, Philips Electronics, CompuAdd, NEC, and other big names in its ranks.

This group defines a multimedia PC as a computer having at least the following:

♪ 80486SX computer operating at 25 MHz

♪ 4M of memory

♪ 160M hard disk

♪ 16-bit digital sound card

♪ Pair of speakers or headphones

♪ Super-VGA (800 x 600) monitor and video card

♪ 1.44M (high-density) 3 1/2-inch disk drive

♪ CD-ROM drive

♪ Multimedia Windows (either Windows 3.0 with Multi-media Extensions for Windows or Windows 3.1)

♪ Keyboard and mouse

♪ MIDI interface and joystick ports

♪ Standard serial and parallel ports

Note: These are based on the MPC Level 2 specifications announced in late April 1993.

Listen Up!

The MPC specifications are the bare minimum. In fact, the MPC Marketing Council sometimes raises these standards a notch or two. If your computer barely meets some of these criteria, such as having a 40M hard disk or only 2M of memory, you may be able to use multimedia, but you probably won't enjoy it. For example, an image may take several seconds to display on an older PC with limited memory.

To display full-motion video images, like those on a TV, you'll need at least a 386 PC with 8M of memory. Also, those images require ample storage space; you'll need at least 100M of disk space... if not more.

A sound card is the backbone for a multimedia-ready PC. In fact, many sound cards include a built-in connection for the CD-ROM drive.

Listen Up!

Pay attention to how a sound card works with the drive. Several sound cards include a CD-ROM connection, but some of these are proprietary, restricting your choice to a handful of drives. For a wider selection, look for a sound card that includes a *SCSI* (small computer systems interface) connector, such as the Pro AudioSpectrum cards from Media Vision. With a SCSI (pronounced "scuzzy") sound board, you can conserve an expansion slot inside your PC for other uses. (In my PC, all eight expansion slots are filled.)

What can you do with an MPC? Most multimedia software packages are designed for education, entertainment, or reference. With a CD-ROM disk's capability of holding so much information (up to 680M!), you can provide volumes of static historical information on one disk.

One of the more impressive CD-ROM disks is Microsoft's Multimedia Beethoven: The Ninth Symphony. Professor Robert Winter, an authority on Beethoven, teaches the user about Beethoven and his Ninth Symphony. Six sections focus on an aspect of the man and his work. For example, the Art of Listening presents the fine points of music appreciation as it pertains to this symphony. You can select and listen to certain passages while the actual notes are displayed on your screen.

Another good example of multimedia is Microsoft's Bookshelf for Windows. This collection of reference books includes animations and actual voices, such as those of John F. Kennedy and Dylan Thomas. The material becomes more compelling

when you hear Dylan Thomas recite his verses as opposed to reading the screen's text yourself.

Compton's Multimedia Encyclopedia for Windows from Britannica Software is included with many CD-ROM drives. This encyclopedia-on-a-disk makes learning much more fun by including animations of a pumping heart or the first moon walk, punctuated with Neil Armstrong's "That's one small step for man" speech.

And this kind of exploration and self-discovery starts with a sound card.

Say It with Sound!

Businesses are discovering that combining graphics, animation, and sound is more impressive, and often less expensive, than a slide show. A sound card adds pizzazz to any presentation or classroom.

A variety of business presentation software and high-end training and authoring packages already exists. And you don't have to be a programmer to get your own show on the road.

For example, Asymetrix Corp.'s Make Your Point, Macromedia's Action for Windows, and others allow you to incorporate multimedia elements in your show. Even such popular software packages as CorelDRAW! and PowerPoint have introduced rudimentary sound and animation features for their presentation files.

Also, Action for Windows allows you to create scenes that correspond to slides in a slide-making application. These scenes contain objects you create, and you can import sounds, graphics, or movies from Macromind Director, a related product.

Action for Windows allows you to create two- and three-dimensional charts. After using a presentation authoring package, you probably won't go back to those black and white overhead transparencies.

Some presentation software packages support MIDI, and you can synchronize sounds with objects. For example, when your company's new product—the Widge 2000—is displayed on the screen, you can play a roaring round of applause. You even can pull in audio from a CD in your CD-ROM drive. Such presentation software programs include clip-media libraries.

Also, learning software and other tasks can be easier with a sound card. Interactive training tools can make learning a less daunting task. Not surprisingly, PC software manufacturers have taken an early lead in this area, reducing customer demand for technical support. Microsoft and Lotus, for example, are already shipping special CD-ROM versions of some of their products. These versions include animated on-line help, replete with music.

Creating an interactive training disk is not as easy as creating a presentation. Whereas presentations are often linear, an interactive training disk must let the student go down any of several learning paths. Affordable products, such as Asymetrix's ToolBook and HSC Interactive, allow you to create interactive training programs. For more money, users can choose from AimTech Corp.'s Icon Author and Macromedia's AuthorWare Professional.

You can even take your show on the road. Some special external sound cards attach to a laptop computer's parallel port to provide audio on the go. Media Vision's Audioport, which is bundled with Lotus Sound, for example, fits in a shirt pocket

and includes a speaker and a microphone port, as well as jacks for external speakers. It sells for $199.

Make Your Own Music

If you're musically inclined, you'll enjoy using a MIDI. Developed in the early 1980s, the musical instrument digital interface essentially is a powerful programming language that lets your computer store and edit or play back music in tandem with a MIDI-compatible electronic musical instrument, typically a keyboard synthesizer. An example of a Windows mixer utility is shown in figure 1.5.

Figure 1.5:

An example of a Windows mixer utility.

The MPC specs described earlier in this chapter call for MIDI support, though many business and general-purpose users do not require the ability to make music.

Listen Up!

Some budget-priced sound cards—such as Creative Labs' Sound Blaster Pro Deluxe or Media Vision's ThunderBOARD—do not provide an interface to MIDI instruments. If you decide to pursue MIDI later, you can purchase a MIDI adapter.

With a MIDI interface, you can compose and edit music for presentations, learn about music theory, or turn your PC into a one-stop music mixing studio.

MIDI makes a musical note sound as if it comes from any of a wide array of instruments. The MPC specifications require a sound card to contain an FM MIDI synthesizer chip and be able to play at least six notes simultaneously. Some companies exceed the specifications: Roland Corporation's $499 SCC-1 GS has more sophisticated MIDI capability, including more realistic musical tones.

To connect a MIDI device to a PC, you need a sound card that has two round serial ports in back—a MIDI input port and a MIDI output port. Besides a keyboard, you'll need sequencing software to modify the tempo, sound, and volume of your recordings or to cut and paste various prerecorded music sequences together.

Unlike other sound files, MIDI messages require little disk space. An hour of stereo music stored in MIDI requires less than 500K. A Windows sound file would require over 1,000 times that.

Sound Check

Software Toolworks has a product called The Miracle Piano Teaching System. This computer-aided system creates the most patient piano instructor you'll ever have. The $479.95 keyboard ships with built-in speakers, headphones, a sustain peddle, and amplifier jacks. There are several hundred lessons and each of them demonstrates new material by playing pieces and illustrating on screen the correct keys to strike.

Since this product includes its own MIDI interface, you don't hook it up to your sound card to use it; it uses the PC's standard serial port. However, you can use the 49-key keyboard with a sound card to act as a MIDI keyboard.

Chapter 1

Screen Savers with Savvy

Your Microsoft Windows screen saver may blank your screen but not your ears.

Sound Check

A *screen saver* is a software program that either blanks your screen or replaces it with moving images after a preset amount of time. Why? If you leave your current work, such as a document, visible on the screen, the monitor's electron beams may permanently etch the static image into the screen's surface. Screen savers often include passwords to protect your work from being seen by prying eyes. For example, Microsoft Windows 3.1 has a built-in screen saver with password protection.

If you don't own a screen saver, you can instead turn off the monitor or dim its brightness when you are away for more than a half-hour.

Screen savers, such as After Dark for Windows and Intermission, now include sounds. In After Dark, the nocturnal module howls and chirps, the aquatic scene bubbles, and the space toasters flap their wings. In Intermission, you'll find a dancing pig and an ant farm.

Throw Your Voice

Virtually all sound cards have an audio input jack. With a microphone, you can record your voice. Using Microsoft Windows 3.1 Sound Recorder, you can play, edit, or record a sound file. These files are saved as WAV files, a type of file format. In the Windows Control Panel, you can assign certain Windows events a specific WAV file. As illustrated by figure 1.6, the starting of Windows could be announced by a loud "Ta-da."

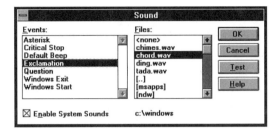

Figure 1.6:
The Sound section of the Windows Control Panel.

By recording your own sounds, you can create your own WAV files and use them for certain events. The standard events are as follows:

♪ Windows start

♪ Windows exit

♪ Default beep

♪ Asterisk

♪ Critical stop

♪ Question

♪ Exclamation

Through the same audio input jack, you can attach your stereo system and record a song as a WAV file. You can also purchase prepackaged WAV files, such as SoundWAV Pro, for under $50. Pre-recorded WAV files can also be found on your local electronic bulletin board or on-line services, such as CompuServe and America Online.

Sound Check

An *on-line service* is simply a gigantic computer that accepts hundreds (if not thousands) of calls from other computers (and the people behind them). For a monthly or hourly fee, you can access the resources of the gigantic computer, such as stock quotes, late-breaking news, soap opera updates, and more. A *bulletin board system*, or BBS, is a smaller imitation of an on-line service. Typically, a BBS is generated by a single PC. Many computer user groups share information among themselves through their own BBS.

Listen Up!

Chapter 12 covers recording, editing, and using WAV files.

Next Best Thing To Being There

Besides creating WAV files, you can record messages as part of your Windows documents and spreadsheets. A business executive, for instance, could pick up a microphone and embed a message in a contract to give his or her secretary explicit instructions. This message is called a *voice annotation* but think of it as a verbal Post-It note.

Voice annotations allow you to embed voice messages, suggestions, or questions within documents and send them to colleagues. To leave such messages, your Windows application must support Windows' *object linking and embedding* (OLE). (Most applications support OLE.) Imagine you're editing a document in Ami Pro and want to insert a voice note by a paragraph that looks questionable. Place the cursor in the text

next to the paragraph, and select <u>E</u>dit, <u>I</u>nsert, New <u>O</u>bject, and Sound Recorder to call up Windows' Sound Recorder. Then click on the Record button and begin speaking. A picture icon of a microphone is inserted in the cell (see fig. 1.7). With a double-click of your mouse, the recorded note can be played back. Chapter 12 discusses how to do this in great detail. Although this capability is welcomed, I doubt voice notes will diminish the use of scribbled notes in the margins and yellow highlighted text.

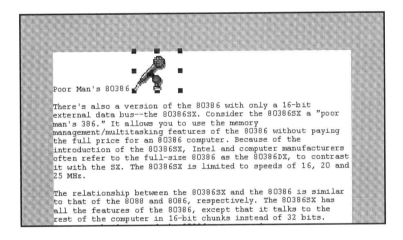

Figure 1.7:
A voice Post-It note is indicated by an icon.

Computer, Take a Note

Some sound cards are capable of voice recognition. Imagine giving your PC voice commands from within Microsoft Windows. For example, Pro AudioStudio 16 from Media Vision includes voice recognition software. You also can get voice recognition for your current sound card. IBM and Dragon Systems are marketing the Dragon Talk-To Plus software

package ($149) for simple voice-command control of Windows applications. Talk-To Plus needs at least a 386SX PC and a Sound Blaster 16 sound card.

Voice-recognition technology is not perfect (but neither is my speaking). Media Vision's ExecuVoice software, for example, can become familiar with a single voice but can adapt to other speakers. Unfortunately, voice recognition technology sometimes is less accurate than baseball players' batting averages (under .300).

Your PC Talks Back

Sound cards can also be used to talk back. Text-to-speech utilities can read back a list of numbers or text to you. (Kind of like a proofreader you don't have to pay.)

Monologue from First Byte, Inc. ($149) is included with the Pro AudioSpectrum sound card. This text-to-speech utility can be loaded in the background while you are using your spreadsheet or word processor. For example, you may be in Lotus 1-2-3 entering columns of numbers. By pressing a hotkey, Monologue begins to read back the numbers you've highlighted. Monologue can also read back an entire file.

You can change the speed and volume of Monologue's voice. You can also change the pitch to resemble a male or female voice. You can even add words to a dictionary of exceptions in which you teach Monologue how to speak "correct" English.

At the time of this writing, there is only one Windows text-to-speech utility available. Monologue for Windows ($149) will read back text you copy to the Windows Clipboard or highlight in an Excel spreadsheet (see fig. 1.8).

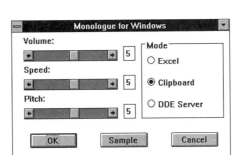

Figure 1.8:

Monologue for Windows reads back what's in the Windows clipboard.

What are the practical uses for a text-to-speech utility? Hearing a letter read aloud may reveal forgotten words or awkward phrases. Accountants can double-check spreadsheet numbers, and busy executives can have their E-mail read to them while they are doing paperwork.

The Best Kind of Multitasking

Microsoft Windows also has the capability to play audio CDs while you are working on something else (see fig. 1.9). As I'm writing this chapter in Ami Pro, I am playing a Billy Joel CD through the Windows Media Player utility. The music can be piped through not only my pair of speakers but also a headphone set plugged into the front of my CD-ROM drive.

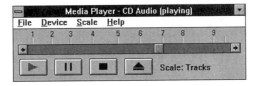

Figure 1.9:

You can play your favorite audio CD while working.

Some sound cards—Sound Blaster Pro, for instance—include a DOS-based CD-player utility. Unlike the Windows utility, you cannot use another program while the CD is playing.

You may not use all of these sound capabilities. By familiarizing yourself with them, you can be open to the possible uses of sound in your everyday work.

Sound Terms

Scanning information about a sound card can be a lesson in confusion. Words like 16-bit, DAC, MIDI port, sampling, and CD-quality are often sprinkled throughout stories about new sound products. Words for the accessories are also confusing: SCSI interface, CD-ROM, data transfer rate, and more.

In this chapter, you learn about:

♪ The definition and makeup of sound, including frequency and amplitude

♪ Basic sound-card terms, such as digital sound and sampling

♪ Differences between 8-bit and 16-bit sound

♪ Terms related to multimedia

♪ Measurements of a good CD-ROM drive

♪ Basic sound formats, such as WAV and MIDI

Chapter 2

You don't need to be an expert linguist to understand a sound-card ad. Certain terms are unique to sound cards whereas others are standard to all types of expansion cards.

Good Vibrations

To understand a sound card, you need to understand sound itself. Every sound is produced by vibrations. Its source may be a crying baby, a guitar, or a doorbell. Whatever its source, vibrations disturb the air, creating sound waves. These waves travel in all directions, expanding in balloon-like fashion from the source of the sound. When these waves reach your ear, they cause vibrations that are perceived as sound.

Some sounds are pleasant whereas others are harsh. The three basic properties of any sound are its pitch, its intensity, and its quality.

Pitch is simply the rate at which vibrations are produced and is measured in the number of Hz (hertz, or cycles per second). One cycle is a complete vibration back and forth. The number of Hz is the frequency of the tone; the higher the frequency, the higher the pitch (see fig. 2.1).

You cannot hear all possible frequencies. Very few people can hear any fewer than 16 Hz or any more than about 20 KHz (1 kilohertz equals 1,000 Hz). In fact, the lowest note on a piano has a frequency of 27 Hz and the highest note a little more than 4 KHz. And frequency-modulation (FM) radio stations broadcast notes up to 15 KHz.

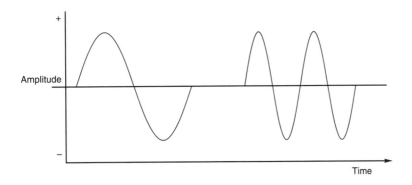

Figure 2.1:
The smaller the frequency, the higher the pitch.

Sound Check

Frequencies beyond our ability to hear are called super-sonic or ultrasonic waves. For example, a "silent" dog whistle is pitched at supersonic frequency and can be heard by dogs but not humans. Extremely high frequen-cies of 100 to 500 KHz can cause strong physical and chemical reactions. These frequencies can force water and oil to emulsify, dust to collect, and gases held in liquids or molten metals to bubble out. In fact, these sounds can destroy certain types of bacteria.

The *intensity* of a sound is called its amplitude. This intensity depends on the strength of the vibrations producing the sound. A piano string, for example, vibrates gently if the key is struck softly. The string swings back and forth in a narrow arc, and the tone it sends out is soft. If the key is struck forcefully, how-ever, the string swings back and forth in a wider arc, sending out a loud (or harsh) tone.

The *loudness* of sounds is measured in decibels (db). The rustle of leaves is rated at 10 db, average street noise at 70, and nearby thunder at 120.

Measuring Up

Sound cards are often measured by two criteria: frequency response (or range) and total harmonic distortion, or THD.

The *frequency response* of a sound card is the range in which an audio system can record or play at a constant and audible amplitude level. Many cards support a range between 30 Hz and 20 KHz. The wider the spread, the better the card.

The *total harmonic distortion* measures a sound card's linearity, the straightness of a frequency-response curve. In laymen's terms, the harmonic distortion is a measure of accurate sound reproduction. Nonlinear elements cause distortion in the form of harmonics. The smaller the percentage of distortion, the better.

Sound Fun

Sound cards first found their way into our computers by adding an audible dimension to computer games. Most sound cards support both of the current entertainment audio standards: AdLib and Sound Blaster. Sound Blaster Pro is a sound card sold by Creative Labs, whereas AdLib Gold is sold by AdLib. To play most games, you must tell your game you have either one or the other sound card. (Some games support only one or the other. Media Vision's ThunderBOARD supports both.) These sound cards vastly improve the sound of the average computer. Instead of silence or a faint buzz, a game's jet engine can mimic real life.

Some sound devices support neither of these game-sound standards. Logitech AudioMan and Microsoft Sound System were meant for business, not fun. (All work and no play makes Bill Gates a dull boy.)

Simple Sampling

Equipped with a sound card, your PC can make noise in three ways: digitizing, synthesizing, and using MIDI.

Digitized sound (also called waveform audio or sampled audio) is the same as that found on an audio compact disc (CD). It's simply recorded audio from a microphone that is converted from the analog sound wave to a digital signal (a series of on or off pulses). This waveform audio uses your PC as a tape recorder. Small computer chips built into your sound card called *analog-to-digital converters* (ADCs) convert analog sound waves into digital bits the computer can understand. When you replay the sounds, *digital-to-analog converters* (DACs) convert the recorded signals back to something audible.

Sound Check

What is analog and digital? Sound is an analog phenomenon, consisting of waves of air pressure reaching your ears like ocean waves riding up on a beach. Computers, however, work only in digital. They see a signal as either on or off; they don't understand shades of gray nor the rise and fall of a police siren's signal. Sound cards provide the piece of machinery needed to translate sounds into digital values and back again. This same technology is used in tapeless answering machines and audio compact discs.

To convert continuously changing analog sound waves into digital signals, the sound waves must be sampled. What is sampling? *Sampling* is the process of turning the original analog sound waves (see fig. 2.2) into digital (on/off) signals that can be saved and later replayed. Sampling is like taking snapshots of a balloon as it is blown up. Each snapshot measures the progress of the balloon's size. For example, at time X, the sound

may be measured with an amplitude of Y. The *sampling rate* is the frequency with which the sound is measured. The higher (or more frequent) this sampling rate, the more accurate the digital sound is to its real-life source. CD-quality sound is measured at 44.1 KHz, or 44,100 times per second.

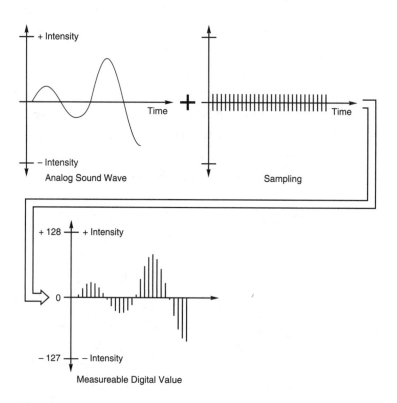

Figure 2.2:

Sampling turns a changing sound wave into measurable digital values.

The sampling rate is only one measure of good sound quality. A sound's resolution is another important factor to consider. *Resolution* is the number of the possible digital values at which a sound sample can be measured. Three sound card resolutions are popular today: 8-bit, 12-bit, and 16-bit. *8-bit audio* means the sound card uses 8 bits to digitize each sound sample. This

translates into 256 (2 to the 8th power) possible digital values at which the sound sample can be measured. A 16-bit sound card can place a sound sample at any of 65,536 values. Like a ruler, the smaller the increments, the more accurate the measurement (see fig. 2.3).

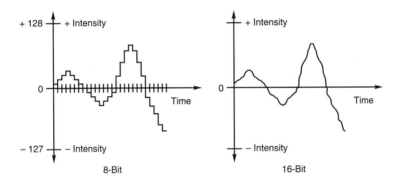

Figure 2.3:

16-bit resolution means more accurate sound reproduction than 8-bit resolution.

Don't think you're missing out if you don't get a 16-bit sound card. Generally, 8-bit audio is adequate for recorded speech whereas 16-bit sound is best for the demands of music.

Listen Up!

8-bit sound is usually recorded in mono whereas 16-bit sound can be recorded in stereo.

Logitech's AudioMan was designed as an 8-bit sound device for business users so they can add voice notes to their Windows work. Likewise, Compaq Computer Corp. is adding 8-bit Business Audio to its computers. Business Audio consists of an

Chapter 2

Analog Devices AD1848 SoundPort, a microphone, a higher-quality system speaker, and software to record and play voice and other sounds under Windows 3.1. You also get utilities to play audio CDs if you have a CD-ROM, and a file manager for your Business Audio sound clips. Business Audio is standard equipment on all Deskpro I and Deskpro M Windows Edition PCs.

Listen Up!

Why handicap your computer with 8-bit sound instead of 16-bit? Using a 16-bit sound card is like driving a Porsche to the nearby convenience store; it's overkill for the task required.

It Hertz

The debate about 8-bit versus 16-bit sound is simply a matter of trading sound quality for disk space. The sampling frequency determines how often the sound card measures the level of the sound being recorded or played back. Basically, you have to sample at about twice the highest frequency that you want to produce, plus an extra 10 percent to keep out unwanted signals. As previously mentioned, human hearing can hear up to 20,000 cycles per second, or 20 KHz. If you double this number and add 10 percent, you get a 44.1 KHz sampling rate, the same sampling rate used by high-fidelity audio CDs. Sixteen-bit sound cards allow you to record at a lower sampling rate and resolution and play back sound files at a higher sampling rate, up to 44.1 KHz.

Sound recorded at 11 KHz (capturing 11,000 samples per second) is fuzzier than audio sampled at 22 KHz. *A sound sampled in 16-bit stereo at 44 KHz (CD-audio quality) takes as much as 10M*

per minute! The same sound sample in 8-bit mono at 11 KHz takes 1/16th the space. Imagine you added a one-minute hi-fi voice note to your Windows spreadsheet. When finished recording, you'd find that its size had quadrupled, if not more!

Multimedia Mania

One phrase on everyone's lips is *multimedia.* Basically, multimedia means the capability to merge voice, images, data, and video on a computer at the same time. Unfortunately, multimedia has become another computer buzzword. To increase their products' allure, many companies tout their merchandise as "multimedia-compatible," which only adds to the confusion.

Today's multimedia products add sound and excitement to your computer. One impetus for the growing number of sound products is Microsoft Windows 3.1. This version fully supports sound. For example, you can have Windows play small sound bites, called WAV files, to indicate when you make a mistake or are entering or exiting the program.

The Multimedia PC (MPC) Marketing Council was formed to generate multimedia standards. This group of hardware and software manufacturers has defined the requirements to turn a regular PC into a multimedia PC. (Chapter 3 covers these MPC requirements in detail.)

8-Bit or 16-Bit Sound?

The original MPC specifications required 8-bit sound. This doesn't mean the sound card must fit into an 8-bit instead of a 16-bit expansion slot. Rather, 8-bit audio means the sound card uses 8 bits to digitize each sound sample. This translates into 256 possible digital values to which the sample can be pegged. This is less quality than the 65,536 values allowed by a 16-bit

sound card. The most recent MPC specs now recommend that you use a 16-bit digital sound card capable of CD-quality sound at 44.1 KHz.

CD-ROM Connection

The other foundation of multimedia is a CD-ROM (compact disc read-only memory) drive. A CD-ROM drive is a cross between a hard disk drive and an audio CD player.

CD-ROM drives provide access to a wealth of text, graphics, sound, video, and animation. A single 4 ¾-inch compact disc, for example, can hold the equivalent information, along with pictures and sounds, of an encyclopedia set—as much as 680M or more of information. Popping a compact disc into the CD-ROM drive is like piling 300,000 pages of information onto your bookshelves.

Listen Up!

Many sound cards double as a CD-ROM controller, or interface, card. However, some sound cards use a proprietary connection that accommodates only certain CD-ROM drives. For a wider selection of drives, consider a sound card that includes a *small computer systems interface* (SCSI) connector. By owning a SCSI sound card, you can save both a slot in your PC and some money on a drive. For example, I own Media Vision's Pro AudioSpectrum sound card that connects to a Sony SCSI CD-ROM drive. I bought both in what's called a *multimedia upgrade kit*. The kit includes the CD-ROM drive, sound card, software drivers to control everything, cables, and, most importantly, instructions on how to connect everything.

 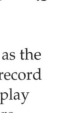

All CD-ROM players read standard CD-ROM disks, just as the CD player in your stereo will play any CD you find in a record store. There's only one caveat: If you eventually want to play CD-ROMs recorded in the emerging extended architecture (XA) format, you may need to upgrade your interface card down the road.

If you want to use multimedia, your CD-ROM drive has one more requirement: it must have an extra audio connection to send sound in analog form from the drive to the sound card.

Like a hard disk, a CD-ROM drive is measured by two criteria: average access speed and data transfer rate. The *average access speed* is how long it takes the CD-ROM drive to find the information you requested. This speed is measured in milliseconds (ms), or thousandths of a second. The *data transfer rate* indicates how fast the found information can be sent to your PC. This rate is measured in kilobytes transferred per second (Kbps).

Make sure the CD-ROM drive you buy meets the MPC performance specifications. The MPC recipe has changed since its debut. A drive should now be capable of sustaining a data transfer rate of 300 Kbps, while claiming no more than 60 percent of main CPU usage.

This 300-Kbps minimum ensures a steady flow of data into the drive's buffer, providing relatively smooth animation instead of jerky screen stutters. For multimedia work, this throughput speed is more important than a drive's access time.

Listen Up!

Most drives' access times hover between 300 and 650 ms, a difference that's hardly detectable when working with one drive as opposed to another. Some inexpensive or portable drives, however, may

continues

continued

have access times as sluggish as 800 ms or more. The most recent MPC requirements suggest a drive with a seek time of 400 ms or less. Some drives include a built-in 8K to 64K buffer, which can perk up performance. The MPC recommends, but does not require, a 64K buffer.

If you love music, a CD-ROM drive also can play CD audio discs. Nearly all drives come with a simple software utility to play audio CDs, and come with audio ports or connectors—usually a headphone jack plus two RCA jacks for plugging in stereo speakers—so you can hear them. In Microsoft Windows, you can use the Media Player to play CDs in your CD-ROM drive *while you are doing other work.*

Doing the Wave

You can use several file formats for storing and editing digitized sound. The most notable is the WAV format supported by Windows 3.1. One audio minute saved to a WAV file requires 2.5M of disk space (see fig. 2.4).

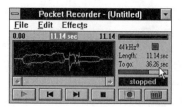

Figure 2.4:
This sound-card utility indicates how much disk space is left for recording.

Listen Up!

You don't need a sound card for digitized sound. Even your PC's built-in, tinny-sounding speaker can play digitized audio with no other hardware. Using special hardware drivers (small software programs), some games can provide digital sound or speech effects. Chapter 3 discusses this.

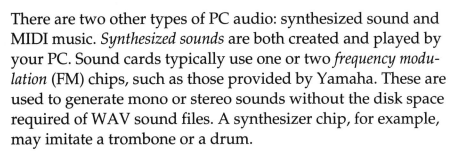

There are two other types of PC audio: synthesized sound and MIDI music. *Synthesized sounds* are both created and played by your PC. Sound cards typically use one or two *frequency modulation* (FM) chips, such as those provided by Yamaha. These are used to generate mono or stereo sounds without the disk space required of WAV sound files. A synthesizer chip, for example, may imitate a trombone or a drum.

The serious musician may prefer a high-end sound card, such as MultiSound from Turtle Beach. MultiSound uses digitized sounds of actual instruments that are preserved in special ROM (read-only memory) chips. FM synthesis is not required. Multisound uses the actual sound of strings and trumpets instead of synthesized music that sounds like strings and trumpets.

MIDI is a step above synthesized sound. The musical instrument digital interface is essentially a programming language that lets your computer store, edit, and play back music in tandem with a MIDI instrument, such as a keyboard synthesizer. Rather than musical sounds, MIDI consists of instructions as to how to play music. A sequencer software program (often included with some sound cards) stores this music to a MIDI file, which requires much less space than waveform audio. This file indicates which instruments to play, what key to press, and

with what gusto to press it. In fact, consider a MIDI file to be like a conductor's musical score. Many sound cards provide a MIDI connector on the back of the sound card. In fact, this interface often doubles as a connector to a joystick. (MIDI is discussed in more detail in Chapter 13.)

Sound Check

The MPC specs insist on MIDI support, although not all of us are musicians. Budget-priced sound cards, such as Microsoft Sound System, Creative Labs' Sound Blaster Pro Basic, and Logitech's AudioMan, do not provide a connection to a MIDI device or interface. However, many companies offer a separate MIDI adapter you can purchase later if you feel a strong desire to be musical.

The Extras

Sound cards come with various jacks, or connectors, to external devices. Most sound cards include a microphone input jack, which allows you to record your voice in a Windows or other sound file. Sound cards also have RCA output jacks for standard headphones or stereo speakers.

By knowing these few simple terms and concepts, you can begin your search for a sound card that fits your needs.

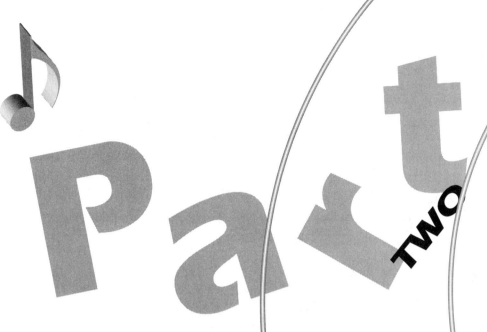

Part TWO

Selecting A Sound Card and Other Equipment

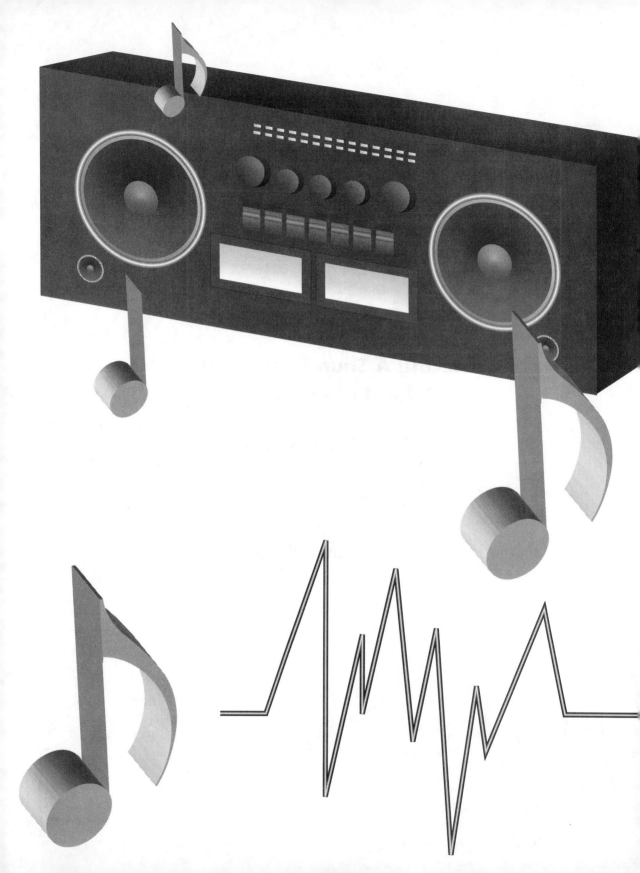

Do You Have What It Takes?

Ideally, adding a sound card should be a plug-and-play operation. Unfortunately, you must consider the various PC hardware items you already own. Sometimes, you may have to "beef up" your system to play sound. Likewise, some people overlook the true expense of a sound-ready system. There are other accessories that many sound-card buyers overlook. (You certainly won't make the same mistake, right?)

In this chapter, you learn about:

- ♪ The details to the multimedia PC (MPC) specifications and what they mean
- ♪ Sound accessories you'll need and connections for them
- ♪ Alternatives to a sound card

One-Slot Solution?

Most sound cards are a type of printed circuit board, or PCB.

Sound Check

A *PCB* is simply a flat piece of fiberglass, usually green, with copper wires etched into its surface and several electronic components mounted on it. This is why sound cards are also called sound boards.

A sound card usually is placed inside your PC into any of several vacant slots. These empty slots are called *expansion slots* or *expansion ports*. Your PC may have between six and eight expansion slots (see fig. 3.1). The circuit boards placed in them are called expansion cards, expansion boards, or add-on cards (see fig. 3.2). In other words, *a sound card is one example of an expansion card*.

Unfortunately, some sound cards may not fit inside your PC because your computer may be of a certain design: either 8-bit or 16-bit.

How do you know which type you have? You plug a sound card into rectangular connectors on your PC's motherboard. (The *motherboard* is the large square circuit board that forms the foundation of your PC.) These connectors are called *edge connectors* because the edge of the sound card is inserted in them.

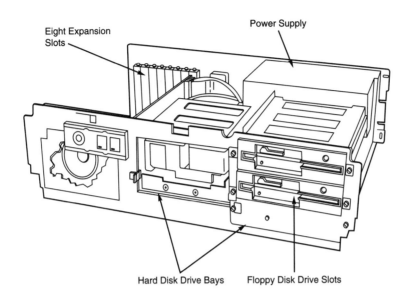

Figure 3.1:
Your PC probably has eight expansion slots.

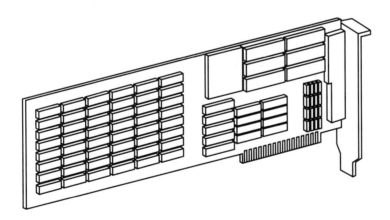

Figure 3.2:
An example of an expansion card.

XT-type PCs, computers that use either an 8088, 8086, or NEC processor, have only one edge connector per expansion slot. One edge connector lets your PC handle only eight bits of information at a time. (A *bit* is a very small unit of information.) A slot with a single edge connector is called an 8-bit slot. 16-bit cards use two edge connectors; 8-bit cards use one, as shown in figure 3.3.

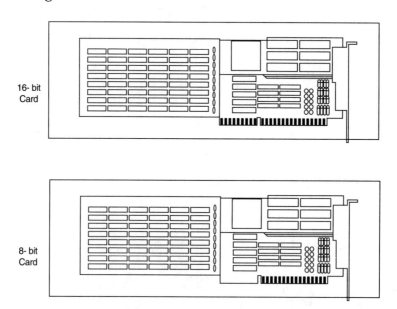

Figure 3.3:

16-bit versus 8-bit cards.

When the AT, or 80286, computer was introduced by IBM in the mid-eighties, some of the connectors were enlarged with an additional edge connector. This second connector allowed expansion cards to take advantage of the 16-bit speed of the 80286 processor found on such computers. A slot with these two edge connectors is called a 16-bit slot. To accommodate both 8-bit and 16-bit expansion cards, the AT computer had a mixture of 8-bit and 16-bit slots. Today's 80386 and 80486 PCs also use this design.

If your motherboard has a second edge connector, the sound card can transfer information more quickly to your PC's brain. In other words, a 16-bit card is faster than an 8-bit card.

You can easily tell if a sound card is an 8-bit or 16-bit card. A 16-bit card has a gap between its two edges, or teeth. An 8-bit card only has one tooth to insert in the single edge connector on the motherboard. If you have an 8-bit computer, you won't be able to use a 16-bit sound card. (*You're one tooth short.*)

Listen Up!

Remember that 8-bit and 16-bit can mean two different things when it comes to sound cards: it can mean either the detail of the sound sampling or the type of expansion slot into which it fits. Sometimes, this confusion can mislead. The Sound Blaster Pro sound card, for example, billed itself as a 16-bit card, but this card could only record and play back 8-bit digital sound samples. It did, however, fit into a 16-bit slot.

It was only until the introduction of Sound Blaster ASP 16 that true 16-bit recording became available. Some customers naturally thought the 16-bit Sound Blaster Pro could sample sounds at 16 bits. (Isn't marketing wonderful?)

Some sound cards require not one but two expansion slots. Sound Blaster 16 ASP has a 20-voice Yamaha YMF-262 chip for MIDI. You can beef up its MIDI abilities by purchasing an optional daughterboard called Wave Blaster. Wave Blaster has a 32-voice E-mu chip. This daughterboard attaches to the Sound Blaster 16 ASP card, but is so unwieldy it prevents you from using the adjacent expansion slot. You may want to place the daughterboard so it occupies the air space of an 8-bit but not a 16-bit slot.

Chapter 3

No Slot Required

If you're intimidated by the thought of installing a sound card inside your computer, and you require only simple sound or want sound on the go, consider an external sound device. (Since such a *sound device* is outside the PC, I won't call it a sound card.)

Such sound devices do not need an expansion slot. The $199 Media Vision Audio Port, for example, connects to your PC's 25-pin parallel port. This is ideal for taking MPC sound on the road. Just plug in and play. Although Audio Port provides 8-bit mono sound, it is ideal for today's notebook computers. Audio Port is self-contained; it has its own speaker and volume control. It operates on four AAA batteries and can be attached to an external speaker and microphone.

Media Vision isn't the only company to provide a portable sound card. Logitech offers AudioMan (see fig. 3.4), a $179 sound card that only gives sound to Windows 3.1. Logitech AudioMan uses two AA batteries and includes a built-in microphone. Unlike Audio Port, AudioMan won't work with DOS-based games that support AdLib- or Sound Blaster-compatible sound. The SoundXchange from Interactive Communications Systems also allows plug-in recording and playback in Windows. You can record a message by picking up the handset or using the built-in microphone.

Listen Up!

Don't think your printer is unavailable when these products are attached. To still print, you connect your printer's cable to these sound products for pass-through printing.

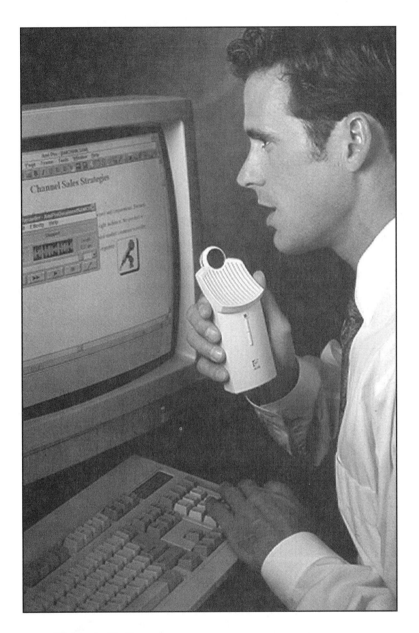

Figure 3.4:
Logitech AudioMan provides sound on the move.

Chapter 3

Look to the MPC

Besides not having the correct expansion slots, your PC may be too limited to fully use a sound card. The specifications defined by the Multimedia PC Marketing Council provide an overview of the MPC-standard PC.

In most cases, a sound card will end up being used for multimedia, the melding of text, graphics, and sound for entertainment and educational uses. The MPC Marketing Council, an arm of the Software Publishers Association, defines a multimedia-capable PC as having at least the following:

♪ Multimedia Windows (either Windows 3.0 with Multimedia Extensions for Windows or Windows 3.1)

♪ 80486SX computer operating at 25 MHz

♪ 4M of memory

♪ 160M hard disk

♪ VGA monitor and video card

♪ 400-millisecond or faster CD-ROM XA-ready drive that can sustain 300 Kbps to your PC without requiring more than 60 percent of your PC's thinking power

♪ 16-bit digital sound card capable of CD-quality sound at 44.1 KHz

♪ 3 1/2-inch high-density disk drive (1.44M)

♪ 101-key keyboard and two- or three-button mouse

♪ MIDI interface and joystick ports

♪ Standard 9- or 25-pin serial port and a 25-pin bi-directional parallel port

♪ Pair of speakers or headphones

Note: These are the MPC Level 2 specifications announced in late April 1993.

Remember that these are minimum multimedia requirements; as a rule of thumb, you may want to double or even triple some of these specifications for reasonable multimedia performance. The following sections examine some of these requirements.

More Windows

If you don't already own Windows 3.1, get it. Microsoft Windows 3.1 was designed for multimedia. In fact, it includes a couple of multimedia "applets" as seen in figure 3.5. (An *applet* is a small utility program that is not considered big enough to be a full-featured application.)

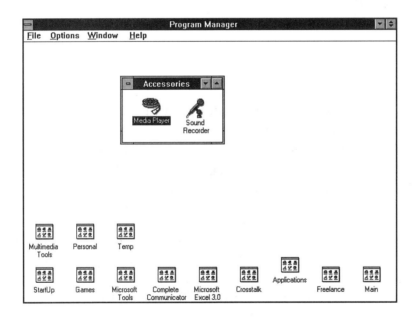

Figure 3.5:
Windows includes some built-in "sound bite-sized" utilities.

Sound Recorder allows you to record, crudely edit, and play back digital sound, or WAV, files. In fact, Windows includes four WAV files to tease you with Windows' sound capabilities.

Media Player, on the other hand, is used to play multimedia files, such as MIDI files. In fact, Windows 3.1 includes a MIDI song called CANYON.MID, a charming two-minute song. The Media Player can also play your audio CDs in the background while you are using other applications. Both applets use VCR-style buttons to play, rewind, and fast forward (see fig. 3.6).

Figure 3.6:
Windows Media Player uses VCR-like buttons.

More Power

A PC with an 80486SX processor operating at 25 MHz is considered the minimum amount of computing power needed to run multimedia software. Ideally, you would want to use a PC with an 80486DX processor at 33 MHz; for demanding multimedia work, such as that involving moving video clips, insist on an 80486DX2/66 MHz.

If you own an 80286 PC, you can still use a sound card. Unfortunately, you will be left to playing DOS-based games and some of the sound utilities included with the sound card. If you want to use the 286 with Microsoft Windows, forget it. The solution is to buy a new PC or install an accelerator card. Accelerator expansion cards, or accelerator boards, can turn an 80286 PC into an 80386SX, which makes your PC compatible with the initial MPC specifications. (Better partially compatible than never?) You simply remove your 80286 processor and plug in the accelerator circuit board. No expansion slot is required for the upgrade.

Listen Up!

80486DX and 80486SX PCs provide ample power for today's multimedia. However, they later can be sped up by adding a DX2 or OverDrive processor. These Intel Corp. upgrade chips allow you to install a single computer chip to greatly increase your PC's speed.

Kingston Technology, Cumulus Corp., and SOTA make accelerator cards. Because each motherboard design is different, these cards only work with certain brands of computers. Cumulus Corp. offers its 386SX card for many 80286 computers, including the Compaq Deskpro 286 and Tandy 3000. Kingston Technology's SX/Now! provides 20 MHz and 25 MHz 80386SX power to Compaq and IBM PS/2 computers (see fig 3.7). SOTA offers its Express/386 accelerator for AT computers in 16-, 20- and 25-MHz versions. These accelerator cards sell for between $300 and $600.

Figure 3.7:

Some accelerator cards, such as Kingston Technology's SX/Now!, plug directly into your 80286's processor socket.

More Memory

The four megabytes of memory recommended in the MPC specifications may let you use your sound card with multimedia, but you certainly won't enjoy it. Consider getting at least 8M of memory, if not 16M. I have 16M on my PC, which allows me to move quickly between several sound applications.

Memory has another use. Some sound utilities use your Windows temporary directory to store files. This temporary directory is usually a RAM drive of about 2M to 8M. If you intend to record large files, you'll require a large RAM drive. (Remember: one minute of CD-quality sound can require up to 11M of storage.)

Sound Check

What's a *RAM disk?* The file RAMDRIVE.SYS is a software utility included with Microsoft DOS that temporarily creates a disk drive in your computer's memory. This RAM drive, or virtual disk, can be created from conventional, extended, or expanded memory. RAM drives are much faster than hard disk drives because your computer can read information much faster from lightning-fast memory than from your PC's hard disk.

More Disk Space

The trouble with digital sound is that it takes up so much space. The sampling rate at which sound is recorded determines how much disk space is consumed. CD-quality sound, for example, is sampled at 44 KHz, requiring almost 11M for every minute recorded. If you reduce the sampling to 8-bit mono at 11 KHz, the file may take 1/16th that space.

This problem is compounded by the software that comes with sound cards. The installation software for many sound cards requires several megabytes. For example, Microsoft Windows Sound System requires 12M of disk space. Third-party collections of sound effects may require an additional 2M to 8M each.

The 160M hard drive suggested by the MPC Marketing Council should be considered just that… a minimum. You may want to multiply this figure by two or even three. Any sound savant would want at least 300M of hard disk space for recording and editing various sound files.

Listen Up!

If you have DOS 6, you may not have to worry about disk space. MS-DOS 6 now includes a disk compression utility called DoubleSpace. This utility can increase the capacity of your hard disk by compressing the files that are on it. Depending on the nature of your files, you may increase your free space by 50 to 100 percent. There are two drawbacks to using DoubleSpace. First, when DoubleSpace is used, it automatically runs in the background as you use your computer, requiring about 40K of your PC's memory. Second, your Windows permanent swap file, which is used to increase the amount of memory available to Windows, must be placed on an uncompressed drive, such as drive D.

More Video

A VGA monitor and video card are recommended by the MPC Marketing Council. However, super-VGA (SVGA) monitors and cards are very popular. What's the difference?

Chapter 3

A video card and matching monitor are measured by its resolution. The resolution is expressed in the number of horizontal and vertical picture elements, or *pixels*, contained in the screen. The greater the number of pixels, the more detailed the images (see figs. 3.8 and 3.9). VGA video cards can produce a maximum resolution of 640 x 480 pixels. They also can display up to 256 colors from a palette of 256,000. (*That's a lot of crayons.*)

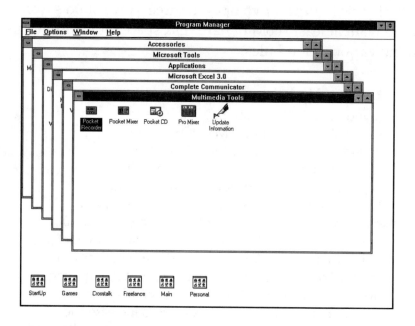

Figure 3.8:
Windows in super-VGA mode.

In 1988, the Video Electronic Standards Association (VESA) announced specifications for super-VGA. SVGA monitors and cards provide a maximum resolution of 800 x 600 pixels and the same colors as VGA. Some SVGA cards (extended VGA) can also display images at 1024 x 768 pixels.

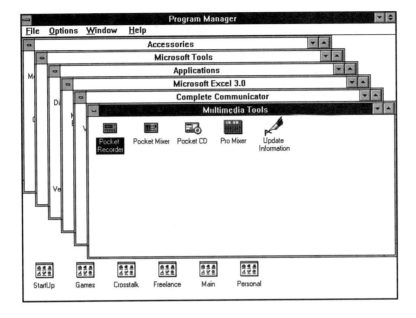

Figure 3.9:

Windows in VGA mode.

Many sound cards support both EGA (the video standard before VGA) and VGA. (Some sound utilities included with these cards support only VGA resolution.) Avoid EGA video cards, since they are limited to 16 colors and can produce images only 62 percent as sharp as VGA cards. Also, many games and all multimedia software require at least VGA resolution.

Sound Check

SVGA is very popular for many reasons. SVGA is convenient for Microsoft Windows, allowing you to get more icons and groups on the screen without having to scroll up or down to make your selections. SVGA is also better for your eyes, since it has higher refresh rate than VGA— about 72 Hz compared to VGA's 60 Hz. By refreshing the screen more often, your eyes will not feel as tired.

continues

continues

Some SVGA cards also support a resolution of 1024 x 768 pixels, but such a high resolution requires a 16-inch or larger monitor to comfortably read the text. On typical 14-inch monitors, this resolution crams too much detail into too small an area. Also, such high resolution slows down your monitor, since the video card must draw all those pixels.

Often, you can select how much memory you want on your video card, such as 256K, 512K, or 1M. Finding 256K on a VGA card is rare; most cards come with at least 512K. The 512K or 1M of memory does not speed up your video card. Rather, it allows your monitor to display more colors and higher resolutions. For 256 colors drawn from a palette of 256,000, you'll need at least 512K of video memory. At 1024 x 768 pixels, you need at least 1M. If you currently don't need this capability, bypass the extra memory. The next generation of video cards will probably provide other features you may need.

Listen Up!

You can speed up Microsoft Windows by picking a lower resolution, such as VGA (640 by 480 pixels), and by using fewer colors. I use super-VGA (800 by 600 pixels) at 16 colors. At this point, I have no daily need for 256 or more colors at the same time.

Some video cards are called Windows accelerator cards because they refresh your screen especially fast. Such video cards have their own on-board computer called a graphics copro-cessor to relieve your PC's main processor from drawing the screen. With an accelerator card installed, your computer can concentrate on other work, rather than handling the pixels, lines, and

other visual data. A variation of the accelerator card works with PCs that use a local bus design. By connecting to the local bus, your video card can work at your PC's top speed, unhindered by the slower *industry-standard architecture* (ISA) computer bus found in typical PCs.

More CD-ROM

Not every CD-ROM drive will work with every sound card. Several sound cards provide a built-in interface for a CD-ROM drive. A built-in CD-ROM connection can save you from buying a separate CD-ROM card, plus it frees up an expansion slot.

Most sound cards, such as those from Media Vision, provide a generic *small computer systems interface* (SCSI) connector along the top side of the card. This allows the sound card to work with any of several drives. For a wider selection of drives, consider a sound card that includes a SCSI connector. The Sound Blaster Pro card uses a proprietary, non-SCSI interface for a Panasonic CD-ROM drive. You cannot attach any CD-ROM drive to it.

All CD-ROM players read all standard CD-ROM disks, just as the CD player in your stereo will play any CD you find in a record store. There's only one caveat: if you eventually want to play CD-ROMs recorded in the emerging extended architecture (XA) format required for an MPC, you may need to upgrade your interface card down the road. CD-ROM XA players are "multiple-session" players that can accept multiple additions to the original recording. Kodak's Photo CD format, for example, relies on CD-ROM XA technology.

As mentioned in Chapter 2, a CD-ROM drive is measured by its average access speed and data transfer rate. The *average access speed* is how long it takes the CD-ROM drive to find the

information you want. Typical speeds range from 250 ms to 400 ms. (The lower the number, the better.) The *data transfer rate* indicates how fast the found information can be sent to your PC. This rate is measured in kilobytes transferred per second (Kbps).

The new MPC Level 2 specs insist on a double-speed drive capable of a data transfer rate of 300 Kbps. (The original MPC specs called for 150 Kbps speed; the new specs build on this.) This 300-Kbps specification speeds the flow of data into the drive's buffer, providing smooth animation and video instead of jerky screen stutters. An example of a drive that meets this criteria is the Toshiba TXM-3401E, which can deliver 332 Kbps. The MPC Level 2 specs recommend a CD-ROM drive with a built-in buffer of 64K. For multimedia work, this throughput speed is more important than a drive's access time. If you already own a CD-ROM drive, does it measure up?

If you want to use multimedia, your CD-ROM drive has one more requirement: it must have an extra audio connection to send sound in analog form from the drive to the sound card.

For an MPC, the drive should provide an output connector and small cable that can feed analog CD audio sound directly to the sound card. (This is above and beyond the larger one that delivers normal CD-ROM data to your PC.) This CD audio cable lets you use the drive/sound card combo to play CD audio disks under software control, or to mix that output with sound from other sources.

If your CD-ROM drive provides a headphone jack and volume control knob, you can listen to CD audio disks without the sound card, but you still need a program to control the drive, and that usually comes with the sound card.

More of Everything

Don't overlook the finer points of the MPC specifications. If you don't have a 3 1/2-inch, high-density (1.44M) disk drive, you may want to consider getting one.

If you add a new floppy drive, your version of DOS must support it. If your version of DOS doesn't support the drive's capacity, you won't be able to format disks and read them. Of course, having the most current version of DOS is best, but DOS 3.3 supports all disk formats except for the new 2.88M size. (Only DOS versions 5 and 6 support the 2.88M disk drive.) If you have DOS 3.2, for example, you cannot add a 3 1/2-inch high-density (1.44M) disk drive.

Similarly, you also need a small program called the *basic input/output system* (BIOS) to support your disk drive. The BIOS is located in ROM computer chips on your motherboard. Many older computers have a BIOS that does not support newer drives. For example, a BIOS dated before 11/15/85 does not support the 3 1/2-inch 1.44M drive. If your BIOS doesn't support your type of floppy drive, you may still be able to use it. Sometimes, DOS may have a workaround solution or the drive controller may have some BIOS chips of its own to support the drive. When BIOS chips are on the controller, they are called BIOS extensions because they are an extension of the BIOS found on your motherboard.

You may also want to make sure you have at least a two-button mouse and a 101-key keyboard. The MPC specifications also call for at least one free communication (serial) port after your mouse is connected. This may mean you need to replace your external modem with an internal one or to connect your mouse to a bus card rather than the serial port. To have a multimedia

PC, you must cover all the bases. A joystick is handy for many multimedia games (see fig. 3.10). Many sound cards include a game port connector. This connector often doubles as a MIDI interface to a keyboard synthesizer or other MIDI device.

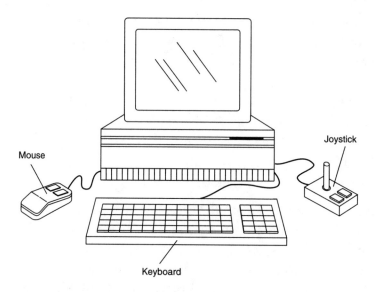

Mouse

Joystick

Keyboard

Figure 3.10:

A mouse, keyboard, and joystick may also be required by your sound card.

Most sound cards do not provide speakers, headphones, or a microphone (although the latest sound cards from Media Vision and Creative Labs are including microphones). These are extra components you'll need to purchase. (These components are discussed in Chapter 5.)

Look Ma, No Card!

If you don't have what it takes for a real sound card, you can improve your PC's built-in speaker. Microsoft has a driver (a small software program) that can improve its sound. PC Speaker (SPEAKER.DRV) allows you to play 8-bit, 11-KHz

sampled sound on almost any PC. The sound quality is scratchy but coherent. You can play Windows WAV files during certain Windows events, such as when you start Windows (ta-da!). I also have used it to play back voice notes embedded in my documents. One disadvantage is that because I am using SPEAKER.DRV instead of a sound card, I cannot record a voice note in my document; without a sound card, there's no jack into which to insert a microphone.

Sound Check

Imagine how you could use PC Speaker: you place voice notes in a Windows file, such as a document or spreadsheet. You then send the file to another Windows user along with PC Speaker. After installing the PC Speaker driver, that person then clicks on each verbal Post-It note to hear your comments. And that person doesn't have to invest in a sound card! You also could use PC Speaker to play back voice notes on your laptop without the aid of a sound card.

Microsoft does not include the SPEAKER.DRV driver with Windows 3.1, but buries it in Data Library 15 of the Zenith forum on CompuServe. I've uncovered it and placed it on the enclosed *Crank It Up!* bonus disk. One reason this driver is not used is that it must consume your PC's attention. For instance, if you were downloading a file in the background while playing a long WAV file, the background task would grind to a halt. On slower PCs, such as 386SX systems, you may hear a hiss during playback. Microsoft does not guarantee that the speaker driver will work with all computer systems.

To install the speaker driver:

1. Place the disk included with this book in drive A or B.

2. Start Microsoft Windows.

Chapter 3

3. Open the Windows Control Panel and click on Drivers.

4. Select <u>A</u>dd from the right-hand list of buttons.

5. Press Enter or OK when the first choice, Unlisted or Updated Driver, is highlighted.

6. Enter the drive letter and path to the speaker driver.

   Using the disk included with this book, type:

   A:\SPEAKER

   in which **A:** is the letter of the floppy drive in which you placed this disk. The driver Sound Driver for PC-Speaker appears in the box.

7. Select OK to add the PC-Speaker driver.

8. From the PC Speaker Setup menu, make your choices (see figure 3.11).

Speed affects the speed at which you play back sound. I recommend you don't change this.

Volume affects the volume, and, in most cases, its setting of 5.0 is adequate. Press the Test button to test and adjust the sound.

Seconds to limit playback places a limit on the amount of time given to play back a sound file. You may want to adjust the limit to "No limit" by placing the scroll bar to the far right. If you kept the limit to a few seconds (the default value), you may not be able to play back the entire sound file if it exceeds the time limit.

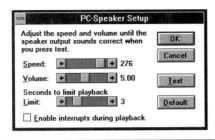

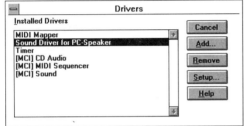

Figure 3.11:

The Microsoft Speaker driver can play Windows WAV files through the built-in speaker. No sound card required!

Enable interrupt during playback allows your system to go somewhat comatose during the playing of a sound file. By default, the PC Speaker driver turns off all of your PC's interrupts so that it gets all of your PC's attention. This provides the best sound quality but causes the mouse cursor, keyboard, and other processes to not respond while a sound file is being played back. If you enable interrupts by placing an X in this box, you can get these processes back at the expense of sound quality, which isn't that good in the first place. I recommend you leave this box unchecked.

Listen Up!

The PC Speaker sound driver is not perfect.
Here are a couple of caveats:

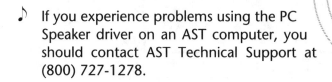

♪ If you experience problems using the PC
Speaker driver on an AST computer, you
should contact AST Technical Support at
(800) 727-1278.

♪ You cannot play WAV files through the Media Player
included with Windows 3.1. Instead, play back WAV
files with the Windows Sound Recorder. The Sound
Recorder is placed in your Accessories Program
Manager group.

♪ If you have a sound card that already plays back
WAV files, you must remove its software driver
before you install the PC Speaker driver. If both are
installed at the same time, the two will fight to play
back the same sound file. You remove your current
sound-card driver from the Control Panel by selecting the Drivers icon. Highlight your installed driver
and then select Remove.

By preparing your PC for a sound life, you can ensure your
chosen sound card will work for you to its fullest. A little more
memory, a little more hard disk space, and perhaps a few other
additions can turn your PC into an MPC, as shown in table 3.1.
The next chapter discusses the various sound cards available
to you.

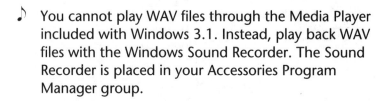

Table 3.1
MPC Minimum versus My Recommendations

Area	MPC Recommendation	My Recommendation
Windows	Multimedia Windows (either Windows 3.0 with Multimedia Extensions for Windows or Windows 3.1)	Windows 3.1
PC	80486SX 25 MHz	80486DX 33 MHz (affordable yet allows later addition of OverDrive chip)
RAM	4M RAM	8M RAM
Hard Disk	160M	240M
Monitor and video card	VGA (640 x 480)	Super-VGA (800 x 600)
CD-ROM drive		
Speed	< 400 ms	<250 ms
Transfer rate	300 Kbps	Ditto
Buffer	No size required	64K buffer
Sound card	16-bit digital sound card with on-board mixing	Ditto
MIDI/Joy-stick Port	MIDI interface and joystick ports	Only if you're musically inclined
High-density floppy	3 1/2-inch disk drive (1.44M)	Ditto
Keyboard	101-key	Ditto
Mouse	Two-button	Three-button
Speakers	A pair of speakers or headphones	Ditto

Chapter 3

Conclusions

The initial MPC Marketing Council specifications for a multi-media-capable PC were too weak and soon outgrown. The MPC Level 2 specifications now seem a bit too high. Foremost, the requirement for an 80486SX PC now seems to alienate the millions of 80386 PCs currently in use (the author's included). Similarly, how many computer users require a 16-bit sound card? Most games are written to be compatible with the 8-bit Sound Blaster or AdLib cards. The double-speed CD-ROM drives provide jitter-free video images on your screen, but how many people can afford the disk space and hardware required to dabble with these images? The one possibility is that the prices of such demanding hardware and software continue to fall to within the credit limit or checkbook balance of the typical computer owner.

Sound à la Card **4**

Selecting a sound card is like buying a car. Many cars have the same features, but some give you more... for a price. Others, like the Yugo, provide affordability but not style. To make your decision, you have to check under the hood or kick the tires. But comparing sound cards is much more difficult than sitting behind the wheel of a Honda or Lexus. What you hear is what you get.

In this chapter, you learn about:

- ♪ The criteria for comparing sound cards
- ♪ Basic categories of sound cards
- ♪ Sound cards for under $100
- ♪ Sound cards designed to plug into your PC
- ♪ Stereo sound cards
- ♪ Windows-only sound cards
- ♪ High-end sound cards for the demanding recording professional

Chapter 4

Hear Ye, Hear Ye

Telling you which sound card to get is like telling you what is good art or good literature. Sound is so subjective. However, the technology in one sound card may be the same as that in another. Case in point: Logitech has licensed Media Vision's multimedia chip sets for its sound cards. The first product resulting from this relationship is Logitech's SoundMan 16, a PC-based, CD-quality sound card. SoundMan 16 is based on the Media Vision 16-bit Spectrum chip set. It also uses Yamaha's high-end OPL3 synthesis chip to imitate musical instruments for MIDI work. At the time of this writing, Media Vision provides its sound technology to over 45 companies.

What are some key features to consider? Look for the following: compatibility, sampling, stereo versus mono, CD-ROM, data compression, external versus internal cards, MIDI interface, bundled software, sound drivers, connectors, and volume control.

Compatibility

Although no official sound-card standards exist, the popular Sound Blaster card has become a de facto standard. Sound Blaster was the first widely distributed sound card, and it's supported by the greatest number of software programs. A sound card billing itself as Sound Blaster-compatible should run virtually any application that supports sound. Many sound cards already support the Multimedia PC (MPC) Level 2 specifications, and allow you to play sound files in Windows, record CD-quality sound, and more. Some sound cards barely fall short of the MPC specs by excluding a MIDI interface. Other compatibility standards to look for are Ad Lib and Pro Audio Spectrum.

Listen Up!

Discover if the applications you plan to run will support your new sound card before you buy it. If you are buying a replacement sound card, make sure it offers the same support as your old card so you can continue running your current programs.

Sampling

The most important sound-card quality is its sampling capability. As mentioned in Chapter 2, *sampling* is the process by which the card converts analog sound signals into a digital format your PC can understand. The sound card changes this digital information back to its original form by using a *digital-to-analog converter* (DAC) chip. For music files, this conversion process is different; the data goes through a MIDI synthesizer that creates sound by blending notes played by different instruments.

The rate at which the card samples (measured in *kilohertz*, or KHz) and the size of its sample (expressed in bits) determine the quality of the sound. The standard sampling rates for sound cards are 11.025, 22.050, and 44.1 KHz, whereas sample sizes are 8, 12, and 16 bits.

Inexpensive monophonic cards generally sample at 8 bits up to speeds of 22.050 KHz, which is fine for recording voice messages. Some stereo-capable cards sample at 8 bits and run at speeds of 22.050 KHz in stereo and up to 44.1 KHz in mono. Other cards can sample 8 bits at 44.1 KHz speeds in both stereo and mono. The latest generation of cards do it all: they can record 16-bit, CD-quality audio at 44.1 KHz.

Chapter 4

Listen Up!

Don't expect a higher-sampling sound card to provide better sound. Very few software programs currently support 16-bit sound. For example, most computer games are capable of sampling only at 8 bits. Even the best-selling Sound Blaster Pro only supports recording at 8 bits. If price is your primary concern, a basic 8-bit card may meet your needs.

If you do buy a card that supports 16-bit sampling, ensure that you have plenty of hard-disk space. The higher the resolution of sampling, the more hard disk required to store the file. The sampling rate also affects file size; sampling at the next higher rate doubles the file size. Some sound cards, such as Sound Blaster 16 ASP, include built-in compression/decompression hardware. Others include software-based compression, but this may slow down your computer.

Stereo versus Mono

You'll also have to consider buying a monophonic or stereophonic sound card. Inexpensive sound cards are monophonic, producing sound from a single source. Still, monophonic cards produce better sound than your PC's speaker.

Stereophonic cards produce many voices, or sounds, concurrently and from two different sources. The more voices a card has, the higher the sound fidelity you'll get. Each stereo chip in a sound card is capable of 11 or more voices. To get 20 or more voices, manufacturers at one time resorted to two FM synthesizer chips. Today, a single chip provides 20 voices, producing truer stereo sound.

A stereo card's number of voices is especially important for music files because the voices correspond to the individual instruments the card can play.

Most sound cards use FM synthesis to imitate the musical instruments played. Most use synthesizer chips developed by Yamaha. The least expensive sound cards use the monophonic 11-voice YM3812 or OPL2 chip. Better sound cards use the stereophonic 20-voice YMF262 or OPL3 chip.

Sound Check

Imitated musical instruments are not as impressive as the real thing. High-end sound cards use digital recordings of real instruments and sound effects. Often, several megabytes of these sound clips are embedded in the card's ROM memory chips. Some sound cards, for example, use the Ensoniq chip set (a type of circuit design) that does wave-table synthesis of musical instruments. Instead of pretending to play a trombone D flat, the Ensoniq chip set has a little digitized recording of an actual instrument playing that note.

If your primary interest in a sound card is for entertainment or for use in an educational or business setting, the monophonic 11-voice chip's quality level may be good enough.

However, if you want better reproduction of sound, buy a sound card that uses the Aria chip set from Sierra Semiconductor. (The related Aria Listener chip set is ideal for voice recognition, such as controlling game and business software.) You may also want to purchase the Wave Blaster daughterboard for Creative Labs' Sound Blaster 16 ASP. Wave Blaster includes a 32-voice E-mu synthesizer chip, which is also used in the MultiSound card from Turtle Beach Systems.

Stereo sound cards vary in sampling rates and sizes. Some stereo cards do not work in mono mode. Also, moving from mono to stereo sound means an increase in the size of the sound files. As with 16-bit resolution, stereo sound is not supported by most software applications. However, a stereo card generates better sound when playing mono software than a mono card can generate.

Another boon to buying the more expensive stereo cards is that they generally come with additional interfaces, such as connections to a SCSI device (like a CD-ROM drive) or a MIDI device (like a keyboard).

CD-ROM

Most stereo sound cards not only provide great sound but also can operate your CD-ROM drive. This means that you should choose your interface with care. Although many cards come with a SCSI port for any SCSI device, such as a CD-ROM drive, others support only a proprietary, or exclusive, CD-ROM interface. If you own a CD-ROM drive, make sure it's compatible with the sound card you plan to buy. If you plan to add a CD-ROM drive or if you expect to upgrade your drive, keep in mind that a proprietary interface will limit your choices. You may be limited to a single CD-ROM brand.

If you're seeking to add both a sound card and a CD-ROM drive, consider *multimedia upgrade kits*. These kits bundle a sound card, CD-ROM drive, CD-ROM titles, software, and cables in an attractively priced package. You can save several hundred dollars by buying a multimedia upgrade kit instead of buying different components. Plus, you have the assurance that the components will work together, especially if you have proper documentation with the kit.

Listen Up!

A family in my neighborhood hired me to help them convert their PC into a multimedia PC. Unfortunately, they had already purchased a sound card and a CD-ROM drive based on the advice of a Canadian friend. Foremost, the CD-ROM drive lacked software drivers and the cables to connect to the sound card. When finished, we discovered that the two were incompatible. After buying a new sound card and $200 of my time, the system finally worked. Although computer literate, I choose a multimedia upgrade kit to ease me into the world of multimedia. Why flirt with incompatibilities and the unknown?

Data Compression

The more-expensive cards produce CD-quality audio, which is sampled at 44.1 KHz. Recorded files at this rate, even that of your own voice, can require up to 11M for every minute of recording. (However, you can select lower sampling rates and 8-bit resolution with these cards.) Because of the demand sound cards place on your disk space, many cards include a data-compression capability. Sound Blaster 16 ASP, for example, includes on-the-fly compression of sound in ratios of 2:1, 3:1, or 4:1.

External versus Internal Cards

Most sound cards are placed inside your PC in an expansion slot. Typically, most sound cards can be configured through software, which bypasses the need to fiddle with jumpers and DIP switches.

Some cards can be plugged into a serial or parallel port instead of an expansion slot. This approach avoids opening your computer entirely and preserves a slot for other uses. If you're leery of working inside your computer, consider an external sound device. Also, an external sound device can be attached to a laptop computer so that it can work on either computer, even when you're on the road. External sound devices generally support 8-bit mono sound.

Listen Up!

Be certain the sound card is compatible with the software you'll be running. For example, Disney Sound Source is a great buy at $49.95, but its proprietary protocol means it doesn't support much software.

Some sound cards do double duty. They may provide a *small computer systems interface* (SCSI) for CD-ROM drives, scanners, and other SCSI-adaptable devices. Some video cards inherit sound card capabilities. The Orchid Fahrenheit VA, for example, doubles as a video-and-sound card for a one-slot solution.

MIDI Interface

The Musical Instrument Digital Interface is a standard for connecting musical instruments to PCs. Many stereo cards come with a MIDI interface, MIDI synthesizer, and sequencing software for composing music. Some cards include only a MIDI interface, so you have to purchase the hardware separately to hook up other MIDI devices. MIDI is covered in detail in Chapter 13.

Bundled Software

Sound cards usually include several sound utilities that immediately begin putting your sound card to work. Most of this software is DOS-based, but Windows-based versions are available with some cards. What could you receive?

♪ Text-to-speech conversion programs.

♪ Programs for playing, editing, and recording audio files.

♪ Cards with MIDI interfaces generally come with sequencer software, which helps you record, edit, and play back MIDI-composed music.

♪ Various sound clips.

Sound Drivers

Most sound cards include universal drivers for DOS and Windows applications. Find out which drivers are included with your chosen card. Windows 3.1 already includes drivers for the most popular sound cards, such as Sound Blaster. Other drivers are available on a separate driver disk available from Microsoft or from Microsoft's Product Support download service. Usually, your sound card includes its own drivers.

Connectors

Most sound cards have the same connectors. These connectors provide ways to pass sound from the sound card to speakers, headphones, and stereo systems, and to receive sound from a microphone, CD player, tape player, or stereo. Typically, your sound card could or should have four types of connectors (see fig. 4.1):

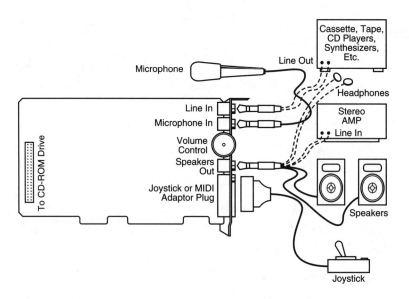

Figure 4.1:

The basic features most sound cards have in common.

♪ **Microphone/stereo input.** The microphone jack is typically a ⅛-inch monaural (as compared to stereo) minijack. A monaural jack combines the single or several sound sources speaking into the microphone and channels them into one carrier wave. (In layman's terms, you won't be able to do stereo recording from the one microphone.)

♪ **Audio-in jack.** This connector hooks up to the audio-out connector from a stereo system or CD-player. This is a ⅛-inch minijack.

♪ **Speaker jack.** What goes into a sound card eventually must come out. The speaker output is a ⅛-inch minijack. Most sound cards have a built-in amplifier, typically providing 4 watts of power per channel. Some sound cards provide separate audio-out jacks that give unamplified sound to your stereo system or amplified speakers.

Listen Up!

Do not connect a mono ⅛-inch miniplug to the speaker output connector. You can short-circuit and damage the amplifier.

♪ **Joystick/MIDI connector.** A 15-pin, D-shaped connector is used to control a joystick or to connect to a MIDI device, such as a keyboard. Sometimes, the joystick port can accommodate two joysticks if you order the optional Y-adapter. To use this connector as a MIDI interface, you'll need to buy the optional MIDI cable. Some sound cards do not provide a MIDI interface. If you're not interested in making music (and spending a few hundred dollars more for the MIDI keyboard), you may want to consider MIDI-less models. Don't worry about the lack of a joystick port either; most PCs include one as part of the input/output (I/O) card. Otherwise, you can buy a separate game card, such as the GameCard III Automatic from CH Products.

Listen Up!

Make sure the card you buy offers all the ports you'll need.

Volume Control

Some sound cards provide a thumbwheel on the back of the card to control its volume. However, this thumbwheel typically

is useless because it becomes difficult to reach after your PC is assembled. Other cards provide a memory-resident utility to increase or decrease the volume. You may have to press, for example, Ctrl-Alt-U to increase the volume. Some cards provide both types of volume controls.

Cheap Sound

Many sound cards are available for under $200. Their sound may not be exquisite, but their price will be music to your ears. These cards are usually monophonic, as compared to their more-expensive stereo brethren.

Disney Sound Source

In its bid to offer "family computing," Walt Disney Computer Software has introduced the Sound Source (see fig. 4.2). This external sound device plugs into your PC's parallel port primarily to provide sound for Disney educational software. Sound Source now is supported by several game manufacturers, including Sierra, Broderbund, Interplay, and Maxis. The latest version of Sound Source is MPC Level 1 compatible, thereby allowing it to play Microsoft Windows WAV files.

Sound Source is the size of a small answering machine. It runs on a single nine-volt battery. Because it is plugged into your PC, you don't have to wrestle with opening up your computer to install this card.

Don't expect rich sound from Sound Source. It is designed as an inexpensive ($49.95 retail) alternative for users who want better sound than what their PC speaker provides. Plus, Sound Source does not have any way to provide audio input. In other words, no microphone jack for recording is provided.

Figure 4.2:

Disney Sound Source provides sound for under $50.

Disney signed an agreement with Packard Bell—Packard Bell claims to be the second-largest U.S. supplier of PC-compatible computers and the number-one supplier in shelf space in the mass-market channel—to offer seven Disney software titles and the Sound Source audio speaker system with Packard Bell systems in the United States and Canada.

Chapter 4

Sound Check

Expect, in the near future, sound to be built into computer *motherboards*—the main circuit board in your PC. ESS Technology, maker of Sound Source, is manufacturing an inexpensive sound chip that many system vendors plan to integrate by the middle of next year. Also, Phoenix Technologies, which makes BIOS chips for motherboards, is licensing the Disney sound technology to add to PCs.

Covox Speech Thing

Speech Thing from Covox, Inc. gives your PC a voice for just under $100 ($99.95). Speech Thing is a fist-sized, 8-bit sound converter (see fig. 4.3). Like Disney Sound Source, Speech Thing plugs into the parallel port of your PC. It attaches in line with your parallel cable so that you can still use your printer. Prerecorded digitized words can be used in your own BASIC programs. An editor adds special effects, new words, and music. The system includes an audio amplifier/speaker with headphone jack, power cable, software, and manual. Also included is the SmoothTalker software, which provides unlimited text-to-speech capability.

Speech Thing is simple to install. You merely plug in the adapter, reconnect your printer cable to the Covox adapter, and copy the sound software to your hard disk. Speech Thing requires a nine-volt battery. A second plug can be used to add a booster speaker, since the power from the parallel port may not be enough to power the current built-in speaker. Many laptop computers, for example, do not supply enough power to the printer port to properly drive the amplified speaker.

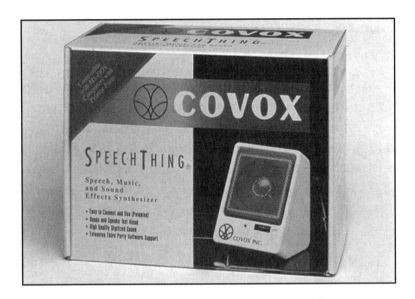

Figure 4.3:

Covox Speech Thing is ideal for simple text-to-speech proofreading.

Besides the hardware itself, you receive a variety of programs, including such useful BASIC files as the SAY utility, which reads special digitized speech files, and the TALK synthesized speech program. Using the supplied software, you can listen to a standard ASCII file using the simple command:

> TALK *filename*

You can also hear single lines of text/symbols entered from the keyboard, such as DOS commands. Once the STDRIVER utility is installed, your computer automatically pronounces DOS commands as you enter them. A second way to use Speech Thing's speech-generation software is to include the supplied BASIC files in your programs. For simple machine-like sound abilities, Speech Thing is just the thing.

Chapter 4

Sound Blaster Deluxe (formerly Sound Blaster 2.0)

Sound Blaster Deluxe from Creative Labs, Inc. is popular; over one million have been sold, according to company officials. The $129.95 product (see fig. 4.4) is an 8-bit card that can play back digital files at sampling rates as high as 44.1 KHz. (The original Sound Blaster had a limit of 23 KHz.) Sound Blaster Deluxe can record at sampling rates as high as 15 KHz. An 11-voice FM synthesizer is used.

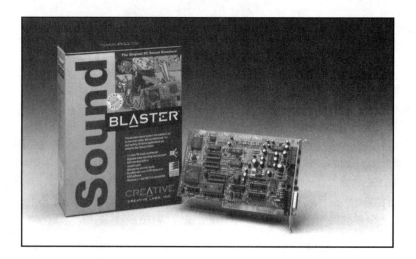

Figure 4.4:

Over 1,000,000 Sound Blasters have been sold.

Its built-in amplifier can provide up to 4 watts of power per channel. It includes a microphone jack, a line-in connector for connection to a stereo system, a volume knob, speaker jack, and a joystick/MIDI connector.

Stereo F/X

ATI Technologies, known for its video cards, developed the audio-only Stereo F/X. Stereo F/X provides simple 8-bit audio capabilities (see fig. 4.5).

Figure 4.5:

ATI Stereo F/X provides inexpensive but clear sound.

The $129 sound card can only sample in 8-bit mode, but its sound-reproduction quality is good if you're only interested in business audio (just voice notes). Stereo F/X can record using a DOS or Windows utility. No SCSI interface is supplied, and VOC files (Sound Blaster format)—but not Windows WAV files—can be compressed. The ATI Stereo F/X is a superior beginner-level sound card. It doesn't offer much in the way of MIDI, but its Sound Blaster and Ad Lib-compatible interface delivers all the system sound you'll need.

Chapter 4

Sound on the Go

Some sound devices, like rubbing alcohol, are meant for external use only. A handful of products are used to add a voice to your laptop computer or share plug-and-play sound between PCs.

Port-Able Sound Plus

Port-Able Sound Plus from Digispeech, Inc. is similar to Logitech AudioMan (described later) but provides richer sound. Port-Able Sound Plus can play back sounds at CD-quality 44.1 KHz but can record up to 11 KHz. The $198.95 device (see fig. 4.6) connects to your parallel port for pass-through printing and includes a built-in unidirectional microphone. It includes a built-in speaker, line-in CD audio, line out headset and speaker ports, software, and cabling.

Figure 4.6:
Port-Able Sound Plus can play back sounds at CD-quality (44.1 KHz).

Lotus Sound multimedia software is included with the product along with Digispeech's own Show & Tell program. Show & Tell allows you to include graphics, audio, and text in presentations created under Windows. It also works with Ad Lib- and Sound Blaster-compatible games. Port-Able Sound Plus uses either six AA batteries or AC power.

SoundXchange Models A and B

InterActive Communications Systems' SoundXchange makes voice annotation as easy as talking on the telephone. In fact, it has the size and appearance of a Princess phone and comes with a bracket for mounting on the side of your monitor or PC.

Like the other portable sound devices, SoundXchange communicates with your PC through a parallel port, with a pass-through plug so you can still use your printer. (A conflict occurs only if a complicated print job and lengthy recording or playback session occur simultaneously.) Once you install its driver in Windows' Control Panel, SoundXchange plays WAV audio files over the base unit's small speaker or, for more privacy, through the handset. Fidelity is no better or worse than that of a standard phone, making it perfectly suitable for voice messages.

SoundXchange is extremely easy to use. You record messages using the handset or the microphone built into the base. A volume control wheel adjusts the amplified speaker, and an output jack allows use of a hands-free headset, available from InterActive. The unit draws power from an external AC adapter.

SoundXchange records only 8-bit audio files, using its own data-compression scheme to compress voice files up to 50 percent. If your audio needs are limited to voice-quality WAV files, SoundXchange fits the bill nicely.

SoundXchange Model B, with its own sound interface and parallel-port plug, lists at $289. If you already have a sound card (such as Microsoft's Windows Sound System) or a computer with built-in sound capabilities (such as Compaq's Deskpro/i), Model A connects to it for $149. Neither unit takes full advantage of the potential of PC audio, but both models do provide a simple, low-cost solution for one of the newest business PC applications.

Sound Cards Go Stereo

The bulk of sound cards can record and play back in stereo. Although stereo sounds require more disk space, you'll hear what you've been missing.

Sound Blaster Pro Deluxe

Creative Labs' $199.95 Sound Blaster Pro Deluxe (formerly Sound Blaster Pro Basic) board is best for those people wanting to add multimedia capabilities to their existing 386 or 486 micros (see fig. 4.7).

Sound Blaster Pro Deluxe fits in a 16-bit expansion slot. It provides 20-channel stereo FM music through a Yamaha OPL3 FM chip. Sound Blaster Pro Deluxe can record and play back in stereo or mono. It can record and play back mono sounds at sampling rates up to 44.1 KHz. Unfortunately, stereo sound sources can be recorded only at 22.05 KHz, not CD-quality.

To conserve disk space, Sound Blaster Pro can decompress digital sound files as they are played back. Unlike Sound Blaster Deluxe, Sound Blaster Pro Deluxe allows you to adjust and mix sounds from the microphone, line-in, CD input, and the digital sound output. This way, you can hear a blend of

sounds, such as music playing in the background while speech and sound effects play in the foreground.

Figure 4.7:
Sound Blaster Pro Deluxe added CD-quality sound but only in mono.

Sound Blaster Pro Deluxe includes a proprietary CD-ROM interface for use with a handful of drives. This card works with the Matsushita CR-521 internal CD-ROM drive or Panasonic-manufactured drives. If you purchase any of the several multimedia upgrade kits offered by Creative Labs, you receive a drive and several discs, saving yourself hundreds of dollars.

A wide array of sound utilities are included, which enable text-to-voice applications, voice and music recording and editing, integration of sound with graphical animation, and control of standard audio CDs.

If interested in MIDI, you can purchase an optional MIDI interface kit. This kit includes Voyetra's Sequencer Plus Pro software and connects to the Sound Blaster Pro Deluxe's joystick port.

Sound Check

Own an IBM PS/2? Micro Channel (PS/2) versions of Sound Blaster Deluxe and Sound Blaster Pro Deluxe are available. They are called Sound Blaster Deluxe MCV (Micro Channel Version) and Sound Blaster Pro Deluxe MCV, respectively.

Sound Blaster 16 ASP

Sound Blaster 16 ASP provides professional-quality sound for under $350 (see fig. 4.8). This sound card from Creative Labs delivers 16-bit stereo sound with a sampling rate of up to 44.1 KHz.

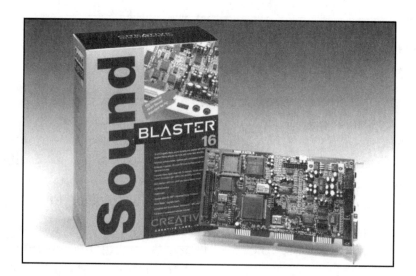

Figure 4.8:

SoundBlaster 16 includes built-in compression.

Sound quality is improved when you add the optional $249.95 Wave Blaster add-on daughterboard, which snaps directly onto

the Sound Blaster 16 card. Wave Blaster acts as a general MIDI wave table synthesizer. When you play back MIDI files, you hear true sampled instrument sounds, not FM-synthesized (imitated) sounds.

What sets Sound Blaster 16 apart from other 16-bit sound cards is its programmable chip, called an *advanced signal processor* (ASP). The ASP compresses and decompress sound files without placing a huge burden on your system's processor. This makes the board ideal for use with multimedia applications in which digitized sound is widely used when your computer's brainpower is required to handle other tasks besides decompressing files. A compression ratio of approximately 4:1 provides an audio signal that sounds virtually the same as the original uncompressed source, while taking up less than 3M per minute.

This sound card provides a library of sound software. For Windows users there's HSC Interactive, a basic multimedia presentation package; Creative WaveStudio for editing and recording WAV files; Creative Soundo'LE for annotating object linking and embedding documents with voice messages; and several other utilities. For DOS users, there's PC Animate Plus animation software and several other voice and music utilities. Some of these utilities are useful whereas others are trivial.

The recording setup lets you choose the audio source (CD audio with an internal connection, line in, microphone, VOC or WAV file, or MIDI) and select which channel goes where on a stereo recording.

For the best sound quality, set Sound Blaster 16 ASP to output your sound at standard levels without amplification. This option creates the highest fidelity signal possible and is CD-quality when recorded at the highest data rate.

Like Sound Blaster Pro Deluxe, Sound Blaster 16 ASP provides a CD-ROM and MIDI/joystick interface.

Pro AudioSpectrum 16

Pro AudioSpectrum 16 (see fig. 4.9) from Media Vision has challenged Creative Labs' Sound Blaster Pro Deluxe. The $299 sound card has been praised for its markedly cleaner high-end sound. With a built-in SCSI interface that is compatible with most CD-ROM drives, Pro AudioSpectrum 16 has gained popularity within multimedia circles.

Figure 4.9:
Pro AudioSpectrum 16 offers good sound at a good price.

Pro AudioSpectrum 16 can sample sound at 44.1 KHz in both stereo and mono. This CD-audio quality has given the company an edge over its competitors.

Chapter 4   **Sound à la Card**   **99**

All of Pro AudioSpectrum's options are software-programmable, and the card comes with several DOS and Windows sound utilities. Pocket Recorder and Pocket Mixer provide recording and mixing features. Pocket Recorder offers better features than the Sound Recorder included with Windows. Pocket Recorder cannot handle cut-and-paste editing, but it allows users to record in stereo with adjustable rate and resolution. Pocket Mixer is an attractive control panel that allows users to set controls and save settings for the board's inputs. A better mixer is also included. The one Achilles' heel of the Pro AudioSpectrum 16 is that it cannot compress sound files to conserve disk space.

Pro AudioStudio 16

Media Vision, Inc. upped the ante in the sound-card market with its Pro AudioStudio 16 (see fig. 4.10). The $349 sound card includes voice recognition software that recognizes 300 words for controlling the Windows desktop with spoken commands.

Pro AudioStudio 16's voice recognition software comes from Dragon Systems, Inc., the same company that provides voice recognition for Microsoft Windows Sound System. This voice recognition program does not depend on the speaker, but the software must be trained to recognize all 300 commands. If you issue a command the software does not recognize, you click on a training icon and speak the word several times before resuming the program.

Pro AudioStudio 16 includes Monologue for Windows, which converts text to speech. This utility can be used for proofreading numbers and other text. This sound card also ships with several other software programs, including a program that automatically installs the card, a Windows tutorial, and a MIDI sequencer for graphically composing music. To edit your sound files, Pro AudioStudio 16 includes a software mixer for combining audio channels and a sound editor for splicing and resizing music sequences.

Figure 4.10:
Pro AudioStudio 16 provides voice recognition and CD-quality recording in stereo.

Pocket Recorder, included with Pro AudioStudio 16, provides compression and decompression so that audio files consume less disk space. Audio files can be compressed at a 4:1 ratio. Recording and playing back sound at rates as high as 44.1 KHz, Pro AudioStudio 16 automatically adjusts to record low-volume sounds as well as loud sounds, and filters out noise.

The card also comes with an FM synthesizer, a game port, and a microphone that sits on top of the computer. A SCSI CD-ROM controller interface included with the card allows users to hook up a CD-ROM drive, saving an expansion slot and additional cost.

SoundMan 16

The $289 SoundMan 16 is the first product resulting from
Logitech's strategic relationship with Media Vision (see fig.
4.11). It uses the Media Vision 16-bit Spectrum chip set and
Yamaha's high-end OPL3 synthesis chip.

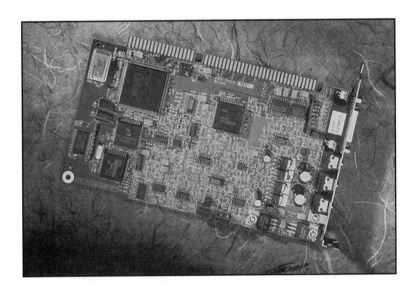

Figure 4.11:
Logitech SoundMan 16 uses some of Media Vision's technology.

SoundMan 16 is a CD-quality (16-bit, 44.1 KHz) sound card. It
can be used to record, mix, edit, and play back sound files in
Windows and DOS. Also, SoundMan 16 includes record and
playback DOS and Windows utilities. It is compatible with
Sound Blaster Pro 1.5 and Ad Lib sound cards. It also includes
a library of MIDI and WAV files. SoundMan 16 includes a
microphone jack, audio in and out jacks, and a joystick/MIDI
connector. It requires a 386SX or faster PC.

SoundMan 16 is ideal for computer users who don't need a CD-ROM interface built into the sound card. SoundMan is easy to install and provides a subset of the powerful utilities included with Media Vision Pro AudioStudio 16. In other words, SoundMan 16 provides clear, straightforward sound capabilities for less money than its competitors.

Sound Producer Pro

Like SoundMan 16, Sound Producer Pro from Orchid Technology provides good voice annotation under Windows. The $199, 8-bit sound card delivers the right combination of features for the growing Windows-based business market (see fig. 4.12). Sound Producer Pro includes a lapel-type microphone, two 5-inch mini-speakers, and third-party sound software for mixing, recording, voice annotating, and playing audio CDs.

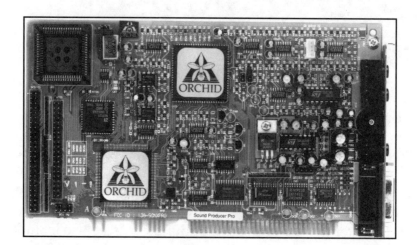

Figure 4.12:
Sound Producer Pro provides affordable 8-bit sound.

Sound Producer Pro requires a 16-bit expansion slot. This sound card uses an 8-bit Aztec FM synthesis sound chip that

supports 20 independent stereo voices. A built-in 4-watt power amplifier drives any speakers or headphones directly. Sound Producer Pro features sampling rates in both playback and record from 4 KHz to 44.1 KHz in mono, and up to 22.05 KHz in stereo. Because this card is meant for adding voice notes to Windows files and not for mixing sound files, the higher sampling rates are not required.

Sound Producer Pro includes ⅛-inch miniconnectors for line-in jacks, microphone, and speakers. A volume control is included along with a combination joystick/MIDI connector. The card includes a connector for attaching a CD audio in connector, a feature lacking in ATI Technologies' Stereo F/X. Orchid's board also contains a CD-ROM interface, making it comparable to Creative Labs' Sound Blaster Pro card.

Sound Producer Pro includes many software utilities, including several packages provided by Voyetra. You'll receive the DOS-based Sound Tracks, CD Player, Sound Master (a mixing and recording utility), Monologue (a text-to-speech synthesizer package), and Sound Producer Pro Mixer, which operates as a TSR. For Windows, Orchid includes WinDAT, a Windows-based mixer, and Orchid Voice Notes, a utility that uses *object linking and embedding* (OLE) to attach voice notes to Windows files.

SOUNDstudio

Cardinal Technologies, Inc. offers a $259 8- and 12-bit stereo card aimed at users who want to upgrade their PC systems to MPC systems. SOUNDstudio is compatible with Windows 3.1 and the Ad Lib standard. It includes an interface for SCSI CD-ROM drives, such as those from Hitachi, NEC, Sony, and Toshiba. For MIDI users, SOUNDstudio includes a 16-bit FM synthesizer that supports the General MIDI specifications. It also offers FM synthesis and 12-bit digital audio.

SOUNDstudio records and plays back audio in 8- and 12-bit resolutions at sample rates up to 44.1 KHz in stereo. You can record 16-bit stereo at 22.05 KHz, but you will have 4 empty bits. It includes connectors for a joystick, microphone, and stereo input and output. It comes with a variety of software.

ViVa Maestro Pro

Modem-maker Computer Peripherals, Inc. entered the sound-card market in late 1992 with its ViVa Maestro Pro multimedia sound card. Maestro Pro also supports the other four standards in PC sound/game boards: the original Sound Blaster, Ad Lib, Disney Sound Source, and Covox Speech Thing. This sound card is compatible with all multimedia games, entertainment, music, and presentation software under both the DOS and Windows environments. ViVa Maestro Pro has a suggested retail price of $229, which includes speakers, seven software programs, and a full set of utility applications.

ViVa Maestro Pro features a 20-voice stereo FM music synthesizer that produces an orchestra of realistic sounds including voice and music. This sound card can play back sounds at CD-quality (44.1 KHz). It plays back and reproduces digitized sounds, such as speech, music, and special sound effects through two 8-bit DAC chips with a sampling rate of 7 KHz.

With ViVa Maestro Pro you get a speaker audio output jack, a microphone input jack, a line input jack, a game port, and an adjustable volume control knob. The stereo microphone input for speech and sound has automatic level control for recording. The game port accepts all standard joysticks, and can be enabled/disabled through software control.

Internal features include two CD-ROM interfaces, an AT bus, the faster SCSI (optional SCSI chip required), CD-audio input, and PC internal-speaker input.

ViVa Maestro Pro's audio mixing and recording capability allows full control over mixing of all audio sources. This stereo digital/analog mixer allows mixing and integration of all audio sources for recording and playback. Like many other sound cards, it has a built-in 4-watt amplifier to directly drive a pair of speakers or headphones. A free pair of stereo speakers are included, or ViVa Maestro Pro can be patched directly into a stereo system.

Any MIDI instrument, synthesizer, or control device can be added to ViVa Maestro Pro with the optional MIDI cable and software package. This allows direct MIDI record and playback from any MIDI device: keyboard, drum machine, sequencer, and so on. A memory-resident, pop-up menu provides volume control although the card itself has a volume knob. Configuration settings and individual volume settings are saved when the card is powered off.

ViVa Maestro 16/16VR

Computer Peripherals also makes ViVa Maestro 16, which sells for $349. ViVa Maestro 16 uses Sierra Semiconductor's Aria chip set for superior reproduction of music. This chip set uses sampled sound rather than FM synthesis for better quality.

Compatible with Sound Blaster and Ad Lib, ViVa Maestro 16 offers playback at 44.1 KHz and records at 44.1 KHz in 8- or 16-bit resolutions. (You record at 12 bits and play back at 16, however.)

The companion $429 ViVa Maestro 16VR is the same as the ViVa Maestro 16 but includes the Aria Listener voice recognition software. The software can recognize the voice of various people and includes a macro facility for creating custom vocabularies.

Chapter 4

UltraSound

Advanced Gravis Computer Technology Ltd. is a Canada-based company that produces UltraSound, a $199.95 sound card introduced in October 1992 (see fig 4.13).

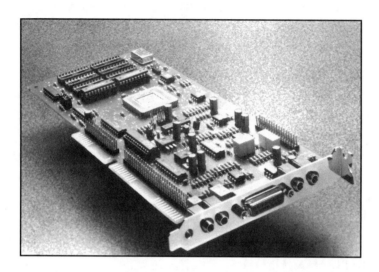

Figure 4.13:
Advanced Gravis's UltraSound uses the Ensoniq chip set for better MIDI sounds.

Sound Check

Logitech owns 43 percent of the outstanding shares of Advanced Gravis.

UltraSound uses the Ensoniq chip set (mentioned earlier) instead of the typical Yamaha chip. This chip set provides wave-table synthesis that is superior to FM synthesis. The result is

extraordinary sound of musical instruments. In other words, Ultrasound uses sampled sounds of actual instruments as the basis for its synthesis, resulting in higher quality and more realistic output. Samples, or patches, can be stored on the hard disk and loaded into the card's onboard memory. This, together with mixer, digital recording and playback, and connectors for a CD-ROM interface, makes it ideal for games and multimedia applications.

Although not supported by all software, UltraSound includes an interpreter that works fairly well with some games. Over 25 game developers, including Electronic Arts, Accolade, and MidiSoft, are writing games for this new sound effect.

UltraSound can do 8-bit recording and can play back at 16-bits and can mix external CD audio, digital audio, and synthesizers. It can generate 32 distinct voices at the same time, versus about 22 from most competing boards. The UltraSound card is compatible with other popular sound cards, such as Sound Blaster and Ad Lib units, and is compatible with multimedia software for Microsoft Windows. It also features a joystick/MIDI port. Interfaces for SCSI, Philips, and Sony CD-ROM drives are available as optional daughtercards.

Sound Check

At the time of this writing, Advanced Gravis was offering the Ultra Air Combat Pak for $249. This collection includes the UltraSound sound card, the Advanced Gravis Analog Pro joystick, and a special version of Electronic Arts' Chuck Yeager's Air Combat.

The $219 UltraChuck Pak includes the sound card and Chuck Yeager's Air Combat. The $229 Ultra Action Pak

continues

continued

includes the sound card, the Advanced Gravis PC
GamePad hand-held controller, and Accolade's
"TestDrive III: The Passion and The Games: Winter
Challenge." When ordering a sound card, ask if any
games are included. Some sound cards include either
full-fledged games or a game sampler.

UltraSound 3D

The $249.95 UltraSound 3D is a follow-up to the Advanced
Gravis UltraSound. UltraSound 3D provides "virtual sound."
With the correct software drivers, Ultra Sound can create the
illusion of sound sources moving about you in three dimen-
sions. This technology should be particularly welcomed by
computer game players.

Advanced Gravis says its UltraSound 3D processes the audio
signal through a technique called *convolution*. New right and
left binaural audio signals are generated to create a wrap-
around sound effect to the human ear. The sound signal is
actually a stereo signal shaped electronically to make the listener hear the sound as three-dimensional.

To get the same virtual-reality effect in other sound cards, you
would need 200 sliders for gain and another 200 sliders for
phase shift per ear and the ability to change all of them in real-
time.

Double Trouble: Video and Sound

If you're not yet interested in buying a new multimedia PC,
consider adding graphics and sound today and a CD-ROM

drive later. Some graphics cards now include sound chips, whereas some sound cards are adding graphics. Either way, you can save money by buying two cards in one as well as conserving an expansion slot.

SOUNDVision

Cardinal Technologies offers SOUNDVision (see fig. 4.14). This video-and-sound card combines 1024-by-768-pixel graphics with 12-bit audio and a SCSI connection for CD-ROM drives. SOUNDVision costs $459 with 1M of video RAM or $419 with 512K RAM. Cardinal uses Yamaha's new CD-quality OPL3 chip set on its $399 SOUNDVision board although the card can only record in 12-bit, not 16-bit audio. Missing the 4 bits, the SOUNDVision's sound quality is not as good as 16-bit sampled sound.

ATI VGAStereo F/X

ATI Technologies, Inc. sells its VGAStereo F/X sound-and-graphics card for an attractive $279. The ATI card (see fig 4.15) combines 8-bit sound with super-VGA (SVGA) display capabilities on a single card.

VGAStereo F/X is like one-stop shopping. It provides not only sound and SVGA graphics but also a quality, three-button, Microsoft-compatible mouse. The only thing missing is a SCSI interface to connect a CD player. The 1M version provides 1024-by-768 resolution with 256 colors and a flicker-free 72-Hz refresh rate.

Figure 4.14:
SOUNDVision video-and -sound card provides good 12-bit audio and sharp graphics.

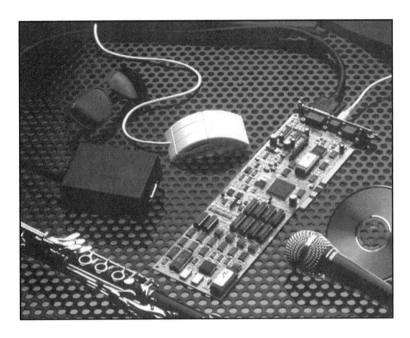

Figure 4.15:
VGAStereo F/X combines a mouse, video card, and sound card in one slot.

The card provides sampling rates of up to 44.1 KHz, automatic level control, and an 11-voice (OPL2) Yamaha FM music synthesizer. ATI VGAStereo F/X is compatible with Ad Lib and Sound Blaster applications. The MIDI box includes In, Out, and Thru ports and a sliding volume control, as well as a standard ⅛-inch port in which to plug a microphone or other external sound sources. Sound files can be compressed to save hard disk space at ratios up to 4:1 (though with some falloff in audio quality).

Although only one audio-in and one audio-out jack is available, the board's 8-watt amplifier lets you connect unamplified speakers or a set of headphones. You get a complete set of audio drivers to use in Windows that installs easily through

the Control Panel. VGAStereo F/X includes a free copy of Voyetra Technologies' sound utilities to record, play, and edit sounds, along with 25 MIDI song files.

Fahrenheit VA

Fahrenheit VA is similar to Orchid's Sound Producer Pro described earlier (see fig. 4.16). It is an 8-bit stereo card suitable for most business uses. Fahrenheit VA is a very fast video and sound card, which uses the S3 86C801 video coprocessor to add zip to your Windows' work. The video coprocessor is a "thinking" video chip that frees your computer from having to draw Windows' screens. A video local (VL) bus version of Fahrenheit VA is also available. Fahrenheit VA/VLB is a VL-bus card that uses S3's 86C805 coprocessor.

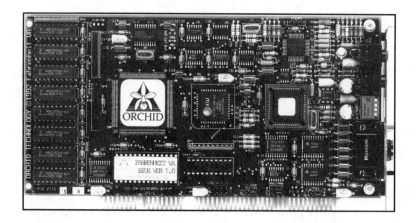

Figure 4.16:
Orchid Fahrenheit VA provides sound while relieving your PC of Windows screen drawing.

Listen Up!

The S3 coprocessor performs many video duties with little help from your computer's central processor. With an accelerator card installed, your computer can concentrate on what it does best—handling data and responding to your needs. In other words, the accelerator card's video coprocessor offloads your computer from handling pixels, lines, and other visual data. That reclaimed power is then utilized for other tasks.

This $299 card includes Orchid's Voice Notes, so you can attach audio messages to any Windows file. An installation disk contains a playback-only version of Voice Notes, and a sound driver can be created to enable systems not equipped with Fahrenheit to play back embedded messages.

Although not armed with fast video RAM (VRAM), Fahrenheit's speed is fast. The included Windows drivers allow it to display 16 million colors at 640×480 resolution, 256 colors at 800×600 and 1024×768 resolution, and 16 colors at 1280×1024 and 1280×980 resolution.

Four switches on the back of the card control monitor refresh rates when jumping between resolutions. Orchid also provides a setup utility along with its Windows drivers that eases the task of changing display preferences.

Thunder & Lightning

Priced at $349, Media Vision's Thunder & Lightning combines 24-bit VGA graphics and 8-bit sound on a single expansion card. With Thunder & Lightning, you can add voice messages to your Windows word processing and spreadsheet files. (You'll need a microphone.)

Figure 4.17:
Thunder & Lightning doubles as a sound-and-video card.

This card offers 8-bit sound recording and playback, good enough for voice notes and simple recordings but certainly less sophisticated than the CD-quality, 16-bit audio possible with more expensive cards.

Thunder & Lightning has an 11-voice synthesizer for playing back 11 different sounds, which is useful for presentations. The card includes various audio I/O ports for connecting an external microphone and speakers. It also includes a MIDI interface.

Compatible with both Sound Blaster and Ad Lib sound boards, this sound card allows you to run software that supports either of these products.

Thunder & Lightning's 24-bit color and 1M of RAM give you an almost infinite palette of 16.8 million colors at standard VGA

(640×480) resolution. At the maximum 1024×768 resolution, you can display 256 colors. The card supports ergonomic Video Electronics Standards Association (VESA)-compliant refresh rates up to 72 Hz. This provides less flicker on your screen and, therefore, less eye fatigue.

This card includes several bundled applications, such as Lotus Sound, which lets you add voice messages to documents in Windows applications. First Byte's Monologue for Windows is included to convert text to speech, and Master Tracks Pro provides MIDI recording and editing capabilities.

TyIn 2000

For the ultimate in one-stop sound, consider TyIn 2000, a combination sound card, voice-mail system, and fax/modem. The $279 TyIn 2000 occupies one 16-bit ISA slot but provides mono 8-bit sound, adequate for voice messages. It can record at a sampling rate of 11.025 KHz but plays back messages at 22.05 KHz.

TyIn 2000 uses an ordinary telephone handset for audio input and output and also supports a Logitech ScanMan hand-held scanner to let you turn hard-copy documents into fax files. The basic package includes the TyIn board, software, and a telephone cable.

Besides acting as a fax/modem, TyIn transforms your computer into a voice-mail system. You can set up multiple mailboxes, each with its own greeting and password for message retrieval.

TyIn's on-screen interface mimics an audio cassette player, with buttons to start recording, stop recording, fast forward, and the like. Also, a delete button removes old messages.

An automatic compression routine creates voice files that use only 3K per second of speech. The clarity of speech depends on the clarity of your connection, sounding about the same as a typical answering machine. You can subsequently embed these messages into any Windows application supporting OLE.

Faxing at 9,600 bps is a breeze with the Fax-It software, which supplies send-and-receive fax capabilities, phone books, automated fax sending, and background receive capabilities. You must load the Scheduler TSR for the program to work, but the installation program automatically plugs a statement into your AUTOEXEC.BAT file.

Windows Sound Only

Some sound cards are targeted at Windows users. Although these cards may not provide all the features you'd want in an MPC, they are affordable and allow you to add voice notes to Windows files and, in some cases, play computer games that require sound.

Windows Sound System

Microsoft Windows Sound System provides Windows sound power at a middle-of-the-road price (see fig. 4.18). It records and plays Windows waveform (WAV) files and plays MIDI sound files. Although not meant for DOS programs, Windows Sound System is Ad Lib-compatible for your computer games.

This $289 short expansion card features an Analog Devices SoundPort chip for waveform audio and a Yamaha OPL3 synthesizer for MIDI music. The SoundPort codec (coder-decoder), which is also used in Compaq's Business Audio-equipped PCs, provides 16-bit, 44.1 KHz (CD-quality) sound.

Many people prefer its sound quality to that of other sound cards. The OPL3 FM synthesizer, found on many popular sound cards, produces stereo music suitable for multimedia presentations and educational use.

Figure 4.18:
Windows Sound System treats "business audio" as serious business.

Windows Sound System includes an inexpensive headphone and a clip-on microphone. It features five jacks: ⅛-inch minijack plugs for microphone in, line in, and headphones out. And whereas most competitors have a single ⅛-inch jack for attaching to speakers, Microsoft Sound System has two RCA output jacks, making it easier to connect external speakers or an amplifier.

The card provides 2 watts of power per channel, which is adequate for headphones or small speakers. For full-room audio, consider amplified speakers or hook the card to your stereo system. Because the sound card omits the typically useless volume control, all audio levels are controlled through recording and volume-control software.

Microsoft includes a suite of attractive software utilities. The SoundFinder productivity application locates, plays, and attaches icons and descriptions to sound files from several sources, including sound files from Apple (AIF), Creative Labs (VOC), and NeXT (SND) systems.

A new Sound *applet* (too wimpy to be called an application) for the Control Panel assigns sounds to more system events, such as expanding or closing windows. An appealing screen blanker plays selectable libraries of sounds ranging from soothing wind chimes to the ambulance sirens of a metropolis at night.

Sound Check

Despite the actual bells and whistles, Microsoft wants Windows Sound System to be known for its voice abilities. For voice notes (or general recording), the Quick Recorder easily captures and edits recorded audio. The recording rate spans from compressed 4-bit 11-KHz monaural sampling for space-conserving voice annotations to 16-bit 44-KHz stereo sampling for high-fidelity sound.

After recording, you can splice out unwanted sections or splice in additional sound. You then can save the results in Windows WAV files or transplant them into OLE-conforming files like Excel or e-mail messages.

Windows Sound System includes speech-recognition software. Using technology developed by Dragon Systems, Inc., the Windows Sound System includes Voice Pilot, which provides voice command/control of the system and related software applications. The system responds to vocal commands like "Next window" or "Cut" and comes with templates for 15 popular applications.

Unfortunately, the success rate of voice recognition is subpar. Users have experienced accuracy of 20 to 50 percent, even after "training" the system. Commands, such as "next," "minimize," or "previous window," are recognized, but failure to recognize other commands may keep you from throwing away your mouse just yet.

The ProofReader utility reads back either Excel or Lotus 1-2-3 for Windows spreadsheet numbers to guarantee accuracy.

ProofReader's customizable vocabulary covers mainly numeric terms and the popular financial, measurement, and spreadsheet terms. The pronunciation and speaking rate are widely adjustable.

Sound Check

Although Microsoft Corp. is a member of the MPC Marketing Council, Sound System does not meet the MPC specifications; it is missing an audio input for CD-ROM drives and a joystick/MIDI connector. Don't expect to play games with this card either; Windows Sound System is not Sound Blaster-compatible, but can be used with games that support the Ad Lib standard.

If your sound needs are business-oriented, neither of these limitations is important. If full multimedia or DOS sound features are important to you, look elsewhere. This is a Windows-based, business audio tool. It doesn't play games but instead rolls up its sleeves and gets down to work.

AudioMan

AudioMan (see fig. 4.19) is Logitech International's flagship product for its "Senseware" product line, designed to give human-like senses, such as sight, sound, and touch, to your computer. Already a large manufacturer of computer mice and hand-held scanners, Logitech will probably become a big player in the sound marketplace.

AudioMan was designed to provide hassle-free addition of voice notes to Windows files. It doesn't do much else; it doesn't provide Sound Blaster-compatible sound to games and cannot work with MIDI devices. The $179 device connects to a standard parallel port but still allows you to print normally. The shaver-shaped device is powered by either two included AA batteries or an AC adapter. An audio output jack handles

headphones, external speakers, or other devices, and an input jack attaches to a CD player or other device. For adding simple voice notes to business documents, AudioMan offers a simple, inexpensive solution.

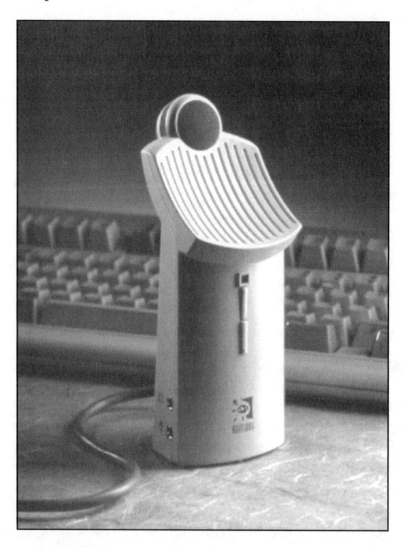

Figure 4.19:
Logitech's AudioMan provides plug-and-play sound for Windows.

Listen Up!

Installing AudioMan is simple; just connect it
to your parallel port. The companion software
requires less than a half-megabyte of disk
space and is installed through either the
Windows Control Panel or Program Manager.
Even if you already have a sound card, you can
install AudioMan. To use AudioMan, open the
AudioMan dialog box from the Control Panel. From
there, you can set the volume or check the charge in
your AA batteries. (You can also use a manual volume
control on AudioMan itself.)

AudioMan's microphone sits on top of its 2-inch concave
speaker. AudioMan records in 8-bit sample rates (mono) at
11 KHz and plays back in 8-bit sample rates at 22 KHz. By
comparison, Microsoft Windows Sound System is capable of
16-bit (stereo) sample sizes at 44.1 KHz. However, Microsoft
Sound System costs over $100 more.

High and Mighty Sounds

Cream-of-the-crop sound cards are primarily used for multimedia and MIDI sound. Their prices range from $400 to $1,000.
Although other sound cards may match their 16-bit, 44.1-KHz
sampled sound, high-end sound cards go beyond CD-quality
sound. They may, for example, provide harmonic distortion
that is one-tenth or less than that of middle-of-the-road sound
cards. Another feature found in such sound cards is the embedding of actual musical instrument sounds in the sound card's
memory chips. When the sound card requires a trombone or
flute in a song, the actual sounds are available. Lesser sound
cards imitate musical instruments through FM synthesis. For
the demanding musician or sound-card maniac, the price is
well worth the performance.

Chapter 4

MultiSound

Turtle Beach Systems' MultiSound digital audio board has been considered the top sound dog among sound cards (see fig 4.20). At $599, it better be. If your multimedia requirements call for high-end audio performance and an extensive selection of top-quality musical instruments onboard, one need look no further than MultiSound.

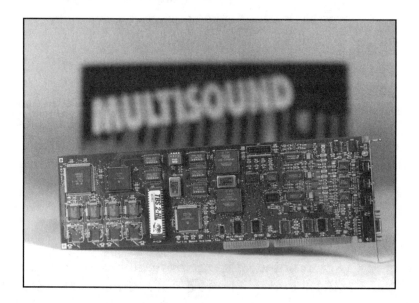

Figure 4.20:
Turtle Beach's MultiSound card gets top honors for sound quality. . .
at a price.

MultiSound has over 8M of sampled instruments and wave-forms stored onboard for virtually instant recall. However, this card doesn't provide Sound Blaster compatibility. Multi-Sound's forte is adding clean, distortion-free music to roll-your-own multimedia presentations.

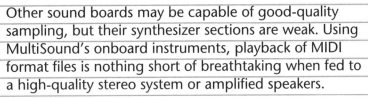

Sound Check

Other sound boards may be capable of good-quality sampling, but their synthesizer sections are weak. Using MultiSound's onboard instruments, playback of MIDI format files is nothing short of breathtaking when fed to a high-quality stereo system or amplified speakers.

MultiSound produces professional-quality digital audio and synthesized music. The board has 16-bit resolution and 44.1-KHz sampling. MultiSound uses an E-mu Proteus chip that produces excellent acoustic instrument sounds and can produce up to 32 voices at the same time. MultiSound has fewer options than other MPC-compatible boards. The only available add-ons are software. Users can hook up a MIDI cable, but the Proteus chip is incompatible with other standards. This short-coming is minor since MultiSound produces professional-quality sound. MultiSound also offers stereo input and output jacks and a knob to control recording level.

The Future: To Be Heard and Not Seen

The sound revolution witnessed in the last year has many participants. This number will only increase. Many of the major players, such as Media Vision, are licensing their technology to other companies who in turn manufacturer sound cards. Because many sound cards use the same sound chips and sound utilities, there's a danger of products having that "me-too" look. As with other computer technologies, sound cards will become a commodity item. You will be able to eventually get very good sound cards for under $200 and eventually under $100.

When selecting a sound card, balance your wallet and your needs. For example, if you aren't musically inclined, you may want to get a sound card that doesn't sport a MIDI interface.

Chapter 4

Conversely, if you want MIDI but not sound for your computer games, consider MultiSound. Table 4.1 may help you make that first purchase.

The following products are indicative of the changes in the marketplace. Each has either been pulled from the market and will be introduced as new and improved or the product will be remarketed by another company.

ThunderBOARD and ThunderBOARD for Windows

Sound-card giant Media Vision competes in the low-end portion of the PC sound market with its $169 ThunderBOARD for Windows (see fig. 4.21). ThunderBOARD (see fig. 4.22) is a lesser version of its Pro AudioSpectrum sound card. At the time of this writing, ThunderBOARD had been pulled from the market. The product will be marketed by a yet unnamed Taiwanese firm that can manufacture the product for less than Media Vision.

ThunderBOARD provides 11-voice mono playback by using a single 8-bit Yamaha digital-to-analog converter (DAC). It includes a microphone jack, volume control, joystick port, and stereo out jacks. ThunderBOARD is versatile; it is compatible with Ad Lib and Sound Blaster audio drivers. It can record and play back sounds up to 22 KHz. For improving game sounds for a low price, ThunderBOARD is a good bet.

Audioport

The $199 Audioport from Media Vision gave laptop computers plug-and-play mono sound (see fig. 4.23). However, Media Vision pulled the plug on this product although it is considering reintroducing it. Audioport plugs into your computer's

parallel port. The size of a hand-held calculator, this device runs on either four AA penlight batteries or an AC adapter (included).

Figure 4.21:
ThunderBOARD for Windows provides good sound to most games.

Audioport supports both digitized sound (WAV) and MIDI files. It has a volume control and an internal speaker. Its output power is only ¼ of a watt, but can be heard even with the volume turned down. For privacy, a headphone jack can be used to drive self-powered speakers. A microphone jack is included (but not a microphone) so that you can make your own recordings. Audioport also supports MIDI.

Figure 4.22:
ThunderBOARD will be marketed by a yet unnamed Taiwanese firm.

Audioport is not the most amazing product. It records in mono at a resolution of 8 bits and a sampling rate of 22 KHz. Other similar cards are providing 16-bit resolution at 44.1 KHz. Perhaps this is why the product was pulled from the market.

Figure 4.23:
Audioport provided sound for laptop owners.

Port Blaster

Creative Labs, maker of Sound Blaster, briefly introduced Port Blaster for on-the-road notebook presentations. The Windows 3.1-compatible device attaches to a laptop's parallel port to provide sound capabilities. It features 8-bit voice sampling and stereo playback. It uses a 20-voice FM synthesizer and a stereo mixer for audio sources, and includes a built-in power amp and speaker. A MIDI interface is also included. Port Blaster retailed for $199. Creative Labs hopes to re-release the product soon.

These are only a few of the fast-moving changes in the sound-card industry. Some products are renamed or repackaged with different and more software games and utilities. Others, like a sonic boom, are here today and gone today.

Table 4.1
Sound Cards at a Glance

Model	Stereo/Mono (S/M)	Maximum Bits, Recording	Maximum Bits, Playback	MIDI Capable	CD-ROM Capable	Sound Blaster Compatible	Ad Lib Compatible	Retail Price
Inexpensive Sound Cards								
Sound Source	M	na	8	N	N	N	N	$49.95
Speech Thing	M	na	8	N	N	N	N	$99.95
Sound Blaster Deluxe	M	8	8	Y	N	Y	Y	$129.95
Stereo F/X	S	8	8	Y	N	Y	Y	$129
ThunderBOARD/ ThunderBOARD for Windows	M	8	8	Y	N	Y	Y	$169
Portable Sound								
Port Blaster	S	8	8	Y	N	Y	Y	$199
Port-Able Sound Plus	S	16	16	N	N	Y	Y	$198.95
SoundXchange Model A and B	M	8	8	N	N	N	N	$149 $289
Stereo Sound Cards								
Sound Blaster Pro Deluxe	S	8	8	Y	Y	Y	Y	$199.95
Sound Blaster 16 ASP	S	16	16	Y	Y	Y	Y	$349.95
Pro Audio Spectrum 16	S	16	16	Y	Y	Y	Y	$299.00
Pro Audio-Studio 16	S	16	16	Y	Y	Y	Y	$349.00
SoundMan 16	S	16	16	Y	N	Y	Y	$289
Sound Producer Pro	S	8	8	N	Y	Y	Y	$199

Model	Stereo/Mono (S/M)	Maximum Bits, Recording	Maximum Bits, Playback	MIDI Capable	CD-ROM Capable	Sound Blaster Compatible	Ad Lib Compatible	Retail Price
Stereo Sound Cards								
SOUNDstudio	S	12	12	Y	Y	N	Y	$259
ViVa Maestro Pro	S	8	8	Y	Y	Y	Y	$229
ViVa Maestro 16 and ViVa Maestro 16VR	S	12	16	Y	Y	Y	Y	$349/$429
UltraSound	S	8	16	Y	Y	Y	Y	$199.95
UltraSound 3D	S	8	16	Y	Y	Y	Y	$249.95
Multipurpose Sound Cards								
SOUNDVision	S	12	12	Y	Y	N	Y	$399
VGA-Stereo F/X	S	8	8	Y	N	Y	Y	$279
Orchid Fahrenheit VA	S	8	8	N	Y	Y	Y	$299
Thunder & Lightning	M	8	8	Y	N	Y	Y	$349
TyIn 2000	M	8	8	N	N	N	N	$279
Windows-Only Sound Cards								
Windows Sound System	S	16	16	N	N	Y	N	$289
AudioMan	M	8	8	N	N	N	N	$179
High-End Sound Cards								
MultiSound	S	16	16	Y	N	N	N	$599

Options Are Extra

Buying a sound card is often not an end in itself. Other accessories will be purchased that unsuspectingly raise the cost of your PC sound system. At the very least, you'll have to invest in a set of speakers or headphones. At most, you may want to purchase a MIDI synthesizer keyboard.

In this chapter, you learn:

- ♪ How to select a set of speakers or headphones
- ♪ How to choose a CD-ROM drive
- ♪ How to choose a microphone
- ♪ How to choose a joystick
- ♪ About the accessories needed to make MIDI musical scores

Listen Up!

The rule of thumb is to buy equipment and accessories that match the quality of your sound card. If, for example, you have a true-blue 16-bit sound card, invest in quality equipment. Your primary criteria should be: *How much money am I willing to pay for this quality?*

Quality Speakers, Quality Sound

Successful business presentations, multimedia applications, and MIDI work demand external high-fidelity stereo speakers. Although you can use standard stereo speakers, consider these obstacles. Stereo speakers are normally too big to fit on or near your desk. A smaller bookshelf speaker would be better. Also, sound cards offer little or no power to drive external speakers. Some cards have small 4-watt amplifiers, not enough to drive quality speakers. Finally, speakers sitting near your display may create magnetic interference, which can distort colors and objects on-screen or jumble the data recorded on your disks nearby.

Listen Up!

Speakers are often an overlooked expense. My first sound card was a $97 ThunderBOARD from Media Vision. I thought the $100 investment would let me sample the sound-card waters without spending too much. Once I received my order, I purchased a pair of bookshelf speakers. To my surprise, I had to invest another $150 for a good pair of Sony speakers.

To solve these problems, computer speakers need to be small, efficient, and self-powered. Also, magnetic shielding needs to be used, either in the form of added layers of insulation in the

speaker cabinet or by electronically canceling out the magnetic distortion.

Listen Up!

Although most computer speakers are magnetically shielded, do not leave recorded tapes, watches, personal credit cards, or floppy disks in front of speakers for long periods of time.

Quality sound depends on quality speakers. A 16-bit sound card may provide better sound to computer speakers, but even an 8-bit sound card sounds great when piped through a good speaker. Conversely, using an inexpensive speaker makes both 8-bit and 16-bit sound cards sound tinny.

Sound Check

Ultimately, choosing the right speakers is a highly subjective affair; the engineering specifications for speakers are dubious and often misleading. The best way to buy a computer speaker is to "audition" them before you buy them.

Picking the Right Speaker

Dozens of speaker models are on the market, ranging from less expensive minispeakers from Sony and Koss to larger self-powered models from companies such as Bose. To evaluate speakers, you need to know the lingo. Speakers are measured by three criteria:

♪ **Frequency response.** Frequency response is a measurement of the range of high and low sounds a speaker can reproduce. The ideal range is from 20 Hz to 20 KHz, the

Chapter 5

range of human hearing. No speaker system reproduces this range perfectly. In fact, few people hear sounds above 18 KHz. An exceptional speaker may cover 30 Hz to 23 KHz. Lesser models may only cover 100 Hz to 20 KHz. Frequency response is the most deceptive specification because identically rated speakers can sound completely different.

♪ **Total Harmonic Distortion (THD).** THD, or just distortion, is an expression of the amount of distortion or noise created by amplifying the signal. Simply put, distortion is the difference between the sound that was sent to the speaker and the sound that we hear. The amount of distortion is measured in percentages. An acceptable level of distortion is that below .1 percent (one-tenth of one percent). For some CD-quality recording equipment, a common standard is .05 percent. Some speakers have a distortion of 10 percent or more. Headphones often have a distortion of about 2 percent or less.

♪ **Watts.** Usually stated as watts per channel, this is the amount of amplification available to drive the speakers. Check that the company means "per channel" (or RMS) and not total power. Many sound cards have built-in amplifiers, providing up to 8 watts per channel. (Most provide 4 watts.) However, the wattage is not enough to provide rich sound. This is why many speakers have built-in amplifiers. With the flick of a switch or the press of a button, these speakers amplify the signals they receive from the sound card. If you do not want to amplify the sound, you typically leave the speaker switch at its "direct" setting. In most cases, you'll want to amplify the signal.

To power computer speakers, two or four C batteries are used. Because these speakers require so much power, you may want to invest in an AC adapter, although more-expensive speakers include one. An AC adapter will prevent you from buying new batteries every few weeks. If yours didn't come with an AC adapter, you can pick one up from your local Radio Shack or hardware store.

You can control your speakers in various ways, depending on their complexity and cost. Typically, each speaker has a volume knob, although some share one volume control. If one speaker is further away than the other, you may want to adjust the volume accordingly. Many computer speakers include a *dynamic bass boost* (DBB) switch. This button provides a more powerful bass and clearer treble, regardless of the volume setting. Others have separate bass and treble boost switches or a three-band equalizer to control low, middle, and high frequencies.

Listen Up!

When you rely on your sound card's power and not your speaker's built-in amplifier, the volume and dynamic bass boost controls do not have an effect. Your speakers are at the mercy of the sound card's power.

Connecting Your Speakers

To connect to your sound card, an ⅛-inch stereo miniplug is connected from the sound-card output jack to one of the speakers. The signal is then split and fed from the first speaker to the remaining one through a separate cable, as shown in figure 5.1.

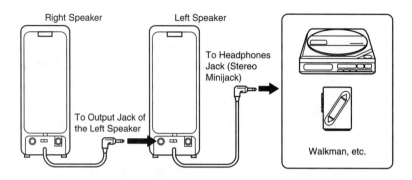

Figure 5.1:
The sound card's signal is split between the two speakers.

Before purchasing a set of speakers, check that the cables between the speakers are long enough for your computer setup. For example, my computer is in a mid-tower case and sits alongside my desk. Of the speakers I tested, only a couple had ample cable length to reach my desk where the speakers sat side by side.

Listen Up!

Beware of speakers that have a tardy built-in "sleep" feature. When such speakers are not in use, they turn themselves off to save electricity. My former pair of speakers had an annoying habit of clipping the first part of a sound after a period of inactivity. Upon starting a game, for example, the first half-second of sound may be lost.

Speaker Choices

Computer speakers and headphones come in a variety of prices. Obviously, the more expensive ones provide better sound. The models discussed next are arranged from highest to lowest price.

Listen Up!

Avoid buying a pair of speakers that costs less than $40 per pair. The quality just isn't there. Instead, you may want to invest in a comfortable set of headphones that provides the same quality as a pair of quality speakers.

ACS300

If you want the very best in computer speakers and can afford them, consider the three-part ACS300 from Altec Lansing Consumer Products.

The $400 ACS300 features two clamshell satellite speakers that provide the midrange and treble part of the sound. A lunch-box size subwoofer delivers the bass. By adjusting the open angle of the clamshells, you can position the speakers precisely, so that none of the sound is muffled on the desktop. You close the clamshells when not using them.

The small size of the satellite speakers ($3 \frac{1}{2} \times 5 \times 7$ inches) allows them to be mounted on a wall or placed beside your monitor or on your desk. Each satellite has a 4-inch woofer and a half-inch dome tweeter. The accompanying subwoofer picks up where the satellite drops off, reproducing bass notes below 120 Hz. The subwoofer, although not magnetically shielded, can be hidden under a desk.

Altec includes a variety of controls, including controls for volume, treble, bass, balance, and *digital signal processing* (DSP) enhancement. The DSP control adjusts the sound to increase the sense of stereo separation. Controls are also provided for mixing and balance; the AB mixing control allows you to preview and set the two sound sources for the best possible combination.

Chapter 5

The ACS300 has a 9-watt-per-channel amplifier and a rated frequency response of 35 Hz to 20 KHz (+ or - 3 decibels), with total harmonic distortion (THD) less than 0.8 percent.

Sound Check

Altec Lansing also offers the ACS200, which lacks the separate subwoofer and retails for $300.

Bose Roommate Computer Monitor

The Bose name has always connotated sound quality. Bose Corp. now offers its $339 Bose Roommate Computer Monitors (see fig. 5.2). Housed in tough 6 x 9 x 6 inch (HWD) molded styrene cabinets, this pair of speakers combines woofer, midrange, and tweeter in the same unit. However, the size makes the speakers a bit clumsy for your desktop. The rugged design makes them ideal for the traveling presenter.

Controls are simple on the Bose Roommate. One volume knob adjusts the level of both speakers; most other adjustments are made automatically, including dynamic equalization to ensure the proper proportion of high and low frequencies at loud and quiet volumes.

Sound Check

Because of doubts about the accuracy of other manufacturers' rated specifications and the questionable value of such specifications, Bose does not provide specifications for their products.

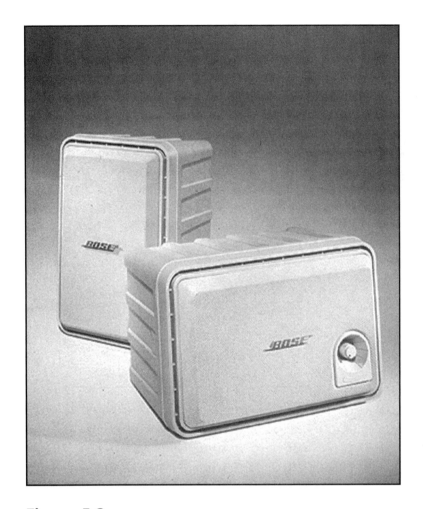

Figure 5.2:
The Bose Roommate Computer Monitor.

Roland MA-12C Micro Monitor

For serious MIDI users and musicians, consider buying the
Roland MA-12C Micro Monitors (see fig. 5.3). These $290
speakers are adaptable and very rugged. Each speaker has
three full-size RCA jack inputs located on the back: a line input

(to be used for a CD player or an audio card), a microphone input, and an instrument hookup—perfect for MIDI users.

Figure 5.3:
Roland's MA-12C Micro Monitor.

Although these speakers lack a headphone jack, Roland is one of the few companies to offer an on/off power button on each speaker.

At 8 ½ x 5 x 6 ¼ inches (HWD), the Roland speakers may be a little large for typical desktops, but the thick plastic speaker cabinets and heavy-duty power cords make them ready for the road. Each speaker has a single driver and an independent 10-watt power amplifier with individual controls for volume, bass, and treble.

Sound Check

Like Bose Corp., Roland doesn't provide ratings for the speakers' frequency response or total harmonic distortion.

Persona PC

Persona PC speakers from Persona Technologies are the best size for computer desks. They measure 9 x 4 x 5 inches (HWD), sitting inconspicuously on your desk or attached, like ears, to the sides of your monitor (see fig. 5.4).

The $230 Persona PCs are three-way speakers. Each contains a 3-inch woofer, a 2-inch midrange driver, and a piezo ribbon tweeter. Persona Technologies rates the speakers' amplifier at 10 watts per channel with 0.5 percent total harmonic distortion.

Each speaker has controls for volume, stereo separation, and bass. The back of each speaker features a jack for a pair of headphones. When you plug in the headphones, the speakers are automatically muted, and you can still adjust the volume with the volume control.

The frequency response of the Persona PCs is rated at 75 Hz to 18 KHz (+ or - 3 decibels). Although this is short of the 20 Hz to 20 KHz audible range of frequencies, virtually no speaker system covers the entire range.

Listen Up!

For better bass response, you can buy the Persona Sub Woofer. This $200 component is equipped with a 25-watt amplifier and covers the bass range from 40 to 150 Hz.

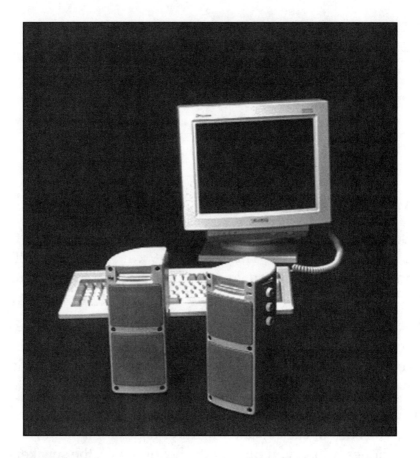

Figure 5.4:
The Persona PC speakers.

Koss HD/6

The Koss HD/6 speakers (see fig. 5.5) provide larger speakers for demanding sound. This model is the largest of the Koss Hard Drivers family of computer speakers. Each HD/6 speaker stands 8 ½ x 4 x 5 inches, powered by a 4-inch dynamic driver. Like all speakers reviewed here, a separate switch can turn off the built-in amplifier, relying on the power of the sound card.

Figure 5.5:
Koss HD/6 speakers.

The frequency response of the HD/6 is 50 Hz to 20 KHz. A *dynamic bass boost* (DBB) switch refines bass and treble, and separate volume controls can mix volume. The HD/6 provides 5 watts of power.

Koss HD/4

The Koss HD/4 speakers (see fig. 5.6) provide a good balance of value and features. The $59.99 mid-size speakers (7 x 4 x 3 ½ inches) include a three-band equalizer. Only one volume control is provided, which only matters when the speakers are not equidistant from the listener.

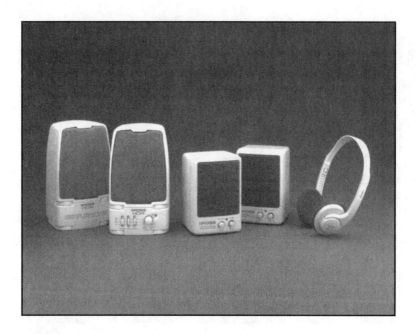

Figure 5.6:

Koss offers a family of affordable PC speakers.

The frequency response of the HD/4 is 50 Hz to 20 KHz. This provides beefy sound on a beer budget. The HD/4 provides 7.2 watts of power.

Koss HD/1

The $39.99 HD/1 speakers from Koss provide the smallest footprint of the Koss speakers (5 x 3 ½ x 3 ½ inches). Each speaker has its own volume control, and separate bass and treble boost switches are included. The Hard Drivers have a frequency response of 50 Hz to 20 KHz. Like the HD/4, the HD/1 speakers provide 7.2 watts of power.

Make Your Selection

Table 5.1 provides some of the specifications on these speakers. This table should not be your only guide to picking a computer speaker. Such other facets as the actual speaker size or harmonic distortion should be considered. Your first criteria should be price, followed by space required for your computer setup.

Table 5.1:
A Comparison of Computer Speakers

Product	Dimensions HxWxD (in.)	Space required (cubic in.)	Headphone jack	Frequency response (Hz)	Watts	Price
ACS300	3.5x5x7	123	Y	35-20,000	9	$400
Bose Roommate Computer Monitor	6x9x6	324	Y	na	na	$339
Roland MA-12C Micro Monitor	8.5x5x6.25	266	N	na	10	$290
Persona PC	9x4x5	180	Y	75-18,000	10	$230
Koss HD/6	8.5x4x5	170	N	50-20,000	5	$99.99
Koss HD/4	7x4x3.5	98	N	50-20,000	7.2	$59.99
Koss HD/1	5x3.5x3.5	61	N	50-20,000	7.2	$39.99

*na—not available

Listen Up!

If you were to shop by specifications alone using this table, you may easily overlook a better-sounding speaker. A speaker's internal quality is not always revealed by specifications but by your ear.

Heady Headphones

Headphones are an option when you can't afford a premium set of speakers. Headphones provide privacy while allowing you to crank up the volume on your sound card. Although dozens are available, one pair of headphones is highlighted next.

Koss HD/2

The Koss HD/2 headphones (see fig. 5.7) provide professional quality sound in a comfortable headset. The HD/2 headphones have a frequency response of 20 Hz to 20 KHz with a distortion of less than .3 percent.

The HD/2 headphones have foam ear cushions, pivoting ear cups, and a covered, adjustable headband to assure the best fit, flexibility, and comfort. Its cord provides ample length to reach floor- or desktop-mounted computers.

Koss Game Phone

For sound-card quality that's affordable, Koss Corp. has introduced the Game Phone, a lightweight headphone designed to bring stereo sound to portable video game and computer systems. The Game Phone also can be used with any portable stereo, cassette, or CD player.

Figure 5.7:
The Koss HD/2 headphones are an alternative to speakers.

At 1.5 ounces, the Game Phone has a frequency response of 20 Hz to 20 KHz. With a distortion level of 1.5 percent, the Game Phone yields adequate but not impressive sound. It costs only $9.95.

Seeking CD-ROM

If you want to enjoy multimedia with your sound card, you'll have to consider a CD-ROM drive.

A CD-ROM drive allows you to access hundreds of megabytes (up to 680M, to be exact) of pictures, text, and sound on a single 4 ¾-inch disc. Popping a CD-ROM disc into the drive is the equivalent of piling 300,000 pages of information onto your bookshelves. All the information of an encyclopedia set, for example, can be stored on a single shiny disc.

Listen Up!

Don't expect a CD-ROM drive to be fast, however. By today's standards, CD-ROM drives are snails. The access time of a top-notch CD-ROM drive is comparable to a floppy drive's, or roughly 20 times slower than a modern hard disk.

Most CD-ROM drives are used by placing the silver disc into a CD-ROM caddy, which in turn slides into the drive. The caddy system isn't the quickest or most convenient, but offers an extra layer of protection against tainting the disc with dust or fingerprints. Some drives offer still another layer of protection, with double doors or automatic seals that keep dust from getting into the drive once a disc is loaded.

Sound Check

Other CD-ROM drives have adopted the caddyless technique used by audio CD players; you simply hold the disc by its edges and place it directly on the drive.

MPC Standards

The new Multimedia PC specifications set up by the MPC Marketing Council require a multimedia-compatible CD-ROM drive to be capable of sustaining a data transfer rate of 300 Kbps. The 300 Kbps minimum allows smoother animation than possible with slower drives.

Like a hard disk, a CD-ROM drive is measured by two criteria: average access speed and data transfer rate. The *average access*

speed is how long it takes the CD-ROM drive to find the information you requested. This speed is measured in milliseconds (ms), or thousandths of a second. The *data transfer rate* indicates how fast the found information can be sent to your PC. This rate is measured in kilobytes transferred per second (Kbps).

Most drives' access times hover between 300 ms and 675 ms. Some inexpensive or portable drives, however, may have access times as sluggish as 800 ms or more. Your CD player should have an average access time of at most 300 ms (the lower the number, the better). The MPC Level 2 specs call for a drive with a seek time less than 400 ms.

To get more speed, companies use various techniques. Some drives include a built-in buffer of 8K to 64K to perk up performance. The MPC Marketing Council recommends that drives have a 64K buffer.

Make sure the CD-ROM drive you buy meets the MPC (Multimedia PC) Level 2 specifications for performance. The MPC recipe has changed since its debut. The MPC now requires a drive capable of sustaining a data transfer rate of 300 Kbps. When operating at 150 Kbps, the drive should claim no more than 40 percent of main CPU usage.

The 300-Kbps minimum ensures a steady flow of data into the drive's buffer, providing relatively smooth animation instead of jerky screen stutters. For multimedia work, this throughput speed is more important than a drive's access time.

To get 300 Kbps, many drives use double-speed technology, which doubles the speed of the drive when reading certain kinds of information from the disc. NEC Corp. calls its version of double-speed MultiSpin. MultiSpin NEC drives whisk along at 300 Kbps for text or graphics, but slow to 150 Kbps so that music and speech sound normal. MultiSpin technology is used in the highly rated NEC CDR-74 drive.

SCSI or Exclusive?

Most CD-ROM drives rely on *Small Computer Systems Interface* (SCSI) adapter cards to work with your PC. Others use proprietary, or exclusive, interfaces; you can only use certain CD-ROM drives with that interface card. Many sound cards provide either a proprietary or SCSI connector for a CD-ROM drive. The Stereo F/X-CD card from ATI Technologies, for example, only works with Mitsumi drives. Similarly, the Sound Blaster Pro works only with Panasonic drives. Other sound cards, such as Pro AudioSpectrum 16, provide SCSI interfaces to accommodate a wider range of drives.

If you use a SCSI drive with your sound card, you can connect up to seven SCSI devices—and not just CD-ROM drives. This is called *daisychaining*. One SCSI controller, for example, lets you connect up to seven hard disks, tape drives, CD-ROM drives, or printers. In other words, you can add up to seven SCSI devices to your computer while using only one expansion slot for the one SCSI controller. With SCSI, you have to worry about such issues as drive ID and termination for each device. You may hear or read horror stories of people who have struggled to get this daisychaining to work, spending hours sorting through the options to get multiple peripherals to cohabitate on a single connection. This task may be easier if you buy a complete SCSI drive kit from a reputable dealer.

In or Out?

Should your CD-ROM drive be an internal or external model? It depends on you. Like modems, CD-ROM drives work the same whether located inside or outside your PC. An external CD-ROM requires an outlet plug and can be shared between several computers. Unlike modems, internal and external

CD-ROM drives usually require an expansion slot, obliging you to crack open your PC's case and install an interface card.

The exceptions are drives that plug into parallel-port adapters, such as Trantor Systems' popular Mini-SCSI Plus parallel-to-SCSI adapter. This Walkman-style approach is the only way to use a CD-ROM with a laptop or notebook PC, though it may not prove up to multimedia performance standards; CD-ROM drives plugged in your parallel port are not as fast as those directly attached to the inside of your computer.

Listen Up!

For an internal drive, you'll need an empty 5 ¼-inch drive bay in which to mount the drive. For an external drive, make sure the adapter cable that connects the drive and interface board is long enough; a few models cheat you with 18-inch or shorter cables that may hardly stretch from the rear to the side of your PC.

X Marks the Spot

Most CD-ROM drives work the same way. They are compatible with the industry-wide CD-ROM data storage format known also as High Sierra (after the Nevada hotel where the standards committee met in 1983) and ISO 9660. Given the proper connector and software, the drive will work equally well with a PC and play practically any CD-ROM disc.

What about tomorrow's CD-ROM standards. After finding a drive that is MPC-compatible, you may want to consider a drive that supports the CD-ROM XA format.

XA stands for *Extended Architecture*, a specification created by Sony, Philips, and Microsoft that governs audio compression

and allows interleaving, or mixing, of audio and computer data. Not many discs take advantage of XA yet, but those that do will be closer to true multimedia than their predecessors. IBM Corp. has been an early backer of CD-ROM XA, supporting the specification as part of its Ultimedia product line. Other drive makers have either recently released XA-ready drives or announced XA upgrade strategies.

Sound Check

You may already be familiar with the CD-ROM XA format and not know it. Kodak's new Photo CD technology uses a CD-ROM XA drive. Photo CD lets you place photographic images on a CD-ROM. Under Photo CD, you can partially fill a disc with images and take it back to the Kodak lab a month later to add more photos. Some CD-ROM XA drives only support Photo CDs recorded in a single session. Other CD-ROM XA drives are multi-session, accepting discs that have been appended with additional photos or other information. The recent MPC Level 2 specifications require a drive to be CD-ROM XA ready and multisession capable.

Hear It All

A CD-ROM drive should include an audio connection to send sound in analog form from the CD-ROM drive to the sound card. Most CD-ROM drives include their own digital-to-analog conversion circuits, which turn a digital signal into CD-quality music. If you don't connect these two, your PC may have to handle the digital music alone. Although feasible, this simply gives your PC extra work that could otherwise be handled by the drive and sound card.

Another advantage of connecting a CD-ROM drive to your sound card is that you can mix sounds from several sources.

For example, I can record my voice to a Windows WAV file and have CD music playing in the background of the recording. This voice-over technique can be used for creating livelier presentations.

Audio Too!

For music lovers, a CD-ROM drive can also play CD audio discs. With few exceptions, nearly all drives come with a simple software utility to play audio CDs, and with audio ports or connectors so you can hear them—usually a headphone jack plus two RCA jacks for plugging in stereo speakers. Note that not all drives can send output to both the headphone and speaker jacks at the same time. And some high-end drives offer separate controls for left and right audio channels.

Listen Up!

If your CD-ROM drive provides a headphone jack and volume control knob, you can listen to CD audio discs without the sound card. I often plug in a headset to hear my favorite audio CD while doing other work.

Audio in a Kit

Multimedia upgrade kits are a convenient way to get a sound card, CD-ROM drive, cables, and software in one package. My first CD-ROM drive was part of a multimedia upgrade kit. Although computer literate, I didn't want to wrestle with getting a CD-ROM drive to work with the sound card. Nor did I want to find that I was missing a piece of software or an important cable that prevented the whole system from working.

Several sound-card manufacturers and mail-order companies offer multimedia upgrade kits. For example, Media Vision's $749 Fusion CD 16 is a collection of multimedia hardware and software that includes the 16-bit Pro AudioSpectrum 16 sound card and a 650-millisecond external SCSI NEC CD-ROM drive. A version with a Sony CD-ROM drive costs $699.

If you're looking for a plug-and-play multimedia sound solution, Media Vision also offers the $1,300 CDPC—a CD-ROM drive, a 16-bit sound card, a MIDI interface, an amplifier, and stereo speakers rolled into one peripheral. It's housed in a handsome art deco case and connects to your PC through an expansion card. It's a simple solution for the multimedia beginner who has a generous budget.

A multimedia upgrade kit may be targeted to just DOS users or Windows users. Media Vision also offers its Pro 16 Multimedia System, which is better suited for Windows. At $1,195, it includes a 16-bit sound card, a faster (280 ms access time) NEC drive, Macromind Action presentation software, Lotus 1-2-3 for Windows with Multimedia SmartHelp, and several Windows and DOS entertainment titles.

These suitcase-sized upgrade kits often include a few CD-ROM titles, such as Compton's "Family Encyclopedia with World Atlas," Broderbund's "Where in the World is Carmen Sandiego?," or Microprose's "Mantis."

Listen Up!

Bundles are a good idea: you can get valuable CD software titles, and everything is designed to work together. By buying everything together, the price is usually lower than buying components separately.

Be sure to evaluate the components in these kits one by one. Don't let anyone slip you a slow CD player by enticing you with good software.

Don't Forget Mr. Microphone

Most sound cards do not include a microphone. You'll need one to record your voice as a WAV file. Selecting a microphone is quite simple. You need one that has a ⅛-inch miniplug for plugging into your sound card's microphone, or audio in, jack. Most microphones have an on/off switch.

Like speakers, a microphone is measured by its frequency range. However, this buying factor is not important since the human voice has a limited range. If you are recording only voices, consider an inexpensive microphone that covers a lesser range of frequencies. An expensive microphone extends its recording capabilities to frequencies outside the voice's range. Why pay for something you won't need?

If you are recording music, invest in an expensive microphone, although an 8-bit sound card can record music as well with an inexpensive microphone as an expensive one.

Your biggest decision is selecting a microphone that suits your recording style. If working in a noisy office, you may want a unidirectional microphone that will prevent extraneous noises from being recorded. An omnidirectional mike would be best for recording a group conversation. If you want to keep your hands free, you may want to shun the traditional handheld microphone for a lapel model.

Sound Check

Some sound cards include a microphone. Media Vision Pro AudioStudio 16, for example, includes a small lapel microphone and a holster in which to place it. The Sound Blaster 16 ASP includes a handheld microphone.

Chapter 5

Joy of Joys

Many sound cards include a joystick, or game, port. (This joystick port often doubles as a connection to a MIDI device.) A joystick is ideally meant for game playing, such as simulating flying a Cessna aircraft (see fig. 5.8). Like a speaker, a joystick is best chosen through hands-on experience.

A joystick includes a fire button on top of a center wand you move in any of eight directions. A second button or pair of buttons are located on the base of the joystick.

Good joysticks have resistance that increases the further you move the center wand from dead center. A joystick is often measured by the life cycle of its buttons. For example, some fire buttons are rated at 10 million clicks. Other features to look for are calibration controls for both X and Y axes.

Some joysticks include suction cups that mount the unit to your desk. If short on desk space, you may prefer a smaller joystick that fits in your hand. If you are left-handed, look for an ambidextrous joystick, not one that is contoured for right-handers.

Some joysticks are especially meant for flight simulation games. ThrustMaster from ThrustMaster, Inc. provides additional buttons for firing and selecting missiles, turning radar on or off, and looking in different directions.

A Mate for Your MIDI

If you are interested in a MIDI to create synthesized music, you'll need to connect your keyboard or another MIDI device to your sound card. The joystick ports on sound cards have unused pins that can be used to send and receive MIDI data. By

connecting a MIDI interface cable to the joystick port, you can connect your PC to a MIDI device. This cable has three connectors: joystick connector, MIDI In connector, and MIDI Out.

Figure 5.8:
CH Products Flightstick is ideal for flying.

Media Vision sells an adapter box (see fig. 5.9) called MIDI Mate ($69.95) for adding Musical Instrument Digital Interface input, output, and throughput connectors to its boards.

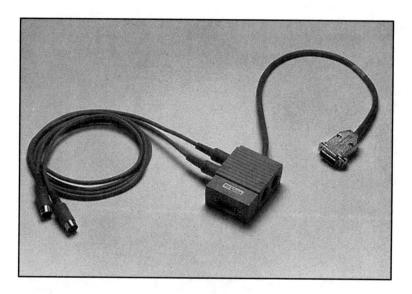

Figure 5.9:
MIDI Mate provides the connection to your MIDI keyboard.

Listen Up!

Since Logitech SoundMan 16 uses some of Media Vision's technology, it uses the same MIDI cable as the Pro AudioSpectrum cards.

Creative Labs offers the MIDI Kit for its Sound Blaster family of sound cards. This kit includes a Voyetra Technologies

sequencer program to record, edit, and play back your MIDI files and an interface cable to attach your sound card to the keyboard.

Synthetic Sound

If you are considering MIDI, you will also have to get a MIDI keyboard synthesizer. To make MIDI scores, you need sequencer software to record, edit, and play back MIDI files. (Some sound cards include sequencing software.) You also need a sound synthesizer, which is included in the sound card. A MIDI keyboard simplifies the creation of musical scores. A MIDI file contains up to 16 channels of music data, so you can record many different instruments and play them back. Using the keyboard, you can enter the notes for various instruments.

To enhance MIDI sounds for the Sound Blaster 16 ASP sound card, consider the $249.95 Wave Blaster from Creative Labs (see fig. 5.10). Wave Blaster attaches to the Sound Blaster ASP 16. When MIDI music is played, it looks to the Wave Blaster for any of 213 CD-quality digitally recorded musical instrument sounds. Without Wave Blaster, Sound Blaster 16 ASP would imitate these sounds through FM synthesis. Using Wave Blaster, music sounds like it's being played by real instruments.

Several MIDI keyboards are available, such as the Roland A-30 or PC-200 MK2 (see fig. 5.11). These keyboards may cost from $395 to over $7,000. Chapter 13 covers the MIDI and these keyboard synthesizers in more detail.

Arming your sound card with these extras allows you to smartly begin making the most of it. Although some of these options cost hundreds of dollars, adding them enhances your enjoyment of your sound-happy system.

Chapter 5

Figure 5.10:
Wave Blaster enhances MIDI sounds for Sound Blaster.

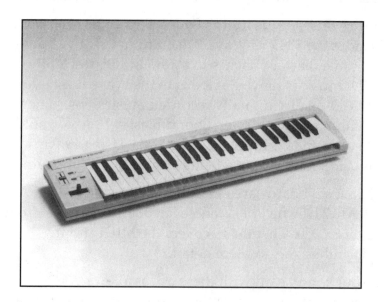

Figure 5.11:
The Roland PC-200 MK2 MIDI keyboard is one MIDI choice.

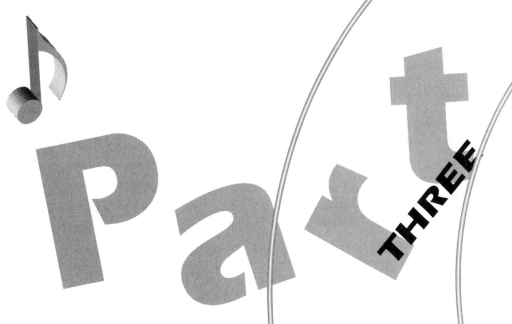

Part THREE

Installing a Sound Card

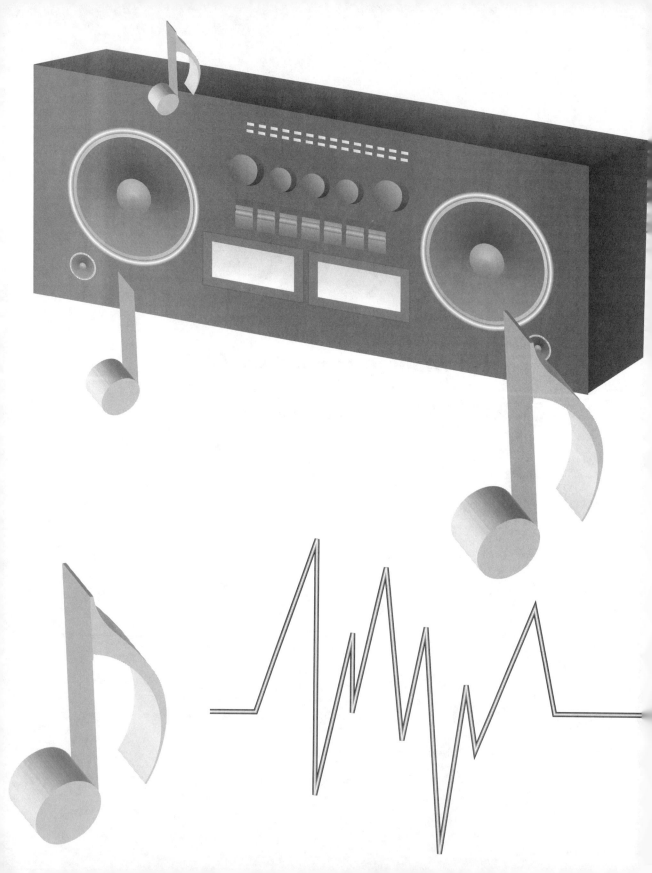

Presto Sound

6

Installing a sound card isn't brain surgery. It's no more difficult than installing an internal modem or a VGA card, but this step may be intimidating until you actually do it. If you are installing an *audio port*, a sound device that attaches to your parallel port, the process is even easier. Simple common sense, and this chapter, can make the process a breeze, not a hurricane.

In this chapter, you learn how to:

- ♪ Open up your computer
- ♪ Handle and insert your sound card
- ♪ Set jumpers and DIP switches
- ♪ Attach a CD-ROM drive

Chapter 6

Say "Aaahhh"

If you want to give your computer a voice, you're going to have to look down its throat. This involves removing the external metal case and adding your sound card. To install a sound card typically requires these steps:

1. Open your computer.

2. Configure your sound card.

3. Install the sound card and attach the CD-ROM drive, if present.

4. Close your computer.

5. Install the sound-card software.

6. Attach your speakers and other sound accessories.

Some manufacturers use an installation procedure different from this. Microsoft's Windows Sound System has you install some of the software first to determine how it can best work in your PC.

When people talk about their computers, they usually are referring to the system unit. The *system unit* is the box that holds your computer's "brain," memory, disk drives, expansion slots, and video card. In other words, it holds the very *guts* of your computer. In most cases, you'll need to crack open the system unit to add a sound card. Your system unit may be either a desktop model or a floor-standing (tower) model.

A Port of Call

The back of the system unit has several interesting features. Plugs for connecting your computer to the electrical outlet are, of course, in the back, as is an opening for the power supply's cooling fan to spew heated air. Notice a row of several narrow rectangular slots. These are called *expansion ports*, which allow you to attach your monitor to its matching video card or a phone line to your fax modem.

Behind each port is an *expansion slot*, a physical connector to your computer's motherboard. Any item that fits in an expansion slot is called an *expansion card* or *add-on card*, such as a VGA or sound card. Some expansion slots may already be filled. Otherwise, the unused expansion slots have metal covers over them.

To install a sound card, you'll need one basic tool: a medium-size Phillips screwdriver. (A pair of needle-nose pliers is convenient to have, but not necessary.) Avoid magnetic-tipped screwdrivers: the magnetic field may damage sensitive electronic components.

Listen Up!

You can get a variety of PC tools bundled in a "PC tool kit" that sells for about $30. I once received such a tool kit after subscribing to *PC World* magazine. If you're lazy like me, get a rechargeable electric screwdriver. Forget acquiring esoteric equipment, such as logic probes or soldering irons; you're a computer user, not a computer technician.

Cracking It Open

Never opened your PC before? Use the following procedure to open up your computer and get accustomed to seeing its "in-nards." Opening your computer is mandatory if you want to take advantage of your computer's capability to evolve and grow. A sound card is just one of many improvements you can do yourself.

To remove your computer's case follow these steps:

1. Turn off and unplug your computer from the electrical outlet.

Listen Up!

Before unplugging anything from the back of your computer, you may want to label each cable with some masking tape so you know to which port it should later be reconnected.

2. Unplug any remaining cables from your computer.

Listen Up!

Various cables are connected to your computer, such as those to the keyboard, modem, monitor, and more. *You may need to loosen a few screws that hold some cables in place.* Grab each cable at its base and pull straight back, not at an angle. If you pull cables at an angle, you can damage or bend the pins at the connection.

3. Gently move your computer to an area where you will have ample room to disassemble it.

   Carry the computer in an embrace. In other words, don't hold the computer at arms length; you could damage your back. Bend at the knees to let your legs do as much of the lifting as possible.

4. With a Phillips screwdriver, remove the screws that hold the case to your system unit.

   Normally, five or six screws secure the case to the rear of your PC (see fig. 6.1). (Actually, I'm down to two screws these days since I do a lot of testing of sound cards and other add-ons.) *Refer to your PC's manual for proper removal.* These screws are on the outside perimeter at the corners and middles. Any other screws are usually meant to hold internal components to the case. For example, four screws hold the power supply in place. Set aside the screws you remove so that they won't be lost.

5. Firmly grasp the computer case from both sides and gently slide it back or forward (depending on the type of computer you have).

On desktop computers, the case usually slides forward. The case also normally includes the *bezel*, the attractive front of your computer. On floor-standing computers, such as tower and mini-tower cases, the case is removed by sliding it backwards, leaving the bezel behind.

Chapter 6

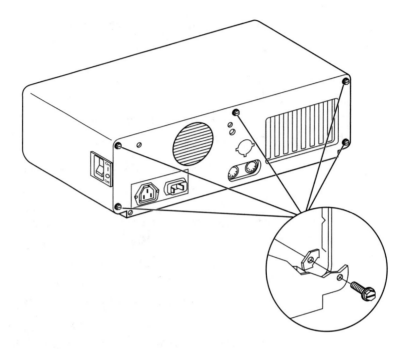

Figure 6.1:
Five or six screws typically free your case for removal.

Listen Up!

As you remove the case, be wary of any resistance; you might be snagging internal cables. Set aside the case where it won't be scratched or marred. Place the case flat on the floor so that it doesn't tip over.

Static Kills

Some of the electronic parts in your computer can be damaged by extremely small amounts of electricity. Before you touch anything inside your computer or the sound card you are installing, drain yourself of any built-up static electricity.

You can discharge static electricity by touching an unpainted, grounded metal object—that is, a metal object in contact with the ground. For example, you can touch the metallic inside of your computer case lying nearby. You also can touch any electrical appliance that has a metal case, such as a lamp or stereo system. You can also touch the computer frame itself. When working on the inside of your computer, ground yourself briefly every few minutes, such as touching your PC's metallic power-supply housing.

Listen Up!

One good way to ground yourself when adding a card is to touch the power supply box inside the computer.

You can reduce static electricity in several ways. Don't wear knit or wool sweaters, avoid fur or furry animals, don't walk on carpet, and don't touch rubber or plastic toys and balloons. Avoid any unnecessary moving around as you work. Avoid rubber-soled shoes—opt for leather. Ideally, removing your shoes and socks provides the best protection, but may be inconvenient or (gulp!) embarrassing.

Listen Up!

You can get extra antistatic protection by using a grounding wrist strap. A *ground strap* is an elastic wristband with a built-in metal plate. You wear the wristband, which you then attach by a wire to a grounded metal object, such as a power-supply case. With a ground strap, you are continually being drained of static electricity.

A Slot for Sound

After the cover is off your PC, notice its six to eight expansion slots. Some of these slots may already be filled by expansion cards. Others are vacant, waiting to be filled.

Expansion slots typically come in two sizes: 8- and 16-bit. An 8-bit slot has a single rectangular connector on the motherboard into which you plug an expansion card. This is called an *edge connector* because the edge of the expansion card is inserted in it. A 16-bit expansion slot uses two edge connectors (see fig. 6.2). Most computers have a mixture of 8- and 16-bit slots.

Sound Check

8-bit versus 16-bit? This is where confusion reigns. The same terms used to describe a type of expansion card also are used to describe the resolution of the sound. 8-bit sound allows a sound sample to be measured at any of 256 values. The higher-quality 16-bit sound card can record sounds at any of 65,536 values. The more accurate the measurement is, the more accurate the sounds are when played back. Some computer owners have been misled by thinking they purchased a 16-bit *resolution* sound card when they actually have purchased a lesser-quality 8-bit sound card that fits into a 16-bit slot.

Customizing Your Card

Usually, you do not have to configure a sound card to work with your PC. This task is often tackled by the sound card's installation software. Sometimes, you have to "tweak" a couple of items before you install your sound card. The following items can be configured on the sound card:

♪ Jumpers

♪ *Dual In-line Package* (DIP) switches

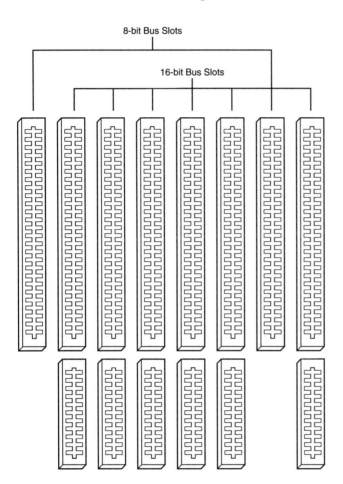

Figure 6.2:
A 16-bit versus 8-bit connector.

Jumpers

Jumpers, or shunts, are commonly used to configure an expansion card (see fig. 6.3). A *jumper* is simply a short piece of wire encased in plastic that lets you make an electrical connection

between two pins on your card. A jumper is easy to remove and change, but you may want to use needle-nosed pliers to grab it. By simply sliding the jumper over two neighboring pins, you connect them, thereby changing the card's settings. On your sound card, jumpers may be indicated by the letter "J" or "JP" followed by a number, such as "J3" or "JP5." Consult your manual.

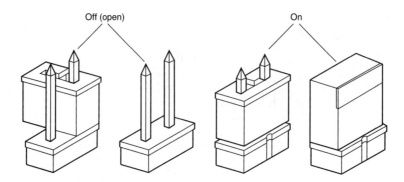

Off (open)   On

Figure 6.3:
A jumper that is off and on.

DIP Switches

You also can configure your expansion card with a DIP switch or one of its variants, such as a *rocker* or *toggle* switch (see fig. 6.4). A DIP switch is simply a small bank of switches. How small? The switches are spaced at 10 switches per inch, although many DIP switches only have four switches. They are easy to spot; they are usually blue or red. Each switch has two positions: on or off. On the switch's plastic face, the word "ON" or "OPEN" may be printed. Don't confuse these two terms: "OPEN" means *off* (an open circuit). By setting each switch to either on or off, you can tell your expansion card to behave a certain way. A four-switch DIP switch, for example, lets an expansion card maker provide up to 24 combinations, although the features you can change on your card are usually fewer.

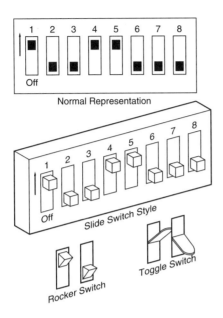

Figure 6.4:
Examples of DIP switches.

These two items allow you to turn the sound card's joystick port on or off, change the "address" where the sound card can be found by its software, and more.

This Joystick or Another?

One option you may be able to change on your sound card is its joystick port. If you already have a joystick (or game) port on your PC, turn off the joystick on the sound card. (You can't have two separate joystick ports.)

Listen Up!

Although you can't have two joystick ports on your PC, you still can use two joysticks at the same time. For example, I have CH Products' Gamecard III installed on my computer. This game card has connectors for two joysticks, so you can fly with a friend.

For example, Sound Blaster 16 ASP uses a jumper called "JYEN" to turn the joystick on or off. To turn the joystick off, remove the jumper connecting the two pins that form JYEN.

Turn Off the Amp

Another thing you may be able to change is whether the sound card's built-in amplifier is on or off. Many sound cards amplify the sound to about four watts to drive your small bookshelf speakers.

Why would you want to turn off this amplifier? If you are using amplified speakers—speakers that have their own amplifiers—you would want to avoid the distortion caused by amplifying an already-amplified signal. (Too many amplifiers spoil the broth.) If you are using the Sound Blaster 16 ASP with an amplified speaker, you can set the jumpers to turn off the sound card's own amplifier, providing better sound reproduction.

In the next section, you configure your sound card as needed.

Listen Up!

Other options can be configured with DIP switches and jumpers. Chapter 9 discusses interrupts, addresses, and DMA channels. These items often are the primary culprits when a sound card fails to work.

MIDI and Base Address

Expansion cards rely on input/output addresses to work. *I/O addresses* are places assigned in your computer's memory where the card can "talk" to different parts of your computer. For example, your keyboard has an address. Sound cards also have

addresses. If two parts of your computer live at the same address, one will have to move.

If you have an expansion card that already uses the address required by your sound card, you'll need to change the address of one or the other.

A sound card may use two addresses: the base I/O address and the address for the Musicial Instrument Digital Interface (MIDI) port. Typically, you won't have to change these addresses. Chapter 9 discusses how to resolve any problems when two cards try to live at the same address.

Excuse Me, May I Interrupt?

Some sound cards also require you to set the interrupts they will use. The *interrupt* (IRQ) is a method used by your sound card to get your computer's attention. Without interrupts, your computer processor would have to finish whatever work it is doing before letting another part of your computer use it.

In the next section, you will change these options before you place the sound card in your PC.

We're Rocking Now!

After your computer is open, you can install your sound card. Simply follow these steps:

1. Select a slot for your sound card.

Your sound card can be either an 8- or 16-bit expansion card. *Select a slot that matches the type of card you have.* For example, you don't want to put a 16-bit card (one with dual edge connectors) into an 8-bit slot (one with a single edge connector). An 8-bit card, however, can fit into either an 8- or 16-bit slot.

If you have several empty slots from which to choose, you may want to place the new card in a slot as far away as possible from the others. This reduces any possible electromagnetic interference—that is, it reduces the possibility of stray radio signals from one card affecting the sound card.

2. Remove the screw that holds the metal cover to the empty expansion slot you've chosen (see fig. 6.5).

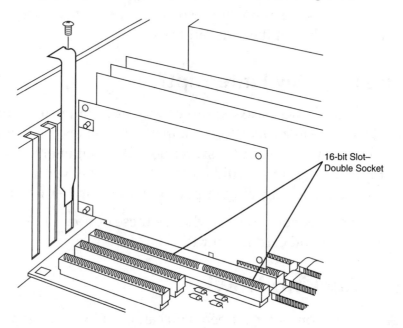

16-bit Slot–
Double Socket

Figure 6.5:
Remove the metal plate to open up the slot you want to use.

Only one screw needs to be removed to free the metal plate from the case. Set aside the screw where it won't be misplaced. Save the metal plate in case you remove the expansion card later. For instance, you may want to sell

your computer and keep some of the expansion cards for your next computer. If you've saved that metal plate, you can replace it over the "gaping" hole.

4. Remove your sound card from its protective packaging.

Expansion cards are shipped in a special gray or silver anti-static bag. First, drain yourself of static electricity by briefly touching your computer's metallic frame. When you open the antistatic bag, carefully hold the card by its metal bracket and edges. *DO NOT touch any of the components on the card* because any static electricity you may have can damage the card. Also, do not touch the gold edge connectors. If you must set the sound card down, place it on its antistatic shipping bag. Never place the sound card on a table or carpet.

5. Configure the sound card.

As mentioned in the previous section, you may have to set jumpers or DIP switches to configure your sound card to work best with your computer. You might, for example, want to turn off your sound card's joystick port because your joystick is already connected elsewhere to your PC. See the instructions that came with your sound card.

6. If an internal CD-ROM drive is to be connected to the sound card, attach its cables.

Some sound cards can also run your CD-ROM drive, especially if the sound card offers a SCSI interface. Attach your CD-ROM's striped ribbon cable to your sound card.

Chapter 6

Listen Up!

The red edge of the CD-ROM cable should be placed on the side of the connector that has the name "0" or "1" printed on the sound card. If you don't, the CD-ROM drive won't work.

The CD-ROM drive also has an audio cable. Connect this cable to the audio connector on the sound card. This connector is configured so that you can't insert it improperly.

7. Insert the card in the edge connector (see fig. 6.6).

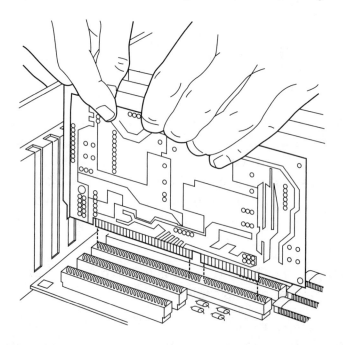

Figure 6.6:
Firmly push the card into its slot.

Touch a metal object nearby, such as the inside of your computer's cover, to drain yourself of static electricity.

Then, holding the card by its metal bracket and edges, place it in the expansion slot.

Rock the expansion card back and forth along its length. In other words, do not twist the card from side to side but rather push down alternately on each end. You may encounter firm resistance as you press on the card; this is natural. Watch the motherboard to gauge how much force to apply. You should not have to push so hard that the motherboard bows downward, almost touching the bottom of the case.

8. Attach the screw to hold the expansion card.

   Tighten the screw to hold the expansion card in place. Do not overtighten this screw; you later may need to remove it. When you are finished installing the sound card, it's time to get your computer up and running again.

9. Put the outer case back on your computer.

   As you slide the case on, avoid snagging any inside wires or cables. Tuck these in as you replace the case.

10. Install and tighten the case screws.

    Use the first two screws to affix the bowed edges of the case, usually the lower left and right sides of the case. Attach the remaining screws to your computer.

Listen Up!

Do not overtighten these screws. Your computer is not a blender; it won't vibrate apart if the screws are not absolutely tight. The possibility exists of tightening the screws so much that their slotted heads may chip or flare out, making it difficult or even impossible for you to remove the case later.

Chapter 6

11. After the case is on, return the computer to its normal location and attach all cables.

Reattaching all the cables and cords to your computer can be a chore, especially if your computer is placed so the back, where the cables are attached, is near a wall.

Listen Up!

One simple trick is to place a permanent mark, such as an "X," on each cable so that you know which end should be up when the cable is attached. Otherwise, you may try inserting the cable upside down, possibly damaging the connector.

Spring Cleaning

As long as you have your computer open, you may want to do some spring cleaning. As the power supply's fan draws cooler air in through your computer, dust becomes an unwelcome visitor. Dust clings to electronic components, giving them unwelcome insulation.

On the outside, use a toothbrush to remove dust from the computer case's vented slots. Brush the exhaust fan plate in the back of the computer to dislodge dirt. Also use the toothbrush on the inside vents of the power supply.

Next, use a makeup or camera lens brush to loosen dirt and dust from your computer's components, such as the computer chips attached to the motherboard. To reduce static electricity, use short, slow strokes to remove the coats of dust.

Listen Up!

Some people use compressed air to blow dust out and away. Make sure that you get computer-grade air, not just air used for camera lenses.

Where Next?

The next few chapters discuss attaching your sound accessories, installing your sound software, and common problems in getting a sound card to work.

Where's That Speaker?

You can connect various types of equipment to your sound card, making it a clearinghouse of sounds. Making these connections is simple if you have the right touch.

In this chapter, you learn:

♪ What the various connections on your sound card are

♪ How to add speakers

♪ How to connect your stereo system

♪ How to connect a joystick or MIDI device

♪ How to connect an external sound device

Chapter 7

A Bunch of Holes

Basically, a sound card is an expansion card with many connectors to the outside world (see fig. 7.1). These connectors are typically ⅛-inch minijacks (or simply "jacks"). Occasionally, a coaxial cable jack is used. These connectors include the following:

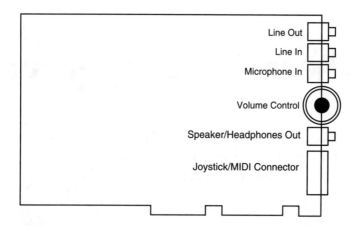

Figure 7.1:

A typical sound card's features.

♪ **Stereo, or audio, line out connector.** The line out connector is used to send sound signals from the sound card to the outside. The cables from the line out connector can be hooked to stereo speakers, a headphone set, or your stereo system. If you hook up your stereo system, you can have amplified sound.

Sound Check

Some sound cards, such as Microsoft's Windows Sound System, provide two jacks for line out. One is for the left channel of the stereo signal; the other is for the right channel.

♪ **Stereo, or audio, line in connector.** The line in connector is used to mix sound signals, which you can then save to your computer's hard disk.

♪ **Microphone, or mono, in connector.** You connect a microphone to this ⅛-inch minijack to record your voice or other sounds to disk. The microphone jack records in mono, not in stereo. Many sound cards use *automatic gain control* (AGC) to improve recordings. The AGC feature adjusts the recording levels on-the-fly. A 500 to 10K ohm dynamic or condenser microphone works best with this jack.

♪ **Speaker/headphone out connector.** Some sound cards do not provide a speaker/headphone connector. Instead, the line out doubles as a way to send stereo signals from the sound card to your stereo system or speakers. When both a speaker/headphone and line out connectors are provided, the speaker/headphone connector provides an amplified signal that can power your headphones or small bookshelf speakers. Most sound cards can provide up to four watts of power to drive your speakers.

Conversely, signals sent through the line out connector are not amplified. This provides the best sound reproduction because the stereo system or amplified speakers will amplify the sounds.

Chapter 7

Listen Up!

A stereo microphone will not work with a sound card's microphone jack. Typically, a microphone is monophonic. You would want a stereo microphone to record a group of singers, for example.

Sound Check

Some inexpensive sound cards use the line in connector rather than a separate microphone jack.

♪ **Joystick/MIDI connector.** The joystick connector is a 15-pin, D-shaped connector. Two of the pins are used to control a MIDI device, such as a keyboard. Many sound-card makers offer an optional MIDI connector. The MIDI Mate from Media Vision, for example, is used by both Logitech SoundMan 16 and Pro AudioStudio 16. This MIDI connector allows you to add a MIDI device and continue using your joystick.

Listen Up!

If you need to run two joysticks to fly with a friend, you often can buy a joystick splitter Y-cable from your sound-card maker. Using Y-cables from other companies may not always work.

♪ **Volume control.** A thumbwheel control is provided on some sound cards, although sophisticated sound cards have no room for such a control. Instead, a combination of keys can be used to adjust the sound. Pro AudioStudio 16 from Media Vision, for example, uses Ctrl-Alt-U and Ctrl-Alt-D to increase and decrease the volume, respectively. Press these three keys together to adjust the volume from within a game, Windows program, or other application.

Listen Up!

If your card has a volume control on the backside of the card, adjust it to mid-level.

Use table 7.1 to check off which connectors your chosen sound card has:

Table 7.1
Which Connectors Does Your Sound Card Have?

Connector	Yes	No
Stereo line, or audio, out		
Stereo line, or audio, in		
Speaker/headphone connector		
Microphone, or mono, in		
Joystick/MIDI connector		
Volume control		

Chapter 7

Use this table in this and later chapters to understand how you need to connect your sound cards to external systems, such as a stereo system or unamplified speakers.

Making the Connection

Now that you are more comfortable with your sound card, you can connect your various sound accessories to it (see fig. 7.2).

Listen Up!

Always turn off your computer and any audio equipment before you connect cables to or disconnect cables from your audio ports. You risk damaging both the computer and your audio equipment with the electrical energy they carry.

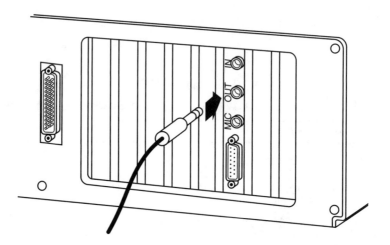

Figure 7.2:
Turn off your PC and audio equipment before connecting cables.

Speakers First

You can connect small speakers to the speaker jack. Typically, sound cards provide four watts of power per channel to drive bookshelf speakers. (Four watts is much smaller than my 50-watt speakers!) Also, these speakers need to be rated at between four and eight ohms.

Listen Up!

If you are using speakers rated for less than four watts, do not turn up the volume on your sound card to the maximum; your speakers may burn out from the overload.

You'll get better results if you plug your sound card into powered speakers—that is, speakers with built-in amplifiers. Another alternative is to patch your sound card into your stereo system for greatly amplified sound. Of course, you'll have to move your PC near your stereo system or vice versa.

As discussed in Chapter 5, powered speakers come in several styles and price ranges. A growing number are designed specifically for multimedia and sound cards. Some offer individual satellite speakers that can be placed anywhere; others come pre-installed in a cabinet that matches your PC case, fitting between the PC and monitor.

Listen Up!

Using an amplified (powered) speaker or your stereo system? Some sound cards, such as Sound Blaster 16 ASP, allow you to turn off the sound card's built-in amplifier. This allows you to send the very best quality signal to the speaker or stereo system for amplification.

Ordinary powered speakers, the kind that you plug in to a Walkman-like portable stereo, also work with multimedia systems, but you may need an adapter cable to match the jack on the sound card to the speaker plugs. For example, you may need a Y-adapter to go from the left and right speaker jacks of your "boombox" to a single ⅛-inch miniplug to your sound card.

True Stereo Sound

If you already have a stereo system and want to connect your sound card directly to it, check the plugs and jacks at both ends of the connection. Most stereos use *pin plugs*—also called *RCA* or *phono plugs*—for input. Although pin plugs are standard on some sound cards, most use miniature ⅛-inch phone plugs, which require an adapter. For example, you can purchase from Radio Shack an audio cable that provides stereo ⅛-inch mini-plugs to phono plugs (Cat. No. 42-2481A).

Listen Up!

Make sure that you get stereo, not mono, plugs, unless your card only supports mono, such as the ThunderBOARD. To ensure that you have enough cable to reach from the back of the PC to your stereo system, get at least a six-foot-long cable.

Hooking up your stereo to a sound card is simply a matter of sliding the plugs into jacks. If your sound card gives you a choice of outputs—speaker/headphone and stereo line out—choose the stereo line out jack for the connection. This gives the best sound quality because the signals from the stereo line out jack are not amplified. The amplification is best left to your stereo system.

Connect this output to the auxiliary input of your stereo receiver, preamp, or integrated amplifier (see fig. 7.3). If your stereo doesn't have an auxiliary input, other input options include—in order of preference—tuner, CD, or tape 2. Do not use phono inputs, however, because the level of the signals will be uneven. On my stereo system, I connected the cable's single stereo miniplug to the sound card's stereo line out jack. Then I connected the two RCA phono plugs to my stereo's tape/VCR 2 playback jacks.

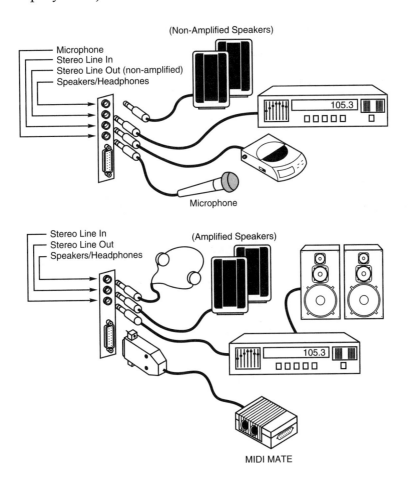

Figure 7.3:
Connecting your stereo system is simple.

Listen Up!

The first time you use your sound card with a stereo system, turn down the volume on your receiver to prevent surprises—and blown speakers. Barely turn up the volume control and then select the proper input (such as Tape/VCR 2) on your stereo receiver. Finally, start your PC. Never increase the volume to more than 3/4 of the way up. Any higher and the sound can become distorted.

Mixing and Matching

Your stereo system cannot only play your sound card through your stereo speakers but also can record sounds from your stereo to your computer. You can even mix sounds from several audio sources, which you then can record to your hard disk through the sound card.

You can, for instance, play subtle, relaxing music from an audio CD player while speaking into the microphone attached to your sound card. You can record the "mix" of these two to your hard disk and later edit it and enhance it.

Chapter 11 discusses the various sound-card utilities to perform such feats. For now, you need to know how to attach your stereo to the sound card so that you can record. On my stereo system, I simply used another audio cable from Radio Shack to connect the Tape/VCR 2 record out jacks to my sound card's stereo in jacks.

Sound Check

Your PC already has several cables connected to it. Adding audio cables makes the problem worse. To prevent these cables from becoming entangled, use garbage bag twist ties to bundle related cables together. You can tie all the new audio cables together, for example. You also can buy special-purpose flex tubing that acts as a conduit for your cables.

You also can make your own cable protector. Buy about 20 feet of flexible plastic tubing about 1 ½ inches in diameter. Cut the tubing to the correct lengths for the groups of cables you're about to enshroud. Thread your cables through the tubes. If several cords need to be put through the tubing or have large connectors, simply slit the tubing lengthwise to accommodate them.

Double Duty

Connecting the joystick is quite simple. Simply slide the 15-pin D-shaped plug into the matching hole. The joystick port on many sound cards often doubles as a connection to a MIDI device, such as a MIDI keyboard. A special MIDI adapter lets you have both connected.

If you intend to use a MIDI keyboard or other MIDI device, you'll also need a MIDI adapter. These adapters use a 15-pin female connector that connects to your sound card's MIDI/joystick connector.

You get such adapters from the manufacturer of your sound card. Media Vision, for example, sells MIDI Mate ($69.95) for its Pro AudioSpectrum line of sound cards. Creative Labs, on the other hand, sells MIDI Kit ($79.95). These adapters often come with MIDI sequencing software. The Creative Labs MIDI kit comes with software from Voyetra Technologies.

Chapter 7

The adapter uses some of the joystick's pins to provide one MIDI in and one MIDI out connection. The MIDI interface on sound cards uses the standard defined by the International MIDI Association. Simply plug in the MIDI adapter to the sound card's MIDI/joystick connector as illustrated in figure 7.4.

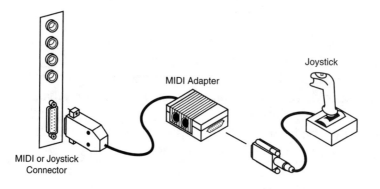

Figure 7.4:
The MIDI adapter lets you still use your joystick.

Dealing with Sound Ports

Sound ports, which clip onto your computer's parallel port, only need a little installation help. The inexpensive Disney Sound Source, for example, has a sound converter plug attached to your PC's parallel port.

To install Sound Source, first remove your parallel printer cable and attach the converter (see fig. 7.5). Next, attach the parallel cable to the converter, and then connect a phone cable to the side of the converter and to the Sound Source.

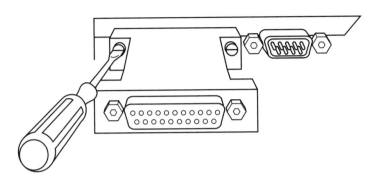

Figure 7.5:

The Disney Sound Source plugs into the sound converter.

With your sound equipment attached, you now can install your sound card's software and explore the world of digital audio, making music and sounds on your PC.

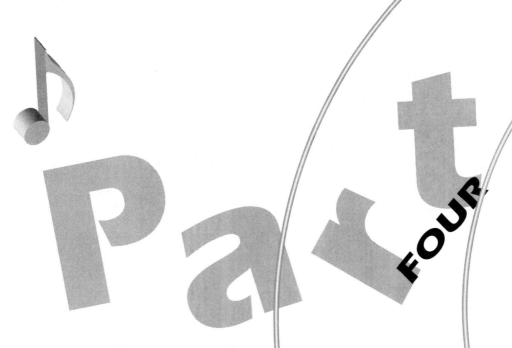

Setting Up the Software

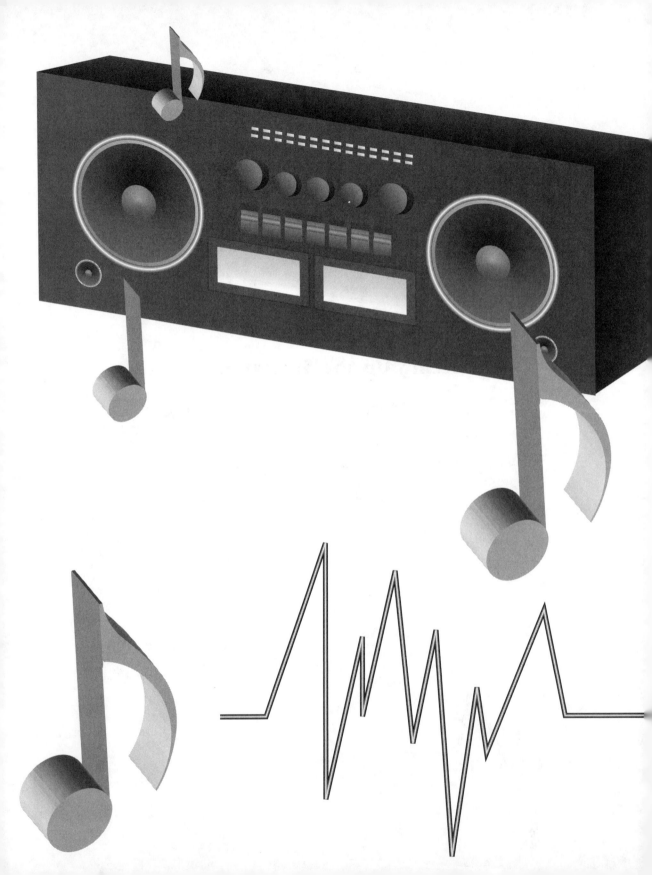

Giving Your Sound Card Its Voice

8

A sound card is a special type of expansion card. It simply doesn't work immediately upon installation. Like many out-of-the-ordinary expansion cards, a sound card requires software to bring it to life. This software uses some of your computer's resources, such as interrupts and DMA channels, to work nimbly and efficiently.

In this chapter, you learn:

♪   What the needs of a sound card are

♪   How to install DOS drivers for your sound card

♪   How to install Windows drivers for your sound card

Basic Requirements

If your PC is to develop a voice, it will need some basic require-ments, such as a DMA channel, an IRQ or two, I/O addresses, and installation software.

The Dastardly DMA

Sound cards often use *direct memory access* (DMA) channels to speed getting information to and from your PC's memory. DMA channels also allow your sound card to play alongside other tasks. By using the DMA controller chips built into your computer, your sound card can bypass the central processor altogether (kind of like eliminating the middleman.)

The number of DMA channels is limited, and not all expansion cards use them. XT-type computers (8088/8086) provide four DMA channels. AT-type (80286, 80386, 80486) computers can use any of eight. Unfortunately, some channels (2 and 4) are reserved for refreshing your computer's memory and control-ling your disk drives (see table 8.1).

Table 8.1
DMA Channels and Purpose

DMA Channel	Purpose
0-1	Unused
2	Used by your floppy disk controller
3	Unused
4	Refreshes your computer's memory
5-7	Available on AT-type and PS/2 comput-ers but usually not used

The original Sound Blaster could be set to DMA channel 0, 1, or 3. Some sound cards, such as Sound Blaster Pro Deluxe, can share a DMA with an expansion card that already uses the same channel.

Interrupt-ions

The *interrupt* (IRQ) may be the source of many sound-card woes. The interrupt is a method used by your sound card to get your computer's attention when it needs it.

Without interrupts, your computer processor would have to finish whatever work it is doing before letting another part of your computer use it. This can be terribly inconvenient. When you type at your keyboard, for example, the keyboard controller chip inside your computer interrupts the processor so that each keystroke can be placed into the keyboard buffer, or storage area. If not for interrupts, your keystrokes would be lost until the processor was finished with its other work.

Like I/O addresses, the number of interrupts is limited. XT-type computers have five interrupts, 2 through 7 (see table 8.2). These interrupts are prioritized, with interrupt 2 being more urgent than interrupt 7. When an interrupt is used, your PC's processor stops dead in its tracks and handles the computer device with that interrupt.

Table 8.2
Interrupts and What They Control

Interrupt	Device	Comments
0	Timer	
1	Keyboard	

continues

Table 8.2
Continued

Interrupt	Device	Comments
2	Unused	Used in AT-type computers as a gateway to IRQ 8/15 or for EGA/VGA video cards.
3	COM2 (second serial port)	Often used for a modem or mouse.
4	COM1 (first serial port)	Often used for a modem or mouse.
5	Hard disk	Hard disk for XT-type computers and some times LPT2 for AT-type computers.
6	FDC (floppy disk drive controller)	
7	LPT1 (first parallel printer port)	May be shared with an expansion card.
8	Clock	Interrupts 8 through 15 are available on AT-type computers only and often not to expansion cards.
9	PC network	
10-12	Unused	
13	Math coprocessor	Used for speeding mathematical calculations, such as in spreadsheet or computer-aided design (CAD) programs.

Interrupt	Device	Comments
14	Hard disk	
15	Unused	

Many sound cards recommend an interrupt of 5 or 7 and sometimes interrupt 10. If interrupt 7 is used, problems can occur if you use the sound card while printing. Otherwise, you should have no problem.

A Forwarding Address

Expansion cards rely on input/output addresses to work. The *I/O address* is a place assigned in your computer's memory where the card can "talk" to different parts of your computer. For example, your keyboard has an address. Sound cards also have addresses. Some I/O addresses are set in stone. A joystick controller (or game card), for example, has a set address of 200-20F.

If you created a totally new expansion card, you would pick an unassigned address. A limited number of I/O addresses are available, however. Your PC, for example, is limited to three printer ports—LPT1, LPT2, and LPT3—and two serial ports—COM1 and COM2. (With DOS 3.3 and later, you also can have COM3 and COM4; however, you must "split" COM1 and COM2 by having them share their interrupt, described next, with these newcomers.) Likewise, you almost always cannot have two video cards; the two will fight to the death for these addresses.

If you have an expansion card that already uses the address required by your sound card, you'll need to change the address of one or the other; they both can't live at the same address. (Who pays for the utilities?)

A sound card may require two addresses: an address for the card itself and an address for its MIDI port. Typically, you won't have to change these addresses. Sound Blaster Pro and Sound Blaster 16 ASP, for example, use several addresses starting at address 220.

Sound Check

If another card in your computer uses the same addresses, interrupt, or DMA channel, problems occur when both cards are being used at the same time. This is called a *device conflict*. Chapter 9 discusses how to solve these. Typically, jumpers or DIP switches (mentioned in Chapter 7) are used to resolve the conflict. Some sound cards allow their interrupt and DMA channels to be changed through software, saving you the job of opening up your computer to make the necessary changes.

Install Away!

All sound cards come with installation software. Installation software performs a variety of tasks, like the following:

- ♪ Analyzes your computer to recommend available DMA channels, IRQ settings, and I/O address changes

- ♪ Sets up Sound Blaster compatibility for computer games

- ♪ Turns your joystick port on or off

- ♪ Enables your MIDI interface

- ♪ Installs the sound-card drivers (small software programs) for Windows and DOS

- ♪ Installs the sound utilities included with your sound card

♪ Modifies your Windows startup files, such as WIN.INI and SYSTEM.INI

♪ Modifies your DOS startup files, such as CONFIG.SYS and AUTOEXEC.BAT

No Driver, No Sound

Of all the tasks the installation software does, the most important one is placing the sound-card device driver program on your hard disk and configuring it.

What's a device driver? A *device driver* (or simply *driver*) is a small software program that tells your computer how to work with an attached device, whether it's a sound card, CD-ROM drive, or other esoteric addition to your PC. For example, MSCDEX.EXE is a driver that helps your PC work with a CD-ROM drive as if it were another drive.

The driver is needed because almost all devices communicate in a slightly different way. Imagine that the device driver is a foreign language interpreter. The interpreter (the driver) must translate what one person says to another person, yet in another language. A device driver handles the translation responsibilities for both parties.

To use your sound card with DOS programs, such as games, you must have a device driver loaded from CONFIG.SYS, your computer's primary startup file. When you start your computer, it looks at the DEVICE= statements in CONFIG.SYS. From these, it determines which drivers it needs to correctly operate your equipment, such as a sound card. It locates the driver and loads it into memory, allowing your PC to quickly communicate with each device when called upon to do so.

Chapter 8

Sound Check

CONFIG.SYS and AUTOEXEC.BAT are simple text files that your PC looks for as it starts. Both of these files customize your PC to work a certain way. These files typically are found in the root (top) directory of your hard disk, such as C:\. The CONFIG.SYS file contains instructions that your PC uses to fine-tune itself and to better work with expansion cards and other devices attached to it. AUTOEXEC.BAT, on the other hand, is simply a list of DOS commands that you could otherwise type at the keyboard. When these commands are placed in the AUTOEXEC.BAT file, they are remembered and played back each time you start your computer. The files SYSTEM.INI and WIN.INI serve a similar purpose for Microsoft Windows.

For many sound cards, you can edit later your CONFIG.SYS file to change its settings without running the installation software again. Chapter 9 discusses this approach in detail.

For Windows sound, your WIN.INI and SYSTEM.INI files also are modified. Your original files usually are saved to new file names so that you can restore them, if needed. Windows Sound System, for instance, renames your original SYSTEM.INI to SYSTEM.WSS.

In Windows, sound-card drivers are added, removed, and configured in the Windows Control Panel, which is found in the Main group (see fig. 8.1). After just installing Windows, only four drivers are listed as follows:

♪ **MIDI Mapper.** A driver that lets you change your MIDI setup to work best with your MIDI and other sound equipment.

♪ **Timer.** A multimedia timer driver, to be described in Chapter 14.

♪ **[MCI] MIDI Sequencer.** A driver to let you record, edit, and play back MIDI files.

♪ **[MCI] Sound.** A driver used to play Windows waveform (WAV) files.

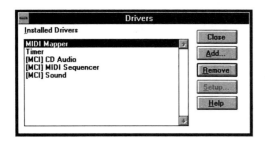

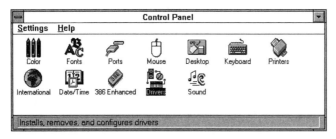

Figure 8.1:

In Windows, drivers are managed from the Control Panel.

Listen Up!

You can learn more about device drivers from your DOS manuals.

Its Own Directory

The installation software often creates a directory for the sound card's various utilities and modifies your CONFIG.SYS or AUTOEXEC.BAT startup files. For example, the directory where the sound card's software is located is usually added to your path: Pro AudioStudio 16 adds the path \PASTUDIO to your PATH statement.

Sound Check

What's a PATH statement? The PATH statement, located in the AUTOEXEC.BAT file, looks like this:

```
PATH C:\DOS;C:\WP5;C:\UTILS;D:\BAT
```

The *PATH statement* tells DOS where to search for your most popular program files. This way, you can type the program's startup command without actually having to go to the directory in which it is located. Your PC looks to your PATH statement to find the program file you requested. For instance, C:\DOS is a path found in almost all PCs. By having the DOS directory as part of your PATH command, you don't have to change to the DOS directory to run frequent commands, such as CHKDSK, XCOPY, FORMAT, and others. Each path is separated by a semicolon (;). When creating your path, always include drive letters with the directory names.

Own a CD-ROM Drive?

If you have a CD-ROM drive, the sound-card installation program also can do the following:

♪ Add MSCDEX.EXE (the DOS CD-ROM driver) to the AUTOEXEC.BAT file

♪ Prepare a CD-ROM drive, if present, to work with your sound card

♪ Install the MCI CD Audio driver (which lets you play audio CDs under Windows)

To bring a CD-ROM player to life, you need to add a device driver to your system's CONFIG.SYS file. With this software driver, your PC recognizes your brand of CD-ROM player. After that, you must run the Microsoft CD-ROM Extensions program—preferably from within your PC's AUTOEXEC.BAT file—so that your computer considers the CD-ROM player like any other disk drive. When it comes to using your CD-ROM player and sound card for multimedia, you handle all other details from within Windows.

Listen Up!

MS-DOS 6 includes a newer MSCDEX.EXE driver, version 2.2. Some sound cards use the version that comes with their installation software. The installation software for my Pro AudioSpectrum Plus sound card, for example, prefers to use the MSCDEX driver it places in its \PROAUDIO directory. Make sure that you're using the most current version!

Sample Setups

The next few sections, look at the installation software of the more popular and newer sound cards, such as:

♪ Microsoft Windows Sound System

♪ Media Vision Pro AudioStudio 16

Chapter 8

♪ Logitech SoundMan 16

♪ Creative Labs Sound Blaster 16 ASP

Microsoft Windows Sound System

Windows Sound System from Microsoft Corp. is the only
sound card that I know of that requires you to run the installation program *before* you install the sound card. Why? The
Sound System's setup program can analyze your PC and select
the best DMA channel, IRQ, and I/O address without the
sound card getting in the way.

The Windows Sound Software follows the style of several
Windows programs. From the Program Manager, select File,
Run, and enter the name of your installation program. Often,
this is **A:SETUP** or **B:SETUP**, depending from which floppy
drive you are installing (see fig. 8.2).

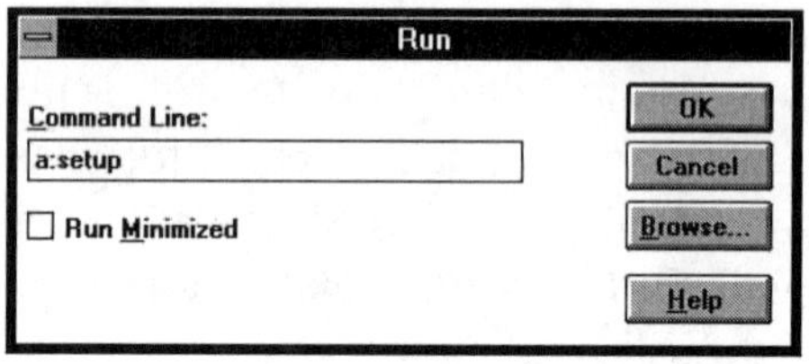

Figure 8.2:
Install the Windows Sound System software from Program Manager.

After starting the Windows Sound System setup program,
select Board Installation. You then can select **A**uto for the
Automatic Board Configuration. After analyzing your PC, the
setup program visually shows you how to set the pair of jumpers on the Windows Sound System card (see fig. 8.3). This pair
of jumpers sets the address at which the card will work. (The
default address is 530.)

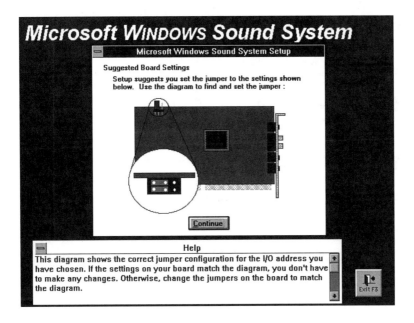

Figure 8.3:

The setup software shows you how to set the jumpers.

After setting the jumpers, you temporarily leave the setup program to install the Windows Sound System card. Turn off your PC and install the card.

Listen Up!

For instructions on installing and handling expansion cards, see Chapter 6.

With the Windows Sound System installed, you then restart Windows. The setup program resumes because it was placed in the Windows Startup group.

With Sound Card installed, select **S**oftware from the main menu and install the disks (see fig. 8.4).

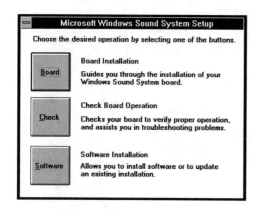

Figure 8.4:

The Windows Sound System Setup software main menu.

Listen Up!

I had trouble installing the Windows Sound System. It seems the Symphony chipset my PC's motherboard uses prevents the sound card from working. A newer set of installation disks and some editing of my SYSTEM.INI file finally got the card working. (Sheesh!)

After these disks are installed, you can return to Windows where a Windows Sound System Setup group is created (see fig. 8.5) or begin a guided tour of the sound card's features. The Windows Sound System software is installed to the directory \SNDSYS.

One thing Windows Sound System does differently from other sound cards is add Volume and Recording icons to your Windows Control Panel (see fig. 8.6). Also, the Sound icon is modified to better work with Windows Sound System. These added controls allow you to adjust the volume for various sound sources during playback and recording, respectively.

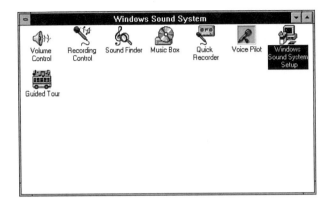

Figure 8.5:

The Windows Sound System group.

Figure 8.6:

The Windows Sound System adds two new choices to the Control Panel.

Pro AudioStudio 16

The Pro AudioStudio 16 software for DOS and Windows is installed entirely from the DOS prompt. You simply type:

```
A: (press Enter)
INSTALL
```

Listen Up!

The Pro AudioStudio 16 installation software only installs the Windows utilities if Windows 3.1 is installed on your PC.

By default, the software utilities and drivers are installed to a directory called \PASTUDIO. You next are asked where Windows 3.1 is installed. The majority of the Pro AudioStudio 16 software is installed; however, two utilities—ExecuVoice and Sound Impressions—must be installed separately. These utilities allow you to give voice commands to your PC and create multimedia shows, respectively.

At the end of the installation, the installation program analyzes your computer to recommend the best DMA, IRQ, and address to work with your system (see fig. 8.7). You'll hear some test sound from your speaker during this process.

```
Pro Audio Studio Quick Start Installation

    Below are the values Quick Start selected for your Pro Audio Studio.
    You will hear a test sound each time an IRQ or DMA channel is tested.

    If you want to change any settings, use the UP and DOWN arrow keys to
    select and press ENTER.  To continue the installation, select 'Complete
    Changes' and press ENTER.

    Installation Information:
       Pro Audio Spectrum DMA:       5
       Pro Audio Spectrum IRQ:       7
       Enable Joystick Port:         NO
       Enable Snd.Blast.Emulation:   YES   Port: 220    IRQ: 5    DMA: 1
       Enable MPU-401 Emulation:     NO    Port: ---    IRQ ---
       Modify C: DOS System Files:   YES
       Modify   WIN System Files:    YES
       Complete Changes:             Accept the configuration shown above




  ENTER=Continue  F3=Exit
```

Figure 8.7:

Pro AudioStudio 16 recommends the best settings.

The software anticipates your choices. For example, if a joystick port is sensed, it sets Enable Joystick Port to NO. Usually, the MPU-401 emulation is turned off. What's that? MPU-401 is the MIDI interface developed by Roland. It was one of the first interfaces designed for the PC. Its design is now regarded as the standard protocol. Unless you intend to add a MIDI device, such as a musical keyboard, leave this choice off by answering NO.

Non-Sound Blaster cards don't want to turn their backs to being Sound Blaster-compatible. This would prevent them from working with many of today's hottest computer games and other software programs. To be Sound Blaster-compatible, these sound cards must switch from their regular mode to the Sound Blaster mode. A portion of the Pro AudioStudio 16 card is set aside to be Sound Blaster-compatible. As you can see in figure 8.7, Sound Blaster emulation is set at address 220 with an interrupt of 5 and a DMA channel of 1.

After you accept your choices, press Enter, and Pro AudioStudio modifies your several startup files, including the Windows files WIN.INI and SYSTEM.INI. When you start Windows, a Multimedia Tools group is located for Pro AudioStudio's various sound utilities (see fig. 8.8). This group includes icons for Pocket Recorder, Pocket Mixer, Pro Mixer, Pocket CD, and other utilities described in Chapter 10.

After installing the Pro AudioStudio 16 software, you can select the Pro AudioStudio Quick Tour icon to learn about the potential uses of this sound card.

Chapter 8

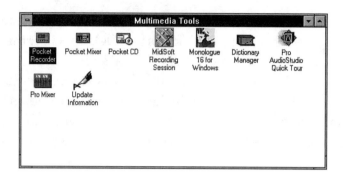

Figure 8.8:
The Multimedia Tools group created for the Pro AudioStudio 16.

Logitech SoundMan 16

The Logitech SoundMan uses some of Media Vision's multimedia chip sets and software found with Pro AudioStudio 16. Instead of reinventing the wheel (I mean, sound card), Logitech has licensed this technology.

Surprisingly, the Logitech software is provided on a single disk. Like Pro AudioStudio 16, the Logitech SoundMan 16 software is installed from the DOS prompt. You simply type the following:

```
A: (press Enter)
INSTALL
```

You first select a directory for the SoundMan software. The standard directory is \SOUNDMAN. The software then recommends some sound-card settings (see fig. 8.9).

You can disable or enable any option. Like Pro AudioStudio 16, you can turn on or off Sound Blaster emulation, the MPU-401 as your MIDI interface, and the sound card's joystick port. You also can set the volume level to any of several levels on a scale of 0 to 100.

```
SoundMan-16
─────────────
                    SoundMan-16 Board Settings Screen

    To change any setting, use the [Up] and [Down] cursor keys to select
    the value to change and press [Enter].  To start the installation,
    select 'Continue' and press [Enter].

    Current Settings:
        SoundMan............... IRQ: 15     DMA: 5
        SoundBlaster........... IRQ: 7      DMA: 1   Port: 220

        SoundBlaster Compatibility:    Enabled
        Joystick Port:                 Enabled
        MPU-401 UART Emulation:        Disabled    Port: 330   IRQ: 2
        Volume Level:                  50

                                     Continue

Press [Enter] to proceed to test these settings
  [F1]=Help   [F3]=Exit                        |
```

Figure 8.9:

The initial Logitech SoundMan settings.

After you have made your choices, the installation software conducts two DMA/IRQ tests for the selected SoundMan 16 and Sound Blaster settings. If you don't hear the chimes, or the software reports that the test failed, you are given the option to change the DMA or IRQ (see fig. 8.10).

```
SoundMan-16
─────────────
    The SoundMan IRQ/DMA Test is POSITIVE...

    If you did not hear anything, the speakers or headphones may
    not be connected to the OUT jack of the board.  The Volume
    may need to be raised.  Try another DMA value as a last resort.

    Select "Continue" to proceed to the SoundBlaster IRQ/DMA Test
    Use the [Up] and [Down] arrows and press [Enter] to select an action.

                        Continue
                        Go Back to Settings

Press [Enter] to continue with the installation
  [F1]=Help   [F3]=Exit                        |
```

Figure 8.10:

You can go back and change the current settings.

After these tests are successful, you then approve the settings that the SoundMan 16 will add to your CONFIG.SYS. This line contains all the DMA, IRQ, volume, and other settings required to bring your sound card to life (see figure 8.11). The software also adds the SoundMan directory to your AUTOEXEC.BAT PATH statement.

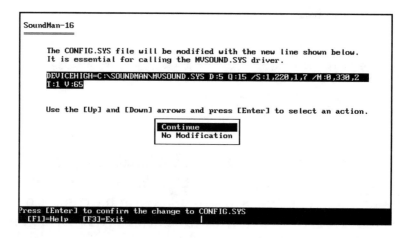

```
SoundMan-16

    The CONFIG.SYS file will be modified with the new line shown below.
    It is essential for calling the MVSOUND.SYS driver.

   DEVICEHIGH=C:\SOUNDMAN\MVSOUND.SYS D:5 Q:15 /S:1,220,1,7 /M:0,330,2
   T:1 V:65

    Use the [Up] and [Down] arrows and press [Enter] to select an action.

                               Continue
                               No Modification


Press [Enter] to confirm the change to CONFIG.SYS
   [F1]=Help   [F3]=Exit                    |
```

Figure 8.11:

A single line in CONFIG.SYS configures your sound card.

After these settings are made, you can exit to DOS or continue with the Windows installation of SoundMan 16. You are reminded to jot down the Sound Blaster settings because some games require this information.

Listen Up!

You don't have to install Logitech SoundMan 16 to work with Windows. You later can install the Windows portion of the SoundMan 16 software from Windows. From the Program Manager, select **F**ile and then **R**un. In the dialog box, type:

    A:WINSTALL (press Enter)

The Windows portion of the installation software asks you into which group you want to place the SoundMan Windows utilities. (The default is SoundMan.) You also are asked (in the destination directory field) where you want to place these utilities and sample sound files (see fig. 8.12).

Figure 8.12:
From Windows, you are asked where you want to install the SoundMan utilities.

Listen Up!

Sound cards are finicky devices. Most come with last-minute instructions, warnings, and lists of known incompatibilities. For example, Logitech SoundMan 16 asks you if you want to view such a README file (see fig. 8.13). I highly recommend that you peruse these text files to see if any of the situations described apply to yours.

Chapter 8

> **Logitech SoundMan-16 Installation**
>
> (!) The readme file contains important information.
> Click OK to read it now.
>
> [OK]   [Cancel]

Figure 8.13:

Always browse the "readme" files provided with your sound card.

After the Logitech SoundMan 16 software is installed, a Windows group is created in which two icons are placed: Pocket Mixer and Pocket Recorder. These are the same sound utilities provided with the Pro AudioStudio 16 card, although Pro AudioStudio includes others.

Sound Blaster 16 ASP

Sound Blaster 16 ASP can also be installed from the DOS prompt only. You type:

```
A:INSTALL (press Enter)
```

The initial screen is chock-full of warnings. The installation software recommends that you turn off your disk-caching software if it uses delayed-writing (most do). If you are using a recent version of Microsoft SMARTdrive (SMARTDRV.EXE), you can turn off disk caching by typing:

```
SMARTDRV C- (press Enter)
```

in which **c** is the drive where you are installing the Sound Blaster software whose disk caching you want to turn off. If you have different disk-caching software, consult its manual.

The installation program also recommends that you view the README file. Finally, you can select the Begin Installation option to install the Sound Blaster 16 ASP software (see fig. 8.14).

```
Copyright (c) Creative Technology Ltd, 1989-1992.    All rights reserved.



                        ┌───────Main Menu───────┐
                        │ View README File       │
                        │ Begin Installation     │
                        │ Common Questions & Answers │
                        │ Exit                   │
                        └────────────────────────┘

                        ┌──────Description───────┐
                        │ This option lets you view the file README.TXT for │
                        │ updated information not included in the manual.   │
                        └────────────────────────┘




                                              [F3] - Exit
```

Figure 8.14:
After viewing the README file, install the Sound Blaster 16 ASP software.

Select a drive in which you want to place the Sound Blaster software. By default, the software is placed in the \SB16 directory. After analyzing your PC, the installation program modifies both your AUTOEXEC.BAT and CONFIG.SYS files (see fig. 8.15). For safety, your original files are saved as AUTOEXEC.B~K and CONFIG.B~K.

```
The following lines will be added to your AUTOEXEC.BAT file.

 SET BLASTER=A220 I5 D1 H5 P330 T6
 SET SOUND=C:\SB16
 C:\SB16\SBCONFIG.EXE /S
 C:\SB16\SB16SET /M:220 /VOC:220 /CD:220 /MIDI:220 /TREBLE:0

The following line will be added to your CONFIG.SYS file.

 DEVICE=C:\SB16\DRV\ASP.SYS /P:220


               Press a key to continue.
```

Figure 8.15:
The installation program alters your PC's startup files.

With the DOS installation finished, you then can start Windows. As Windows loads, Sound Blaster's installation program for Windows immediately begins. With your permission, the Windows drivers automatically are added to the Windows Control Panel. A Sound Blaster 16 group is added alongside your other Windows groups, and icons for the various Sound Blaster 16 utilities are created (see fig. 8.16).

Figure 8.16:

The Sound Blaster 16 group is created for you automatically.

No Winners

Of the four sound cards I installed, all presented one or more setup problems. Thankfully, installation software is definitely getting more sophisticated. No longer do you have to analyze the possible IRQs, DMAs, and I/O addresses that your PC uses before installing the sound card. Microsoft Sound System, for example, even shows you how to set your jumpers after analyzing your system for available addresses. This more-intelligent method of installing software is certainly a step in the right direction.

Still, sound cards simply are the victims of the ever-changing PC design which is kept an "industry standard" through cooperation among cutthroat competitors. (One friend likened the PC architecture to a house of cards that could collapse at any moment.) Windows Sound System, for example, did not work with my PC because it used a Symphony chip set (a type of motherboard design). I had to wait for new software drivers from Microsoft and then edit my SYSTEM.INI file.

How many computer users are able or willing to face these troubles? In the next chapter, you can decide how far you'll go to fix sound-card problems.

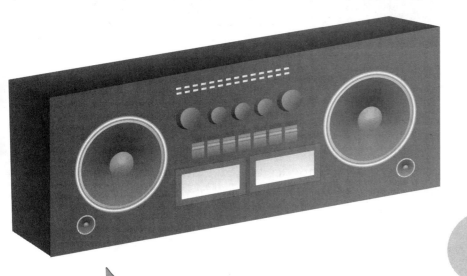

Interrupts, Addresses, and Other Hazards

Not everything sounds great in sound-card paradise. Installing a sound card requires selecting IRQ numbers, a base I/O address, or DMA channels that don't conflict with other devices. Picking the right combination of these is like walking through a minefield without a map: you never know when something is going to blow. Most cards come already configured to use an otherwise idle set of ports, but problems occasionally arise. Troubleshooting can mean changing board jumpers or switches, or even re-configuring your other cards. No one said life was fair.

In this chapter, you learn:

♪ What the anatomy of a hardware conflict is

♪ How to resolve common sound-card problems

♪ How to seek free help from friends and others

♪ How to work best with a technical support department

Conflict, Conflict

To get your sound card working requires the deductive abilities of a Sherlock Holmes, the patience of a St. Peter, and the technical wizardry of Peter Norton. (If you don't have these, don't worry, just read on.)

Whereas installing a video card or modem is a breeze, installing a sound card is a hurricane. All the sound cards I have ever installed posed one daunting snafu or another. Of the several sound cards I received for this book, each posed a problem—I mean, challenge.

Why Fight?

The most common problem for sound cards is that they fight with other devices installed in your PC. You may notice that your sound card simply doesn't work, repeats the same sounds over and over, or causes your PC to freeze in Windows or DOS. This situation is called a *device*, or *hardware, conflict*. What are they fighting over? The same signal lines or channels used for talking to your PC. The sources of conflict are threefold:

♪ **Interrupt requests (IRQs).** IRQs are used to "interrupt" your PC and get its attention.

♪ **Direct memory access (DMA) channels.** DMA channels are a way to move information directly to your PC's memory, bypassing your PC's central brain. DMA channels allow sound to play while your PC is doing other work.

♪ **Input/output (I/O) addresses.** An I/O address in your PC is used to channel information between your sound card and your PC. The address usually mentioned in a sound-card manual is the starting address. Actually, your sound card can require several addresses, which together are called an *address segment*.

Your potential for problems is doubled or trebled because many sound cards also use an IRQ, DMA, and I/O address for the Sound Blaster-compatible or MIDI portions of their cards. For example, Pro AudioStudio 16 by default uses DMA 5 and IRQ 7 for itself, and DMA 1 and IRQ 5 for Sound Blaster compatibility. Also, you can have separate DMA and IRQ settings when your sound card is used with Windows (described in Chapter 12).

Most sound cards include installation software that analyzes your PC and attempts to find settings not yet assigned to other devices. Although fairly reliable, this analysis is not complete because it is not always possible to detect a device unless it is operating during the analysis.

Resolving Interrupt Problems

Your sound card may support any of several IRQs (see table 9.1). Many of the 16 IRQs are reserved for parts of your PC, such as the keyboard (IRQ2). Some sound cards work only with certain IRQs. For example, the Windows Sound System supports IRQs 7, 9, 10, and 11 (the default), whereas Logitech SoundMan 16 can use either 2, 3, 5, 7, 10, 11, 12, or 15. The primary symptom of an interrupt conflict is that a sound skips, playing continuously.

Table 9.1
Interrupts and What They Control

Interrupt	Device	Comments
0	Timer	
1	Keyboard	
2	Unused	Used in AT-type computers as a gateway to IRQ 8/15 or for EGA/VGA video cards.
3	COM2 (second serial port)	Often used for a modem or mouse.
4	COM1 (first serial port)	Often used for a modem or mouse.
5	Hard disk	Hard disk for XT-type computers and sometimes LPT2 for AT-type computers.
6	FDC (floppy disk drive controller)	
7	LPT1 (first parallel printer port)	May be shared with an expansion card.
8	Clock	Interrupts 8 through 15 are available on AT-type computers only and often not to expansion cards.
9	PC network	
10–12	Unused	

Interrupt	Device	Comments
13	Math co-processor	Used for speeding mathematical calculations, such as in spreadsheet or computer-aided design (CAD) programs.
14	Hard disk	
15	Unused	

Directing the DMAs

Your sound card also supports several DMA channels (see table 9.2). Many of the eight DMAs are reserved for parts of your PC, such as your floppy disk controller (DMA 2). DMA channels 5, 6, and 7 are used to provide the best performance under Windows. The primary symptom of a DMA conflict is that you hear no sound at all.

Table 9.2
DMA Channels and Purpose

DMA Channel	Purpose
0	Unused
1	Often reserved for Sound Blaster compatibility
2	Used by your floppy disk controller
3	Unused
4	Refreshes your computer's memory
5	Unused
6	Unused
7	Unused

Chapter 9

Deduction, Watson!

The best way to find your hardware conflict is to locate all the documentation for your PC and its various devices, such as a tape drive interface card, CD-ROM drive, and so on. Use table 9.3 to list the DMA, IRQ, and address that each uses. I've started the list for you. By deduction and the following procedure, you can find which device is causing the problem.

Microsoft Windows 3.1 and DOS6 include a DOS diagnostic utility called MSD.EXE. This utility provides detailed information about your PC, including which interrupts are used. To run it, type:

```
MSD
```

Table 9.3
Hardware Configuration

Device	DMA	IRQ	I/O Address
Timer	na	0	
Keyboard	na	1	
COM1	na	4	
COM2	na	3	
LPT1	na	7	
Memory refresh	4	na	
Floppy disk	2	6	
Hard disk (ATs, PS/2s)	na	14	
Math co-processor	na	13	
PC network	na	9	

Chapter 9

Device	DMA	IRQ	I/O Address
EGA/VGA card	na	2	

Hardware conflicts are normally caused by the following:

♪ Network interface cards

♪ Tape drive interface cards

♪ Special printer controllers (such as a PostScript controllers

♪ SCSI or other device controllers

♪ Scanner interface cards

How do you find which device is in conflict with your sound card? Temporarily remove all your expansion cards except your sound card and other essential cards (such as your video card). Then, add each removed card one at a time until your sound card no longer works. The last card added is the trouble-maker.

Listen Up!

If you own Sound Blaster 16 ASP, run the TESTSB16 diagnostic utility as you remove each card. If TESTSB16 works, the last card removed is the culprit.

Curing the Patient

After you have found the card causing the conflict, either switch the settings for the other device conflicting with your sound card or change the settings of the sound card. In either case, you will have to change the IRQ, DMA, or I/O address. To do this requires setting jumpers or DIP switches or using your sound card's setup software to change its settings.

♪ For the SoundMan 16, you must go to the \SOUNDMAN directory and type:

SETUP (press Enter)

♪ For the Sound Blaster 16 ASP, go to the \SB16 directory and type:

SBCONFIG (press Enter)

♪ For Pro AudioStudio 16, go to the \PASTUDIO directory and type:

INSTALL (press Enter)

Changing the settings of your sound card is simple when your sound card works under DOS. (Chapter 12 describes how Windows works with sound cards.) If you know how to edit your CONFIG.SYS or AUTOEXEC.BAT files, you can make the changes yourself.

For the Logitech SoundMan 16 and Pro AudioStudio 16 sound cards, the same naming conventions are used. For both, the sound driver is loaded in the CONFIG.SYS file. This line may look like this:

```
DEVICEHIGH=C:\SOUNDMAN\MVSOUND.SYS D:5 Q:15 /S:1,220,1,7
/M:1,330,2 J:0 V:65
```

or

```
DEVICE=C:\PASTUDIO\MVSOUND.SYS D:5 Q:7 S:1,220,1,5
M:1,330,2 J:0
```

What does each switch mean?

D:# sets the DMA channel for the sound card. A different value is used for the sound card to be Sound Blaster-compatible. Popular values are 0, 3, 5, 6, and 7.

Q:# sets the IRQ. Popular values are 2, 3, 5, and 7.

S:w,x,y,z sets the Sound Blaster-compatible portion of these sound cards.

> The first value, w, sets whether the Sound Blaster compatibility is on (1) or off (0). Typically, you want this on to use the card with your computer games. The next value, x, sets the base I/O address for Sound Blaster compatibility. Typically, this value is 220. The third value, y, sets the DMA channel to be used. DMA 1 is used. The last value, z, sets the interrupt to be used. Use either 5 or 7.

M:x,y,z sets the MIDI-compatible MPU-401 emulation.

> The first value, x, turns on (1) or off (0) this MIDI portion of your sound card. The next value, y, sets the I/O address used for MPU-401 emulation. Possible choices are either 300 or 330. The last value, z, is the interrupt used for MPU-401. Possible IRQs are either 2, 3, 5, or 7.

T:# sets the timing of the card. Keep this set to 1.

J:# turns on (1) or off (0) the game port on the sound card (described later).

V:# sets the volume on a scale of 1 to 100.

If you are installing Pro AudioStudio 16, you also must edit your AUTOEXEC.BAT file. An *environment variable* is used to turn on Sound Blaster compatibility. This line looks like this:

```
SET BLASTER=A220 D1 I5 T3
```

What does each of these switches mean? **A220** is the Sound Blaster-compatible address, **D1** is the DMA channel, **I5** is the interrupt, and **T3** is the timing. These settings should match the settings in the **S:#** switch mentioned earlier.

If you own Sound Blaster 16 ASP, you also can edit the AUTOEXEC.BAT file. Two lines in AUTOEXEC.BAT may look like this:

```
SET BLASTER=A220 I5 D1 H5 P330 T6
SET SOUND=C:\SB16
```

The BLASTER environment variable helps your PC locate and use the software drivers for Sound Blaster 16 ASP. The BLASTER environment variable sets the I/O address, IRQ, and DMA. These settings were selected through the Sound Blaster's jumpers.

What does each setting mean?

A220 is the base I/O address 220. Other choices are 240, 260, and 280.

I5 specifies IRQ 5. Other choices are 2, 7, and 10.

D1 specifies DMA channel 1 as the 8-bit DMA channel. Other choices are 0 and 3.

H5 specifies the DMA channel 5 as the 16-bit channel. Other choices are 6 and 7.

T6 specifies the type of sound card; do not change this.

Common Symptoms

Just as symptoms accompany the common cold, certain symptoms indicate sound-card problems. Use the following sections to diagnose problems.

No Sound

If you don't hear anything from your sound card, consider these solutions:

♪ Are the speakers connected? Check that you plugged in the speakers to your sound card's stereo line out or speaker jack.

♪ If you are using amplified speakers, are they powered on? Check the strength of the batteries or the adapter's connection to the electrical outlet.

Listen Up!

I once owned a pair of Sony amplified speakers. An avid computer game player, I needed a new set of batteries every week. The first time the batteries ran out, I was surprised when I couldn't hear any sound. The batteries had become so drained that they could not drive the speaker.

♪ Are the speakers stereo? Check that the plug inserted into the jack is a stereo plug, not mono.

Chapter 9

♪ Are mixer settings high enough? Many sound cards include a mixer control for DOS and Microsoft Windows. The mixer controls the settings for various sound devices, such as a microphone or CD player. Your sound card may have controls for both record and playback. Increase the master volume or speaker volume when you are in play mode, as shown in figure 9.1. In DOS, you can adjust the setting either by modifying your CONFIG.SYS file or pressing keys. Both Logitech SoundMan 16 and Pro AudioStudio 16 control the volume by keystrokes. Press Ctrl-Alt-U to increase the volume or Ctrl-Alt-D to decrease it.

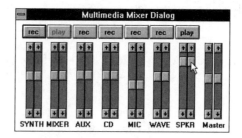

Figure 9.1:
Increasing the speaker may solve your problem.

Adjusting the volume through CONFIG.SYS is a little trickier. As part of the line that loads your sound card's device driver, you may see a switch that sets the initial volume each time your PC starts. For SoundMan 16, this line may look like this:

```
DEVICEHIGH=C:\SOUNDMAN\MVSOUND.SYS D:5 Q:15
/S:1,220,1,7 /M:1,330,2 J:0 T:1 V:65
```

The last switch, V:65, sets the volume on a scale of 1 to 100. You can edit this line to increase or decrease the initial volume; the higher the number, the louder the card.

♪ Have you used your sound card's setup or diagnostic software to test and adjust the volume of your sound card? Such software usually includes sample sounds that play. Sound Blaster 16 ASP, for instance, includes TESTSB16.

♪ Have you tried a hard reset? Turn off your computer for one minute, and then turn it back on. Such a *hard reset* (as opposed to pressing the reset button or Ctrl-Alt-Del) may clear the problem.

♪ Do you lack sound in your computer game? Check that the game works with your sound card. For example, some games may require the exact settings to be Sound Blaster-compatible.

One-Sided Sound

You may hear sound coming from one speaker only.

♪ Are you using a mono plug in the stereo jack? A common mistake is to connect a mono plug to the sound card's speaker or stereo out jacks. Seen from the side, a stereo connector has two darker stripes. A mono connector has only one stripe (see fig. 9.2).

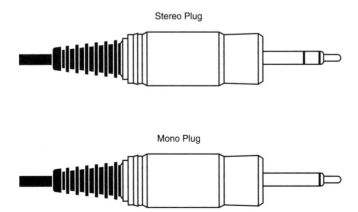

Figure 9.2:

A mono versus stereo speaker plug.

Chapter 9

Listen Up!

If you plug a mono plug into a stereo speaker jack, you may permanently damage your sound card.

♪ Is the driver loaded? Some sound cards provide only left-channel sound if the driver is not loaded in the CONFIG.SYS file. Again, run your sound card's setup software.

Volume Is Low

If you can barely hear your sound card, try these solutions:

♪ Are the mixer settings too low? Again, adjust the volume level in your DOS or Windows mixer. If your sound card uses keystrokes to adjust the volume, use them.

♪ Is the initial volume too low? Some sound cards provide volume settings as part of the line in CONFIG.SYS that loads the sound-card driver. The number regarding the volume may be set too low.

♪ Are the speakers too weak? Some speakers may need more power than your sound card can produce. Try other speakers or put a stereo amplifier between your sound card and speakers.

Scratchy Sound

If you hear scratchy sound from your sound card, try the following:

♪ Is your sound card near other expansion cards? A sound card may be picking up electrical interference from other

expansion cards inside your PC. Move the sound card to an expansion slot as far away as possible from other cards.

♪ Are your speakers too close to your monitor? The speakers may pick up electrical noise from your video monitor. Move them farther away.

Your Computer Won't Start

If your computer won't start at all, you may not have inserted the sound card completely into its slot. Turn off your PC, and then press firmly on the card until it is seated correctly.

Parity Error or Other Lockups

Your computer may give you a memory parity error message or may simply crash. Several things can cause this:

♪ Is there a DMA conflict? When your computer "crashes," it most likely is caused by the sound card using the same DMA channel as another device, such as a disk, tape drive, or scanner. Use your sound-card setup software to change the DMA channel.

♪ Is there an I/O address conflict? Another card may be using some of the I/O addresses used by your sound card. Try to remove some of the other cards to see if that resolves the conflict. If so, change the address of either that card or your sound card.

♪ Are you using the wrong DMA channels? Some sound cards work better with 16-bit DMA channels, such as 5, 6, or 7. Some computers, however, don't work well with them. Try using DMA 3, if available.

Chapter 9

♪ Are you using DMA 1 for Sound Blaster compatibility? Many games require Sound Blaster compatibility set to DMA 1. This can cause conflicts with other cards. Try to change the other boards, unless you can set the game to another DMA.

♪ Should you try another Sound Blaster I/O port? You can change the I/O address required for Sound Blaster compatibility. The default setting is 220. Check that your game can accept a different value.

Joystick Won't Work

If your joystick doesn't work, try the following procedure:

♪ Are you using two game ports? If you already have a game port installed in your PC, the joystick port provided on your sound card may conflict with it. To resolve this conflict, disable the joystick port on your sound card, or disable the one already in your PC. On the Logitech SoundMan 16 and Pro AudioStudio 16 sound cards, the joystick can be turned on or off with a simple change to the device driver line in CONFIG.SYS. For example, the following line is for Pro AudioStudio 16:

```
DEVICE=C:\PASTUDIO\MVSOUND.SYS D:5 Q:7 S:1,220,1,5
M:1,330,2 J:0
```

The last switch, J:0, is used to turn the joystick on or off. On is J:1 and off is J:0. If you have a separate game card or joystick port, change this setting to J:0.

♪ Is your computer too fast? Some faster computers get confused by inexpensive game ports. During the heat of battle, for example, you may find yourself flying upside

down or spiraling out of control. This is one sign that your game port is inadequate. A dedicated game card, such as CH Products GameCard III, can work with faster computers. Such game cards include software to calibrate your joystick and dual ports to let you enjoy a game with a friend. Another solution is to run your computer at a slower speed, which is usually done by pressing some type of turbo button on your PC.

Call the Built-In Doctor

Some sound cards include a diagnostic program. Sound Blaster 16 ASP includes the DOS utility TESTSB16. TESTSB16 tests and provides information about your Sound Blaster's settings. TESTSB16 has the following two tests:

♪ **Hardware configuration.** This utility checks for potential hardware conflicts.

♪ **Audio output.** This test checks the output of synthesized music and digitized sounds. Make sure that your speakers are connected, powered on (if amplified), and that the volume is adjusted on both the speakers and the Sound Blaster card itself.

To run this diagnostic program, simply type the following:

TESTSB16 (press Enter)

During the audio output portion of the test, four sounds of various complexity are played. If you do not hear the 8- or 16-bit digitized sounds, you may have either an IRQ or a DMA conflict. By using SBCONFIG.EXE, you can change these settings.

Chapter 9

Unsolvable Problems

Unfortunately, some sound-card problems cannot be solved. Your PC may be of a certain design that your sound card cannot support. For example, I initially could not get Windows Sound System to work with my PC. It worked, but it played the WAV files either at chipmunk speed or with garbage disposal-like quality. A call to Microsoft's technical support staff helped to decipher the problem. The Windows Sound System was not tested with a PC that uses the Symphony chipset, a type of motherboard design. Apparently, this chipset handles the DMA channel differently from other motherboard designs. The solution was to wait for new software drivers and manually edit the SYSTEM.INI file.

Listen Up!

I found that four sound cards I reviewed did not fully work with my PC. One company even told me to return the sound card as defective. After some late-night tinkering, I found the answer. In my PC's AMI BIOS setup program, the choice for the Timing Parameter Selection was set to 1, the best-case value. (Somehow, this value affects the DMA timing.) After changing the value to 0, all four sound cards worked properly. I certainly was surprised; my previous 8-bit sound card never posed any difficulties.

My main point here is that you shouldn't be frustrated if your sound card doesn't immediately work. The PC "standard" is based loosely upon cooperation among a handful of companies. Something as simple as one vendor's BIOS or motherboard design can make the standard nonstandard.

Help!

The preceding sections dealt with techniques to isolate and fix common sound-card problems. When you're hit with the uncommon sound-card problem, you need to find uncommon help. Pick up the phone and call the sound-card technical support.

Free Help—The Best Kind!

When your PC is under the weather, several sources of free help are available. Neighbors or co-workers, for instance, may have some experience with sound cards or at least DMAs, IRQs, and I/O addresses. They can provide a helping hand. At the very least, they can provide a shoulder upon which you can cry.

A local computer-user's group is a wonderful source of help. These groups typically meet once a month. The meetings often consist of a demonstration by a vendor. Also, these groups normally have an "open access" portion to their meeting to answer any questions members have. For a $30 to $100 per year membership fee, these groups provide ample sources of information, including a newsletter that lists people to contact who have specific areas of expertise.

You can enlarge your universe of helpful friends by using a local *bulletin board system* (BBS) or on-line service, such as PRODIGY or CompuServe. (This is only if your PC is operational enough to use these services; if not, use a friend's PC.) These services have electronic bulletin boards through which you can leave public messages asking for help.

I used to oversee PRODIGY service's Computer Club bulletin board. Over 10,000 messages were placed daily on this one

board alone! Often, people who left messages didn't provide enough up-front information. They would simply write: "HELP! My printer won't print. Can you help me?" To enable these people to help you, provide the following information in your first message:

♪ Brand and type of PC you have, such as an AST Research 386/33.

♪ Amount of memory you have.

♪ Peripherals attached to this PC, such as a laser printer, modem, and so on.

♪ Version of DOS you are using. (To find out which version you have, type **VER** at the DOS prompt.)

♪ Software you were using when the problem occurred.

♪ Any recent changes leading up to the problem.

With this information, you can start a dialog with those who can help you. Check daily for replies to your message. Those who want to help may need further information from you before they can offer a solution.

Seeking Support

Some help you've already paid for. The technical support staff of the company that made your sound card provides help over the phone and on some of the on-line services, such as CompuServe. Because you usually pay for this call (although Media Vision has a toll-free number), make sure that you have exhausted your other sources, including the manual.

Before you call a technical support department, prepare yourself for the help you are about to receive by performing these tasks:

♪ If your PC includes a diagnostic disk, use it before you call. Even if the diagnostic routine doesn't give you enough information to fix the problem yourself, you can at least boast to the technician that you did use it and can provide the technician with the information.

♪ Try to isolate the problem. For example, look for patterns. Does the problem happen only when you use a particular program or at certain times of the day? What exactly were you doing when the problem occurred? For example, one sound card I tested became mute in DOS games only after I had exited Windows.

♪ Watch for error codes. Jot down any error codes that flash on your screen. These codes can be invaluable to a trained technician.

♪ If the problem occurs when you are running a particular software program, reinstall it from the original disks. Very often, the problem was caused by a file copied incorrectly from the disks.

♪ Know the version of DOS running on your PC. Simply type **VER** to discover which version of DOS you are using. Your PC will respond with a message such as
`MS-DOS Version 6.0`.

♪ Print copies of the AUTOEXEC.BAT and CONFIG.SYS files that start up your computer. From the DOS prompt, type **TYPE C:\AUTOEXEC.BAT >PRN** and **TYPE C:\CONFIG.SYS >PRN**. Having these on paper in front of you can expedite the solution.

♪ If your problem is related to Microsoft Windows, print copies of your WIN.INI and SYSTEM.INI files. Use the same technique as printing copies of your AUTOEXEC.BAT and CONFIG.SYS files. Type

`TYPE C:\WINDOWS\WIN.INI >PRN` and `TYPE C:\WINDOWS`
`\SYSTEM.INI >PRN`. You can also use Windows' SysEdit
utility to display these files. In fact, this utility can also
print your CONFIG.SYS and AUTOEXEC.BAT files. To
print each file, select **P**rint from the **F**ile pulldown menu,
or press Alt-F and then P (print).

♪ Run the DOS utility CHKDSK and write down the
information that appears on your screen. This will give
you and the technician a quick check of total and available drive space, and total and free memory. To use
CHKDSK, type `CHKDSK`. To send the results to the printer,
type `CHKDSK >PRN`.

♪ Have some simple tools available. A simple flat-blade
screwdriver or Phillips-head screwdriver may be required to remove your PC's cover.

Making the Call

Solving your sound-card problem by phone is difficult. It also
can be costly because you often pay for the call. Most likely,
you will have to wait to speak with a technician.

Listen Up!
Avoid being on the phone too long. I once
waited 35 minutes to speak to a technician. If
you find the delay unbearable, you may be
offered a chance to leave a voice mail message. Don't expect an immediate reply to your
message. I once left a voice mail call for help and
received a return call... three days later.

Follow these tips to make the most of these resources:

♪ Make sure that you're sitting at the computer when you call. The technician will rely on you to try lots of things, such as turning the PC off and back on again, typing commands, and unplugging and replugging cables and connectors. You can't do these if you're away from your PC.

♪ Be willing to invest enough time to solve the problem. Don't place the call right before lunch, an appointment, or the end of the work day. If a technician invests the time to answer your call for help, you should stay on the line until the problem is solved.

♪ Get the name of the technician, in case you have to call back. If you've spent 45 minutes describing your problem, then working through it to an apparent solution— and the next day, the problem hits again—you'll save a great deal of time and grief by being able to ask for the same person who helped you previously.

♪ Call between 9:30 and 11:30 a.m., or between 2:30 and 4 p.m. These two times are when the number of calls are fewest. The technicians will have plenty of time to think carefully about your problem. Unless you have an emergency, wait to call during these times. The better service can be worth the delay.

♪ If you have a noncritical problem, fax the details of your problem and your computer's setup information to the tech support department. Include a note asking one of the technicians to call you on a certain day and time to work things out. With the information you provide up front, the technician can research your problem, try to

duplicate it on a test machine, and come up with good answers before calling you. Provide a fax number, if possible, so that if the answer is simple, the technician can send you a solution sooner.

Getting Better, But...

In the last year, technical support for sound cards has significantly improved. I've found my waiting times cut in half. Also, most companies now offer extensive electronic support, such as CompuServe or America Online.

The recent improvements in the installation software, in which your PC is scrutinized before setting the DMA, IRQ, and other vital information, make installing a sound card a little less bloody. With falling prices, increasing sound quality, and growing popularity, sound cards would be even more welcome with easier, trouble-free installation.

Using Your Sound Card

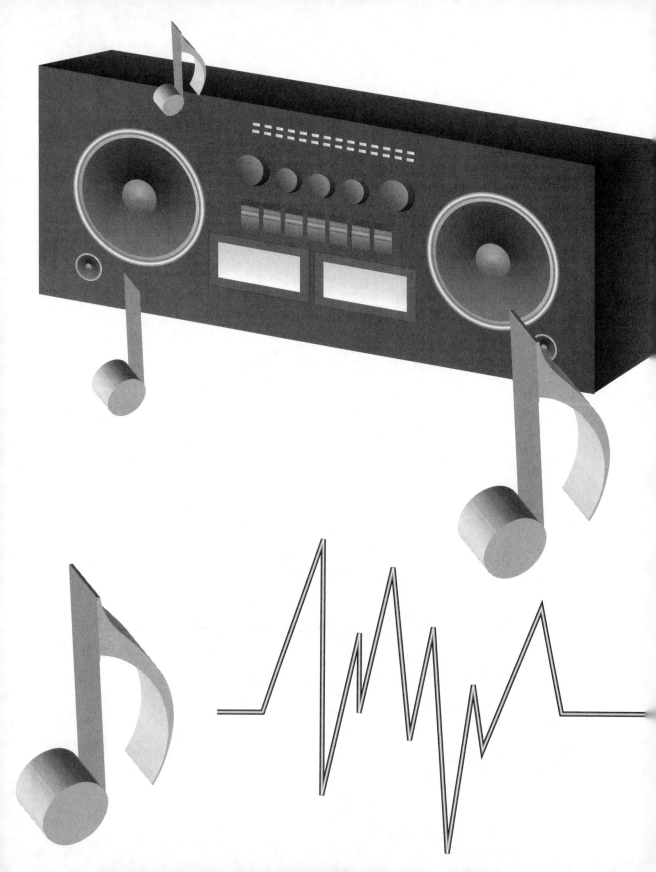

10 Games with a Rumble and a Roar!

Sound cards were made to play games. Instead of firing your cannons with a muffled "plink" from your PC's internal speaker, you can use a sound card to truly hear those deafening cannons roar.

In this chapter, you learn:

- ♪ How sound cards improve games
- ♪ About the history of game sound
- ♪ About common sound card and game problems
- ♪ Techniques to improve your game's sound
- ♪ About the impact of CD-ROM drives on game sound

Chapter 10

Pick a Card, Any Card

Many computer games support sound cards, but do they support yours? Most computer games provide support for the big three sound standards: Sound Blaster, AdLib, and Roland MT-32. You may know what Sound Blaster and AdLib are, but what is Roland MT-32? The MT-32 was a popular MIDI synthesizer developed by Roland Corp. By selecting MT-32, you can play exquisite sound with most computer games. Many other MIDI synthesizers are compatible with the MT-32.

Your computer game may also support IBM sound (your PC speaker) or Tandy sound (see fig. 10.1). The Tandy 1000 computers had a built-in sound chip it inherited from the IBM PCjr. This sound chip had a digital-to-audio converter that provided up to three voices. Today's sound cards provide up to 20 voices.

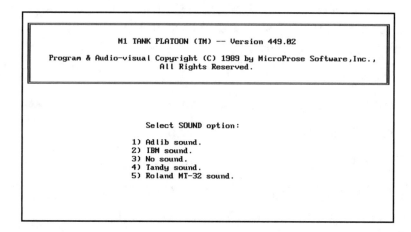

Figure 10.1:
The basic sound-card choices in M-1 Tank Platoon.

Some games support more than the basic three. Some support newer, more-sophisticated versions of Sound Blaster, Voice Master from Covox, ATI Stereo F/X, Disney Sound Source, and the Pro AudioSpectrum family of sound cards. At worst, you can always fall back on your PC's internal speaker (yuck).

If offered, select your exact sound-card model. Some games offer extensive lists (see fig. 10.2). If you add a sound card to an already-installed game, your game will still insist on using your PC speaker or no speaker at all. You need to use the game's setup or installation program to make the switch.

Listen Up!

In some cases, you may have to reinstall the game to have it recognize your new sound hardware.

```
                    Hardware Setup Options:

                    Sound Device:
                    ( ) No sound
                    ( ) PC Speaker
                    ( ) AdLib sound card
                    ( ) COVOX Sound Master
                    ( ) SoundBlaster      (orig.)
                    ( ) SoundBlaster Pro (early)
                    ( ) SoundBlaster Pro (later)
                    ( ) Pro Audio Spectrum
                    (•) Pro Audio Spectrum Plus/16
                    ( ) Roland MT-32/LAPC-1

Use ARROW keys and SPACE bar to select.  Press ENTER when done.

<  OK  >                                        <Cancel>
```

Figure 10.2:
A list of sound cards supported by game developer Sierra On-Line.

Chapter 10

How Sound Cards Improve Game Play

Sound cards can improve games in three ways: musical scores (for background music), digitized voices (for dialogue), and sound effects (for explosions and so forth). Because of their design, some sound cards cannot provide all three. AdLib sound cards, for example, cannot play digitized voices but, instead, are known for playing background music and other effects.

Scene-setting music has been a part of computer games for a long time. Until game developers learned compression techniques, only snippets were used. Later, games became more operatic with entire scores (such as the opening of "Wing Commander"). "Rocket Ranger," a graphic adventure from now-defunct Cinemaware, was an early standout.

With a Sound Blaster (or compatible) sound card, you get not only background music but also digitized voices. For example, a Sound Blaster card lets you hear air traffic control messages in Microsoft Flight Simulator.

The sound you get from a given card depends on not only the sound card but also the effort the game developer has put into those sound effects. For instance, Sierra On-Line in the past has concentrated on making beautiful music with Roland's MT-32. The music, however, doesn't sound as good when other sound cards are selected. Other games generate quite acceptable music for AdLib sound cards. The sound quality is often proportional to a company's experience working with a particular sound card. Some companies program music and digital audio to play to a sound card's strong suit.

Sound Check

The types of games you play also influence how good the sounds are that they generate. Most simulation games—games that simulate real life—have crude sounds, such as screeching tires, explosions, and engine noises. In most cases, these sounds add sufficient enjoyment. Some games go beyond the basics; "Falcon 3.0" from Spectrum Holobyte adds radio chatter and background music. For strategy and sports games, high-quality sound is not as important, except, of course, for the roar of the crowd or background music.

The History of Game Sound

Sound effects and musical scores have been used in games with varying levels of success. Years ago, sophisticated sound effects enhanced computer games. Before sound cards, game makers tried to provide good sound through the PC's internal speaker. RealSound from Access Software was partially successful in providing digitized speech and other effects from the PC speaker. Access' "Mean Streets," a science-fiction role-playing game developed in the late eighties, won acclaim for the way it put the spoken word on a standard PC. For once, you could actually understand the speech without a sound card.

Sound Check

RealSound never became popular, thanks to the inexpensive and feature-laden sound cards from AdLib Inc. (AdLib) and Creative Labs (Sound Blaster).

RealSound, however, hasn't died. "Microsoft Golf for Windows" uses it. Birds and other wildlife chirp periodically (you'll want to turn off this option once you tire of the novelty), and spectators and announcers comment on the action. You'll never tire of those cries of "Nice bird!" when you finish a hole a stroke ahead.

The first sound card was introduced in August 1987 by AdLib Inc. However, AdLib president Martin Prevel had to convince game developers to change their software to accommodate the novel product. When Taito of America released one of the very first games that directly supported the AdLib card, the game-sound revolution was on.

Soon after the AdLib card, Creative Labs (then called Creative Technology) introduced its Game Blaster. Game Blaster was AdLib-compatible and could play 12 stereo instruments simultaneously compared to AdLib's 11 mono instruments. Game Blaster had one chink in its armor; the sound card used AM synthesis instead of FM synthesis. Preferring the Game Blaster over the AdLib card was like preferring AM radio to FM. Even in stereo, Game Blaster didn't sound that good. Game Blaster quickly faded and was superseded by Sound Blaster (code-named the "Killer Card") which was introduced in November 1989.

Unlike the AdLib card, Sound Blaster had a built-in joystick port, a MIDI interface, and, most importantly, *analog-to-digital* (ADC) and *digital-to-analog* (DAC) converters. The result was that instead of just playing music in a game, the sound card could now perform dialogue and sound effects, such as explosions.

Not Perfect

Sound cards do not work perfectly with every game. Many card and sound-driver combinations will result in hesitation between the animation and sound. In some cases, a sound card can prevent you from even installing a game. The game's installation software may halt because of the sound card's presence. For example, game developer MicroProse suggests you type INSTALL-S if you want to turn off the installation

software's capability to recognize your sound card. This auto-detection feature sometimes causes a computer to halt unexpectedly.

Listen Up!

Another problem with games is that you may not be able to control the sound, except through your speakers. The Logitech SoundMan 16 and Media Vision Pro AudioStudio 16 cards, for example, use Ctrl-Alt-U and Ctrl-Alt-D to increase and decrease the volume, respectively. Many games take complete control of your PC, including the keyboard, preventing these commands from working. The only alternative is to adjust your speaker volume by hand.

Some games now work properly when your computer works at top speed or uses an internal/external memory cache. For example, "Falcon 3.0" may produce "popping" sounds or "LHX" or "Ultima VI" may produce distorted or noisy sound effects. If so, you can press your PC's turbo button (if you have one) to slow the computer to match your game.

Sound Blaster Settings

Some Sound Blaster-compatible cards are not considered entirely Sound Blaster-compatible by some games. Some games expect the Sound Blaster-compatible sound card to be using IRQ 7 whereas other games find the IRQ automatically. If the game program can't find the IRQ, your game will start but then lock up. If you can change a game's IRQ setting using the game's installation program, ensure that the setting matches the IRQ value your sound card uses for Sound Blaster-compatibility. Similarly, some games expect your Sound Blaster-compatible sound card to be using DMA channel 1. If your sound card is using a different DMA channel, your sound card may not produce sound effects but will still play the music portion of the game.

The I/O address is another installation pitfall. Sound Blaster uses an I/O address of 220. Some games allow other values to be set, whereas others do not. Check that the value you have set is the one used by your game. The usual symptom of an I/O address conflict is that the game doesn't even recognize the sound card.

Listen Up!

Confused by terms such as DMA and IRQ? Consult Chapters 8 and 9 for more information on these terms and their importance.

Some Sound Blaster-compatible games look to an environment variable in your AUTOEXEC.BAT startup file, such as:

```
SET BLASTER=A220 I5 D1 T3
```

in which A220 is the I/O address, I5 is the interrupt, D1 is the DMA channel, and T3 is a timer parameter that reduces noise. Other games do not look for this variable but allow you to change the Sound Blaster settings through an installation program or by changing a game file. Other games are more rigid and expect the standard Sound Blaster settings.

With the popular "Wing Commander," for example, your computer may lock up or not play any digital audio because of incorrect settings. In this case, you have to turn on speech from "Wing Commander's" INSTALL program. Second, your system must have ample expanded memory. Finally, you should check the WC2.CFG file. This file looks like this:

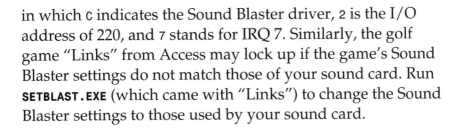

V A904 C27

in which C indicates the Sound Blaster driver, 2 is the I/O address of 220, and 7 stands for IRQ 7. Similarly, the golf game "Links" from Access may lock up if the game's Sound Blaster settings do not match those of your sound card. Run **SETBLAST.EXE** (which came with "Links") to change the Sound Blaster settings to those used by your sound card.

Send More Memory!

The Achilles' heel of many games, which affects sound cards, is memory requirements. Many recent games require at least 600K of free conventional memory to run, and others require expanded memory to create full sound effects. "Falcon 3.0," for example, allows you to fly an F-16 without joining the Air Force. Although "Falcon 3.0" includes exquisite video sequences and exciting real-time combat, its large memory requirements limit its appeal. This flight simulator requires expanded memory if you want speech-synthesized radio chatter. To help out, Spectrum HoloByte includes instructions for making a separate boot disk to optimize memory.

Sound Check

What's conventional and expanded memory? You are already familiar with *conventional memory*; it is the memory into which you load your DOS games or other software. Conventional memory, also known as base or low memory, is any memory below 1M. *Extended memory* (XMS) is memory above 1M. This memory is usually not directly available to your computer, except through special programs, such as Microsoft Windows or disk-caching software. *Expanded memory* (EMS) is, for the most part, converted extended memory.

continues

continued

> The total amount of memory you own is different than how much you have free. Why? Part of the operating system must occupy your PC's conventional memory. Also, your sound-card driver, such as MVSOUND.SYS, and other device drivers require memory. All of these eat away at your total conventional memory. After DOS and these other programs are loaded, the remaining memory is called *free memory*. This remaining memory is what's available to load your game.

If you are using Logitech SoundMan 16 or the Media Vision Pro AudioStudio 16, you can add the /U switch to the line that loads the sound-card driver MVSOUND.SYS. This line in CONFIG.SYS may look like this:

```
DEVICE=C:\SOUNDMAN\MVSOUND.SYS D:5 Q:15 /S:1,220,1,7 /M:0,330,2 J:0 T:1 V:65 /U
```

The /U switch at the end unloads the sound driver from your PC's memory once the card is activated. One disadvantage of unloading the driver is that you can't change the volume level later.

Superior Sound

If you want the very best sound in your computer games, follow these tips:

♪ First, connect your sound card to your stereo system. Playing your sound card through an amplified stereo will give you lifelike sound. Your tank's engines will rumble as loud as the real thing, and you'll feel your jet's afterburners kick in. For more information on connecting your sound card to a stereo system, consult Chapter 7.

♪ If you can't route your sound card to a stereo system, invest in a good pair of computer speakers (covered in

Chapter 5). Don't buy an inexpensive pair; consider spending at least $100 for the pair. If this is beyond your budget, you can buy a good set of headphones for under $30. You will not only get good sound but also avoid disturbing others nearby.

Listen Up!

Avoid playing your games too loudly. You may develop temporary or permanent hearing loss or impairment. Before putting on any set of headphones, hold them away from your ears to avoid injury from unexpected noise or static. If your sound card has a volume control, turn it down before you put on your headphones.

♪ If your sound card is both AdLib- and Sound Blaster-compatible, instruct your game's installation or setup program that you have a Sound Blaster-compatible sound card. This setting provides you with digitized voices and other audio goodies in the game.

♪ If you own Sound Blaster 16 ASP, consider getting the optional Wave Blaster. Wave Blaster is a daughterboard that connects to the Sound Blaster card. Instead of using FM synthesis to imitate musical instruments, Wave Blaster includes actual recorded instruments. This can provide exceptional, lifelike music.

Listen Up!

The DMA channel your sound card is using may also affect game play. Some experts I spoke to recommend you set your sound card to use DMA 5, rather than 6 or 7.

♪ A 16-bit sound card, like Sound Blaster 16 ASP, can actually make an 8-bit game sound worse. You may hear unwanted "hissing" sounds in some games. Some sound cards include a treble control to cut down this high-pitched hiss. Set the treble level listed in your AUTOEXEC.BAT file to zero. This line may look like this:

```
C:\SB16\SB16SET /M:220 /VOC:220 /CD:220 /MIDI:220 /TREBLE:0
```

After restarting your PC, your older 8-bit games will sound better.

Proper Timing

Sound Blaster 16 ASP, Logitech Soundman 16, and Pro AudioStudio 16 (and other sound cards) use a timing switch. You can change this switch to reduce noise the sound card picks up from your PC's internal timer.

In Sound Blaster cards, a line in your AUTOEXEC.BAT may look like this:

```
SET BLASTER=A220 I5 D1 T3
```

For Logitech SoundMan and Media Vision Pro AudioStudio 16, a line in CONFIG.SYS may look like this:

```
DEVICEHIGH=C:\SOUNDMAN\MVSOUND.SYS D:5 Q:15 /S:1,220,1,7 /M:0,330,2 J:0 T:1 V:65
```

For both, the number after the T switch (T3 or T:1, respectively), select a timing parameter. If you hear excessive electrical static from your speakers, change this value to a different number, from 1 to 6. Whenever you change your AUTOEXEC.BAT or CONFIG.SYS files, remember to restart your computer so that the new timing parameter will go into effect.

Games on a Disc

If you have a CD-ROM player, you can buy a plethora of games that have earth-shaking sounds and musical scores (see fig. 10.3). Although multimedia is often considered a term in pursuit of a technology, or a technology looking for a market, the truth is that it's been part of games for a long time.

Figure 10.3:
Digitized sound enhances the latest games, such as "The Dig" from LucasArts.

CD-ROM discs hold such enormous amounts of data that they can replace games that require up to 10 floppy disks during installation. CD-ROM discs give game developers almost unlimited space (up to 680M per disc!) to add such game features as: more elaborate sound effects, album-like sound tracks, detailed graphical bitmapped or object-oriented backgrounds, and more talk. CD-ROM games will bring millions of more users into the computer game-playing fold.

Chapter 10

The new MPC Level 2 specifications (see Chapter 3) provide a new level of game-playing sophistication. A 486SX PC with 4M RAM and a 160M hard disk should provide ample power for game playing. The double-speed, 300 Kbps CD-ROM drive mandated by the new specifications will provide faster retrieval of game information from the disc.

Sound Check

Most CD games are simply retreads of games that originated on floppy. In some cases, the CD is simply a substitute-delivery medium that replaces what would have been dozens of disks. "Stellar 7" from Dynamix, for instance, which was first available only on floppy disks, was made available later on CD-ROM.

Or consider the CD version of "Secret Weapons of the Luftwaffe," a World War II flight simulator that pits American planes against futuristic Nazi jet- and rocket-propelled aircraft. The CD holds not only the game itself but also the contents of several second-purchase packages which add planes to both sides' rosters. The only thing different about the CD version of Secret Weapons is the media itself—what's on the compact disc is identical to what you get when you buy the floppy-based game and the extra aircraft disks.

What Comes on CD

Despite the advantages of a CD, such as providing more graphics and sounds on a single disc, many game developers are not making full use of this technology. Nevertheless, some CD versions of games do give you more. "Battle Chess" tacks on some extras not found on the floppy-disk version. This chess

game uses the CD to pour on additional digitized sound effects, much more music, and over 100M of graphics. When you play "Battle Chess MPC," the pieces still fight over their chessboard territory, as they do in the disk version. Now, though, you actually hear grunts and groans as a Knight takes on a Pawn, for instance, or the metallic sound of sword on shield, or the occasional voice. The background musical score swells at the right places. The sheer size of these baubles demands use of a CD-ROM.

"Where in the World is Carmen Sandiego? Deluxe Edition" is another example of a CD game that provides additional sounds. This version allows kids to visit more countries, interact with more characters, and work with more clues than the floppy version. The CD version includes folk tunes, spoken foreign-language clues, and digitized photographs of the game's locations.

"7th Guest," a ghost-story adventure game from Virgin, will occupy at least two compact discs. This game uses much digitized video, actors' voices, creepy music, and plenty of audio effects.

With few exceptions, multimedia games that mix some or all of the following—sound, graphics, speech, music, or video—are little more than beefed-up versions of existing titles. Rarely is the software publisher willing to stake new development costs on something as risky as CD on the PC. Many gamesters will wonder, why should I pay $80 to $100 for a game? We will probably consider CD-based games as simply an alternative delivery vehicle for our games. Hopefully, those games especially designed to take advantage of the CD (such as holding plenty of digitized sound) will cause game players to acquire CD-ROM drives.

Chapter 10

No CD Required?

Although more and more games are available on CD-ROM discs, not every publisher is rushing to put its wares on the shiny platter. Some games work just fine without a CD-ROM drive. "Wing Commander II," the sequel to Origin Systems' wildly popular space flight-simulation/role-playing adventure, is one of the best examples of floppy-based multimedia.

This space opera lets you pilot several different ships in a battle against the evil, feline Kilrathi, and combines the action of a flight simulator with just enough plot to urge you to the next combat mission (see fig. 10.4).

Figure 10.4:
The feline fiend in "Wing Commander II."

The graphics in "Wing Commander II" are stunning, with colorful explosions of ships in space, detailed cockpits, and high-resolution backgrounds. The opening sequence, which shows the destruction of the humans' space carrier by the

Kilrathi, is about as cinematic as games get. Music sweeps through the game to set the science fiction mood, and sound effects add nicely to the battles. Figure 10.5 puts you in the cockpit.

Figure 10.5:
From your "Wing Commander II" cockpit, you can defend the Earth.

You watch the plot unfold as a third-party observer (camera-like in places). If you have a Sound Blaster sound card and buy the $19.95 Speech Accessory Pack add-on, you'll hear radio messages as you dogfight. (Reportedly, Origin has sold more than 55,000 copies of the Speech Accessory Pack, illustrating the extent of interest in multimedia and the number of sound cards installed on PCs.)

Whether on CD-ROM or floppy disks, all games will be judged by the same criteria: depth of play, length of play, and quality of the imaginary world. My bet is that a sound card and a CD-ROM drive can provide these using flashier sound, narration, music, graphics, and animation.

Recording Studio on a Disk

Sound cards come with several sound utilities. Without these utilities, sound cards would mainly be limited to game playing. These utilities, however, often consume several megabytes of space. How do you separate the wheat from the chaff? This chapter explores DOS utilities; Chapter 12 covers Windows utilities.

In this chapter, you learn:

- ♪ How to use your sound card's testing utility
- ♪ How to record and play back sound files
- ♪ How to use your sound card's DOS-based mixer
- ♪ How to play music and text files
- ♪ How to play audio CDs with a DOS-based utility

Chapter 11

This Is a Test

Your sound card may come with several DOS utilities for recording, manipulating, and playing back sound and music files. Some sound cards include testing software. Sound Blaster 16 ASP, for example, includes the Sound Blaster 16 Test Program (see fig. 11.1). This program tests various features of your sound card, such as the base I/O address, IRQ, and DMA channels being used. If the tests are successful, the test utility plays some sample music and sounds. This Sound Blaster test utility is started by switching to the \SB16 directory and typing **TESTSB16**.

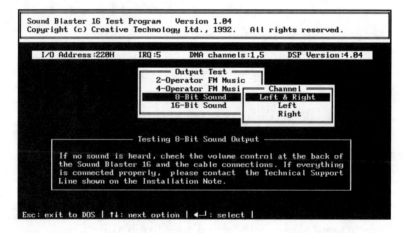

Figure 11.1:
Some sound cards include built-in test utilities.

After checking your I/O address, DMA channel, and IRQ, then test your sound (see fig. 11.1).

Listen Up!

If you don't hear any sounds, turn up the volume control on your sound card, or use the keystrokes that control your sound card (such as Ctrl-Alt-U on Logitech SoundMan 16 and Media Vision Pro AudioStudio 16).

If you use Sound Blaster 16 ASP, you have another utility that lists the versions of the various Creative Labs drivers. This can be useful when you call technical support for help. This utility is found in the \VOCUTIL subdirectory. Simply type the following command:

\SB16\VOCUTIL\READDRV

If no path to the driver is entered (as shown in the preceding example), READDRV looks to the BLASTER environment variable in your AUTOEXEC.BAT file for the location of the drivers. The screen reports the name, version, address, IRQ, and DMA that each Sound Blaster driver uses (see fig. 11.2).

```
Creative Driver Reader Utility    Version 1.05
Copyright (c) Creative Labs, Inc., 1991-1992. All right reserved.
Copyright (c) Creative Technology Ltd, 1992. All rights reserved

C:\SB16\DRV

File :          CT-VOICE.DRV Creative Sound Blaster 16
Version :       3.05 Release 01
BaseAddr :      220
Interrupt :     5
DMA :           1

File :          CTVDSK.DRV Creative Sound Blaster 16
Version :       3.03 Release 01
BaseAddr :      220
Interrupt :     5
DMA :           1

File :          AUXDRV.DRV Creative Sound Blaster 16
Version :       3.00 Release 01
BaseAddr :      220

File :          CTWDSK.DRV Creative Sound Blaster 16
Version :       3.03 Release 00
--- Press any key to continue ---
```

Figure 11.2:
READDRV shows your driver versions.

Chapter 11

Letting Your Voice Be Heard

Besides testing utilities, your sound card may include DOS utilities that record and play back sound files. The Sound Blaster family of sound cards uses a file format called VOC, named after the three-letter extension such files use. These utilities can also support the *waveform audio* (WAV) format. The WAV format is used by Microsoft Windows.

Sound Blaster includes the following utilities:

♪ **VREC.EXE.** Records voice in the VOC format.

♪ **VPLAY.EXE.** Plays back recorded VOC files.

♪ **VOC02N.EXE.** Converts version 1.10 voice files to the newer 1.20.

♪ **VOCN20.EXE.** Converts version 1.20 voice files to 1.10.

♪ **VOC_HDR.EXE.** Adds a VOC header to a file containing raw sound data. After the header is added, you can play the file by using VPLAY.EXE.

♪ **JOINTVOC.EXE.** Joins or combines several voice files.

♪ **WPLAY.EXE.** Plays WAV files.

♪ **WREC.EXE.** Records WAV files.

Pro AudioStudio includes just two utilities:

♪ **PLAYFILE.EXE.** Plays a VOC or WAV file.

♪ **RECFILE.EXE.** Records a VOC or WAV file.

Recording a File

Recording a file from the DOS prompt is simple. Sound Blaster's VREC and WREC utilities are virtually identical.

You can record to your hard disk from a microphone or other sound source, such as a stereo. The length of the recording is limited by your hard-disk space. If you want to record a VOC file, for instance, type the command:

```
VREC filename.VOC
```

In the preceding line, *filename* is the name of your VOC file. You can add various switches to tailor your mini-recording session, such as the following example illustrates:

```
VREC TEST.VOC /B:32 /A:MIC /R:16 /S:44100 /M:MONO
```

What are all these choices?

/B:xx reserves memory during recording so that nothing is lost. The default size for this double-buffering is 16K, but can be set from 2 to 32.

/A:xx selects the recording source, such as MIC (microphone), CD (audio CD), LINE (stereo line in), or FM (FM music). You can record from several sources by using a plus sign (+) to combine the sources. For example, /A:MIC+CD records from the microphone and an attached CD.

/R:xx sets the recording resolution at either 8 or 16 bits. The default is 8, which is fine for recording the human voice.

/S:xx sets the sampling rate. For VREC, you can set the sampling rate from 5KHz to 44.1KHz. For WREC, you are limited to 11KHz, 22.05KHz, or 44.1KHz. The higher the sampling rate, the more accurate the sound; but more disk space is required.

/M:xx selects the recording mode. Use MONO if recording from a monaural source or STEREO if recording from a stereo source. For instance, select MONO if you are recording from a microphone; MONO is the default.

Chapter 11

/T:xx sets the length of the recording time in seconds, up to 65,535 (18 hours).

/Q specifies a "quiet" screen so that no information is displayed on the screen during recording.

/X=command line runs another DOS program as soon as the recording starts.

In the preceding example, the VOC file TEST.VOC was recorded by using the maximum buffer of 32K (**/B:32**) through a microphone (**/A:MIC**) at a resolution of 16 bits (**/R:16**) and sampling rate of 44.1 KHz (**/S:44100**).

RECFILE.EXE used by Pro AudioStudio 16 is simpler; you type:

```
RECFILE filename.ext Rxxxxx Dx Ix S 16
```

filename.ext is the name of the file you are recording. The file is saved to the format of the extension you use. If, for instance, the filename is TEST.WAV, the file is saved as a WAV file.

Rxxxxx sets the sampling rate of the recording from 6KHz to 44.1KHz.

Dx and **Ix** switches specify the number of the DMA channel and IRQ, respectively; these are optional.

S switch forces the recording to be stereo; the default is mono.

16 switch is used to record at a resolution of 16 bits. Without this switch, the recording is done with 8 bits.

Playing a File

After you've recorded a WAV or VOC file, you can then play it back. For Sound Blaster 16 ASP, simply type the command:

```
xPLAY filename
```

x is either V for VOC files or W for WAV files.

filename is the name of the file you recorded. You don't need to include the file's three-letter extension.

For Pro AudioStudio 16, you can type:

```
PLAYFILE filename Dx Ix S Sxxx 16 Rxxxxx
```

filename can be either a WAV or VOC file.

The same switches used in recording can be used for playback. If the stereo (S) switch is used, a mono file is played back through both speakers.

S*xxx* switch adjusts the speed of the file, in which *xxx* ranges from 0 (silence) to 200 (double-speed).

Joined at the Hip

Sound Blaster 16 ASP includes a utility to join several voice files together. The following line joins the two voice files FILE1.VOC and FILE2.VOC together to form FILE3.VOC:

```
JOINTVOC /TFILE3 FILE1.VOC FILE2.VOC
```

You can also include a moment of silence between each joined file by using the /S:*xx* switch, in which *xx* represents tenths of a second. In the following example, a one-second pause is added between the two joined files.

```
JOINTVOC /TACCIDENT.VOC SCREECH.VOC /S:10 CRASH.VOC
```

You can also have a file repeat a certain number of times during the joining process. The repeat switch (/R:*xx*) applies to all files until the repeat end (/RE) command is encountered. In the

Chapter 11

following example, the first two files repeat five times, but the third file does not repeat because the repeat end command precedes it:

```
JOINTVOC /TOUTPUT.VOC FILE1.VOC /R5 FILE2.VOC /RE
FILE3.VOC
```

Converting Files

Sound cards often include utilities to turn one sound file format into that of another. Sound Blaster 16 ASP includes VOC2WAV and WAV2VOC to convert VOC files to WAV files and WAV files to VOC files, respectively. Using this command is quite simple, as the following example illustrates:

```
VOC2WAV VOCFILE WAVFILE
```

You don't need to include the extension for the file formats. During the conversion process, you can use switches to fine-tune the conversion. When converting VOC to WAV files, you can use the following switches:

/Cxx sets files to mono (1) or stereo (2). The default is mono.

/Rxx sets the sampling rate to 11, 22, or 44 KHz. The default is 22.

/Sxx converts silence in the VOC file to the WAV file data block. If set to ON, the silence is converted. The default is OFF.

/Lxx repeats the VOC file according to its built-in repeat count. The default is OFF.

To convert a stereo TEST.VOC file to a mono WAV file sampled at 11.025 KHz, type:

```
VOC2WAV TEST.VOC TEST.WAV /R11 /C1
```

When waveform (WAV) files are turned into VOC files, you also have some extra choices available:

/8 turns 16-bit WAV files into 8-bit VOC files. The default converts the WAV file by using the same number of bits as the original WAV file.

/M converts stereo WAV files to mono VOC files. The default converts the WAV file using the same number of channels as the original WAV file.

Listen Up!

You can use DOS wildcards (such as * or ?) to convert several files at the same time. The following line, for instance, converts all WAV files to VOC files of the same name:

```
WAV2VOC *.WAV
```

Mixing It Up

Sound cards typically include mixer software. A *mixer* allows you to control the volume, gain, and tone of various audio sources. You can, for example, set the recording levels of your microphone and CD player for a voiceover.

Listen Up!

If your DOS mouse driver is loaded, you can use your mouse to make your selections.

A mixer lets you set various settings, including:

  ♪ *Automatic Gain Control* (AGC) to automatically set the microphone's recording level

♪   Master volume

♪   Treble and bass

♪   PC speaker volume (if you attached your PC speaker to your sound card)

♪   CD volume

♪   MIDI volume

♪   Digitized voice volume

♪   Stereo line-input volume

♪   Gain controls to amplify recording levels for both output and input

♪   Left and right volume levels independently

Listen Up!

I was stymied when I used the Sound Blaster's VREC.EXE utility to record my voice. After one use, I could no longer record. Why? The Automatic Gain Control was on and reduced the microphone volume to almost nothing after my booming voice was used on the microphone. By going to the mixer, I saw my mistake when the mike's volume was set to zero.

With a mixer, you can set recording levels and sources, such as recording from a CD at one volume level and playing out to your stereo system at another.

SoundBlaster 16 ASP uses the SB16SET.EXE file as its mixer. To use it, switch to the \SB16 directory and type:

```
SB16SET
```

You can also use SB16SET to set mixer settings from the DOS prompt without ever viewing the program. Although this is a

nice feature to use in a batch file, the lines can cause your
screen to look like Egyptian hieroglyphics, as follows:

```
SB16SET /M:100,75 /VOC:100,100 /CD:200,200 /FM:150,150
/BASS:200,200 /TREBLE:50,50 /AGC:ON /OPGAIN:4,4
/OPSW:ON...
```

You can also have your Sound Blaster mixer as a pop-up,
memory-resident program called SB16MIX. After SB16MIX is
loaded, you can call up the mixer at any time, even while you
are using another program. To load SB16MIX, go to the \SB16
directory and type:

SB16MIX

After you type the preceding command, use the mixer by
pressing Alt-1. This mixer requires a hefty 64K of memory.
To put away the mixer and free up this memory, type the
command:

SB16MIX /U

Listen Up!

SB16MIX and SB16SET are examples of
memory-resident programs or *terminate-and-
stay-resident* (TSR) programs. TSRs are small
programs that are loaded into memory so
they can be instantly popped up over your
current program or otherwise perform work behind the scenes. Some popular TSRs display pop-up
calendars or calculators.

You can remove terminate-and-stay-resident (TSR)
programs from memory only in the reverse order as they
were added. For example, if you load Sound Blaster's
SBMIDI memory-resident utility followed by the
SB16MIX TSR utility, you must remove SB16MIX first,
and then SBMIDI.

Pro AudioStudio 16 also has a mixer—the PAS Mixer (PAS.EXE). Like Sound Blaster 16 ASP, you can use this mixer full-screen or make your selections from a single command. To use the full-screen version of the mixer, type:

PAS *

After the mixer is displayed, you can make your selections (see fig. 11.3). The mixer is the whole screen shot. You can mix and match the volumes of different parts of your sound card, of which the FM Synthesizer is but one. By pressing the Enter key on a choice, you can set different volume levels for play and for play and record. You also can use special effects by pressing F2 (see fig 11.4). From this screen, you can enable RealSound, which is used by some games.

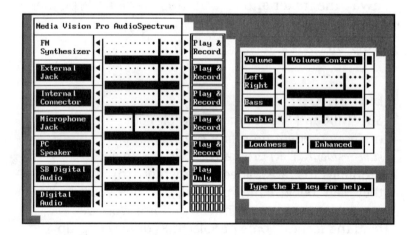

Figure 11.3:
A mixer lets you change recording levels.

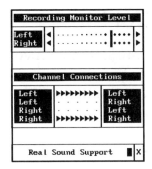

Figure 11.4:
With the Pro AudioStudio 16 mixer, you can turn channels on or off or enable RealSound.

By using the mixer, you can, for example, sing along with an internal CD player but only record your voice. How do you do this? Adjust the volume for the microphone jack, but turn off the volume for the other audio sources, such as digital audio. Use the internal connector to create a good balance.

Listen Up!

The Recording Monitor Level and Master Volume Control affect only what you hear, not what you record. The volume level for recording is set by each slide control.

One advantage of the PAS Mixer is that you can make your settings and save them to a function key. By pressing Shift along with F5, F6, F7, or F8, you can save your current settings to that function key. To retrieve the memorized setting, simply press that function key.

Making Beautiful Music

You can also play music files with your sound card. Depending on the card you purchased, you can play MIDI, CMF, or MOD files. Some sound cards include DOS software utilities that let you play your favorite audio CDs. Some include built-in organ keyboards.

Playing MIDI Files

Almost all sound cards play MIDI files, either from the DOS prompt or from Windows. Such MIDI files often end with the extension MID, such as REGGAE.MID. Chapter 13 discusses MIDI in detail.

For Sound Blaster, you must first load the SBMIDI driver into memory before playing MIDI files. Switch to the SB16 directory and then type:

```
SBMIDI
```

Next, switch to the PLAYMIDI directory by typing:

```
CD PLAYMIDI
```

To play a MID file, type:

```
PLAYMIDI filename
```

In the preceding line, *filename* is the name of your MID file.

Listen Up!

The SBMIDI driver requires 13K of memory. To remove it when you are finished, type the command:

```
SBMIDI /U
```

The driver is unloaded from your PC's memory, freeing it for other work.

You can use switches to enhance the sound of the MID files, such as the following:

/FMT:*type* sets PlayMIDI to use either the Basic or Extended MIDI format. The default is the Extended MIDI format in which all 16 channels are used.

/DRUM:*channel* defines the drum channel; the default is 10.

The following line, for example, plays the MID file REGGAE in the Basic MIDI format, which does not sound as good as the Extended format:

```
PLAYMIDI REGGAE /FMT:BASIC
```

Playing CMF Files

Sound Blaster 16 ASP also can play CMF files, a Creative Labs format similar to MIDI. The utility PlayCMF is included to play these CMF files. Like PlayMIDI, you must install a memory-resident driver before using PlayCMF. Switch to the \SB16 directory, and type:

```
SBFMDRV
```

Next, switch to the PLAYMIDI directory by typing:

```
CD PLAYCMF
```

To play a CMF file, type the following command in which **filename** is the name of your CMF file:

```
PLAYCMF filename
```

Listen Up!

The SBFMDRV driver requires 5K of memory.
To remove it when you are finished, type:

```
SBFMDRV /U
```

The driver is unloaded from your PC's memory,
freeing it for other work.

Blasting Away with Sound Modules

Pro AudioStudio 16 includes a utility called TrakBlaster Pro.
This entertaining program allows you to playback sound modules (files ending with a MOD extension). With TrakBlaster Pro,
you can play back high-quality digital music.

TrakBlaster Pro is mesmerizing. If you have a VGA monitor,
you can visually see the four stereo channels and a spectrum
analyzer (see fig. 11.5). *MOD files* are files that use the
SOUNDTRACKER format, created for the Commodore Amiga
computer.

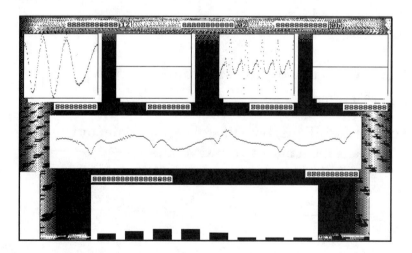

Figure 11.5:
TrakBlaster Pro lets you visually see the music.

Listen Up!

A VGA adapter with at least 256K of memory is required to use TrakBlaster Pro in its graphics mode. Also, TrakBlaster may not work with Novell's DR-DOS.

To configure TrakBlaster Pro to work best with your PC, run TBCONFIG.EXE (see fig. 11.6). You can set the sampling rate to either 32 or 44.1 KHz. If you do not have a VGA monitor, select your display mode as Text.

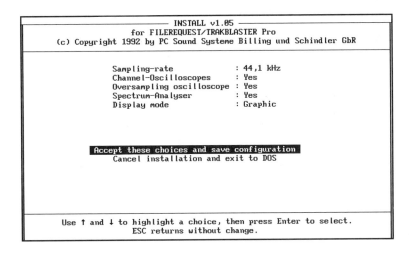

Figure 11.6:

Configure TrakBlaster with TBCONFIG.EXE.

If you have an 80286 PC operating at 8 MHz, select a sampling frequency of 32 KHz and turn all features off. For an 80386 PC operating at 33 MHz, turn all features on and select a sampling frequency of 32 KHz. For an 80386 PC operating at 40 MHz or an 80486 or faster computer, set the sampling frequency to 44.1 KHz and turn on all features.

When finished, highlight the options Accept these choices and save configuration. The configuration information is saved to the file TRAKPRO.CFG.

TrakBlaster is in the \PASTUDIO\TBPRO directory. To use it, switch to the directory and type:

TBPRO

The batch file TBPRO.BAT runs. Press the Spacebar to bypass the TrakBlaster opening screen. From the subsequent screen, select the directory where your MOD files are located. TrakBlaster includes a few MOD files in the MODULES directory (see fig. 11.7). Highlight the MODULES directory and press Enter. Then, select a MOD file to play. While playing the file, you can use the +/- keys to skip tracks.

```
─────────── FILEREQUEST v1.05 ───────────
            for TRAKBLASTER Professional / MediaVision
     (c) Copyright 1992 by PC Sound Systeme Billing und Schindler GbR
Programmed by H. Juettner                      Graphics by F. Trappmann

 [..]          noname  .mod   prelude .mod   short   .mod   sll2    .mod
 v42    .mod




















Path: C:\PASTUDIO\TBPRO\MODULES                    Mask: *.MOD
ESC: Exit         ENTER: Play selected file(s)   SPACE: (Un)Select file
M: New file mask   +/- : (Un)Select all files    Arrow-Keys: Move Bar
```

Figure 11.7:

A few sample MOD files are included with TrackBlaster Pro.

Grinding Away

If you're musically inclined but can't afford MIDI equipment, consider FM Organ bundled with Sound Blaster 16 ASP. It

provides an organ grinder on disk that lets you play musical pieces. To start the organ, switch to the PRO-ORG directory by typing:

```
CD \SB16\PRO_ORG
```

Next, type:

```
PRO_ORG
```

With PRO_ORG, you can play a song, save it to disk, and replay it later. Like any organ, keys are arranged in groups of 12 (five black and seven white keys). Each group is an octave. FM Organ has seven octaves. Four octaves are available at any one time. Use the left/right arrow keys to access the others.

FM Organ relies on function keys (see fig. 11.8). By pressing F6, you can load an existing song. Highlight the song you want to listen to and press Enter. Press PgUp/PgDn to see the screens of songs (see fig. 11.9). After selecting a song, press F4 to play it. Press Esc to stop playing.

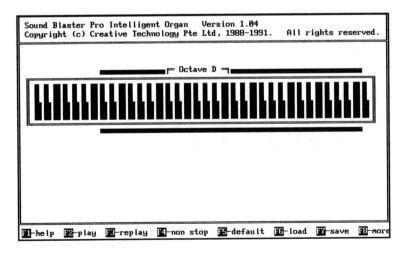

Figure 11.8:

The FM Organ relies on function keys for playing.

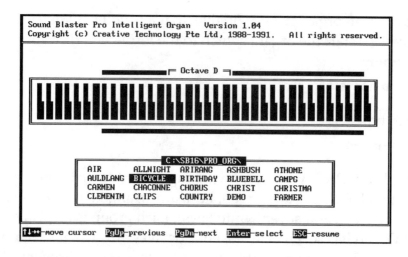

Figure 11.9:

You can pick from several organ songs.

FM Organ also can teach you to play a song. First, use F6 to choose a song. Next, press F8, and then F1 (Learn). If you press F2, the organ shows you which keys to press (see fig. 11.10).

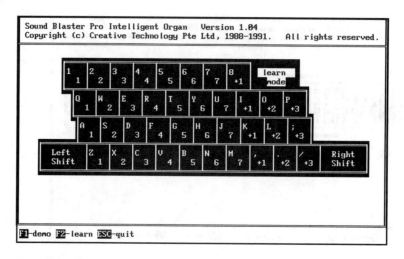

Figure 11.10:

The FM Organ can teach you to play a simple song.

Making a song is just as easy. If you press F5, you can see the default settings. By pressing the letter T, you give your composition a name. Press Enter to return to the main screen. You can then play the melody to the background music.

With FM Organ, you can change the rhythm, instrument, volume, and octave of the music.

Sound Check

FM Organ supports the MIDI interface of the Sound Blaster 16 ASP card. You can then play FM Organ by using a real organ, not your PC's keyboard. After you attach the MIDI keyboard, select MIDI Toggle from the FM Organ program. This switch turns on the MIDI support in FM Organ to support the real keyboard.

Built-In Proofreader

Both Pro AudioStudio 16 and Sound Blaster 16 ASP include text-to-speech utilities. Such utilities turn text you type from the keyboard (or provide as an ASCII file) into spoken words. This can be handy for proofreading material or just having fun with the "HAL-like" computer voice.

Sound Blaster 16 ASP uses SBTALKER as its text-to-speech synthesizer. SBTALKER has the following two facets:

♪ **Read.** This program reads ASCII text files or text entered from the keyboard or communication ports.

♪ **Dr. Sbaitso.** Dr. Sbaitso is a fun program that attempts to converse with you in English.

SBTALKER is installed from a different disk from the other Sound Blaster software. The batch file SBTALK.BAT must be run before either Read or Dr. Sbaitso is used. SBTALK loads a large 189K program into your PC's expanded or conventional memory.

Here, Read This!

The Read program can read text back to you. To use it, type the following command in which text is any text you want the program to say:

READ *text*

If you simply type **READ**, you can enter several lines of text to be read back as you press the Enter key. (Press Ctrl-Z or Ctrl-C to exit the program.) To have Read read from an ASCII text file, simply type :

READ *<filename*

In the preceding command, *filename* is the name of the ASCII text file you want read. The text is read back to you. To see the text as it is read, add a /W switch at the end as follows:

READ <SBTEST.TXT /W

To cancel reading the entire file, press Esc.

The Doctor Is In

Dr. Sbaitso acts as a psychiatrist attempting to solve your personal problems. After running SBTALK, type the following command:

SBAITSO2 /S /40

The /**S** switch runs the program in stereo mode; the /**40** switch runs the program in 40-column wide mode (see fig. 11.11). As you type phrases to Dr. Sbaitso, the program may ask you for more information. To have the good doctor repeat a response,

press R. Several commands are available to change the pitch, volume, speed, tone, and other values.

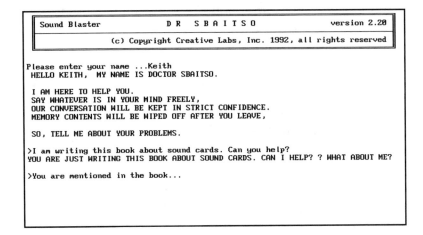

Figure 11.11:
Dr. Sbaitso attempts to solve your problems.

Sound Check

Many sound cards include a Windows text-to-speech utility. A popular utility is Monologue for Windows from First Byte (described fully in Chapter 12). A popular use of Monologue is to have it read the text you highlight in your Windows program and copy it (Ctrl-C) to the Windows Clipboard. Monologue also reads the numbers in Microsoft Excel spreadsheet cells. A DOS version of Monologue is also available with some sound cards.

A Built-In CD

Some sound cards include a DOS utility to play audio CDs in your PC's CD-ROM drive (if you own one). If your CD-ROM drive uses the Microsoft MSCDEX.EXE CD-ROM extensions, it can play audio CDs.

Sound Check

You don't need a utility to play audio CDs from Windows. Microsoft Windows includes the Media Player to do so. However, some sound-card manufacturers include a superior utility for playing CDs under Windows. This is discussed fully in Chapter 12.

Pro AudioStudio 16 includes the Music Box (MUSICBOX.EXE) to play audio CDs. After placing an audio CD in your CD-ROM drive, simply go to the \PASTUDIO directory and type:

```
MUSICBOX
```

The Music Box menu appears (see fig. 11.12). If you haven't inserted a CD yet, the LED window will say "no CD"; otherwise, the Music Box displays the total playing time of the inserted CD. If your DOS mouse driver is active, you can click on your choices. If not, you can use the keyboard keys listed in parentheses in the following list of functions. The Music Box uses the same VCR-like buttons as a conventional CD player.

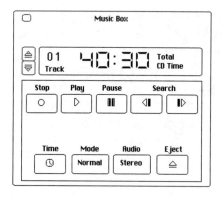

Figure 11.12:

The Music Box plays audio CDs from DOS.

The Music Box can be used to do various functions, including the following:

Play (P) plays a CD.

Time (T) changes the time to elapsed time for the current track, time remaining on the current track, or remaining CD playing time.

Stop (S) stops playing.

Pause (Spacebar) pauses playing.

Search (right/left arrow keys) forwards or reverses playing.

Mode (M) allows you to switch between random play, continuous play, and normal play.

Eject (E) ejects the current CD so that you can insert another.

You can have Music Box load as a memory-resident (TSR) program so that you can play audio CDs while using another DOS program. The TSR requires 18K of memory. To load the Music Box as a memory-resident program, type:

```
MUSICBOX /R
```

The standard hotkey to "pop up" the Music Box at any time is Left Ctrl-Left Shift-Tab, although you can change this. You can then use the keystrokes to change your CD player. To exit Music Box, press Esc.

Sound Check

Logitech SoundMan 16 includes some of the same DOS utilities as the Media Vision Pro AudioStudio 16 card. SoundMan includes RECFILE.EXE, PLAYFILE.EXE, and the PAS Mixer.

Chapter 11

The Death of DOS?

Don't expect the DOS utilities included with your sound card to get any better. With the proliferation of Windows, many sound-card makers are shunning DOS utilities for Windows equivalents. For example, Pro AudioStudio 16 now includes Monologue for Windows. Media Vision's prior sound cards included Monologue for DOS.

DOS-based utilities are for new sound-card buyers who don't (yet) own Windows. The DOS software trinkets included with sound cards provide crude record and playback functions, giving the buyer an immediate, but not sophisticated, use for the new sound card. With a sampling of a sound card's capabilities, the buyer can move on to the more powerful Windows utilities.

Pane-Less Windows Sound

An increasing number of sound cards come bundled with Windows sound utilities. Expect more of these useful and entertaining utilities to be offered in the near future. This chapter explores Windows sound utilities and shows you how:

- ♪ Windows delivers sound
- ♪ To use Windows OLE and DDE
- ♪ To record a voice Post-It note in your Windows file
- ♪ To record and play back sound files
- ♪ To use your sound card's Windows mixer
- ♪ To play music files, such as MID and RMI files
- ♪ Your sound card can proofread your text or numbers
- ♪ To have your sound card recognize your voice
- ♪ To play audio CDs from Windows

Chapter 12

Windows Sound

Microsoft Windows 3.1 was meant to be seen. . . and heard. This version of Windows jump started the interest of PC users in multimedia—the melding of graphics and sound. Windows 3.1 provides affordable, powerful sound to the average user.

By working under the Windows environment, compatibility problems common in DOS are eased. Add a sound card and install the correct drivers, and you will be able to record and play back all sorts of music and sound in all sorts of applications. The installation of CD-ROM drives is also simplified. Moreover, because the system can use new drivers as they become available, you will be able to install new equipment that hasn't yet been invented.

Applet a Day

Windows 3.1 comes with two multimedia applets: Media Player and Sound Recorder. (An *applet* is a software program that is not powerful enough to be considered a full application.) Both are installed in the Windows Accessories group (see fig. 12.1).

Figure 12.1:
Windows includes two sound utilities.

Media Player allows you to open and play a file that is supported by one of the installed multimedia drivers. For example,

you can use Media Player to play audio CDs in a PC's CD-ROM drive. A typical installation of Windows includes drivers for MIDI and sound (WAV) files, even if no hardware is present to let you hear them. To hear them, you need a sound card or a special driver for your PC's speaker. The sound-card drivers are referenced in your SYSTEM.INI file in two adjacent sections: [mci] and [drivers]. These sections may look like this:

```
[mci]
WaveAudio=mciwave.drv
Sequencer=mciseq.drv
[drivers]
timer=timer.drv
midimapper=midimap.drv
```

Sound Check

What is MCI? No, it's not the large phone company. Microsoft furnishes a high-level script language called *Media Control Interface* (MCI) that plays audio and video sequences without the need for programming. The Windows 3.1 Media Player can play MCI scripts.

Although Media Player is versatile, it is not as full-featured as other dedicated software utilities. Media Player, for example, can play audio CDs, but it cannot do continuous play or random shuffling of the tracks. Other software programs do a much better job.

Control Me

The Control Panel is the place for adding and removing the sound card, CD-ROM, and other drivers. If, for example, you want to play CD audio on your PC, use Control Panel to load a CD audio driver. Some sound-card installation routines modify

Control Panel. The Windows Sound System, for example, adds Volume and Recording icons to the Control Panel (see fig. 12.2). In addition, the Sound dialog box (click on the Sound icon) includes new features.

Figure 12.2:

The Windows Sound System adds new features to the Control Panel.

Sound Check

Windows 3.1 supplies drivers for Ad Lib, Creative Labs SoundBlaster 1.0 and 1.5, Media Vision THUNDERBoard, MIDI Mapper, Roland LAPC-1 and MPU401, Timer, MIDI Sequencer, MIDI Sound, and CD Audio.

Imagine you are adding a CD audio driver to play audio CDs in your Windows-compatible CD-ROM drive. To install the CD audio driver:

1. Start Microsoft Windows.

2. Open Control Panel from the Main group and double-click on Drivers (see fig. 12.3).

   The Installed Drivers dialog box appears and shows you the multimedia drivers already installed in your version of Windows.

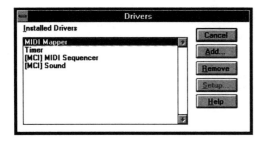

Figure 12.3:
You may have to install sound-card drivers using the Control Panel.

3. Select **A**dd from the right-hand list of buttons.

4. Choose [MCI] CD Audio from the list.

   If a driver is already present on your computer, you will be asked if you want the current driver or want to replace it with a new one.

Listen Up!

The top choice, Unlisted or Updated Driver, allows you to add drivers supplied by hardware manufacturers. If your driver isn't listed in the rest of the window, select this choice—often the necessary process.

5. Insert the requested Windows disk in your floppy disk drive and press Enter.

6. After the driver is added, a confirmation message appears (see fig. 12.4).

Figure 12.4:
You'll be told if the driver was installed correctly.

7. Click on OK and exit the Control Panel.

Listen Up!
You must exit Windows and restart it for any changes to take effect.

Some sound cards can accept separate settings under Windows and DOS (see fig. 12.5). Some Windows programs may operate better under Windows with different DMA settings (such as DMA 5, 6, or 7). When using a DOS program, you can select separate DMA and IRQ settings for the best performance (that is, DMA 1 or 3, IRQ 2, 3, 5, or 7). With separate DOS and Windows sound-card settings, you may be able to play a DOS game that uses a sound card from within Windows. From the Control Panel, highlight your driver and select **S**etup. You can then pick the best IRQ and DMA.

Media Player

If you install a CD-ROM drive, you can use it to play audio CDs, but you may not have a way to access the music on the CD. Although some sound cards include Windows audio CD software, you can always use the Media Player included with

Windows. Start the Media Player, which is in the Accessories group, then choose Device, CD Audio (see fig. 12.6).

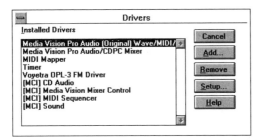

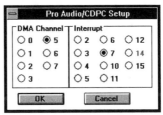

Figure 12.5:

You can set a different DMA channel and IRQ for Windows sound than your DOS sound.

Figure 12.6:

The Media Player can play audio CDs and more.

Listen Up!

If you don't yet own a sound card, you can listen to audio CDs through the drive's headphone jack and the Media Player. To hear the music through your speakers, you must install a sound card.

Insert an audio CD in your CD-ROM drive (most CD-ROM drives require that you put the CD disc into a CD-ROM caddy). Media Player instantly reads the CD and displays the CD playing time (see fig. 12.7). If you open the **S**cale menu, you can select T**r**acks to see the individual tracks.

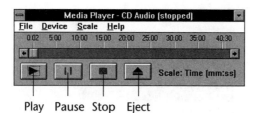

Play   Pause   Stop   Eject

Figure 12.7:
The Media Player shows how long the audio CD will play.

The Media Player uses VCR-like controls, which appear as the international symbols used on most audio devices:

♪ Play

♪ Pause

♪ Stop

♪ Eject

The scroll bar above these controls can be used to move to a different part of the CD.

Media Player can also play other media. If you select **D**evice, **M**IDI Sequencer, you can load the delightful CANYON.MID song included with Windows (see fig. 12.8). CANYON.MID is an example of a MIDI song. Once the song is loaded, press the play button.

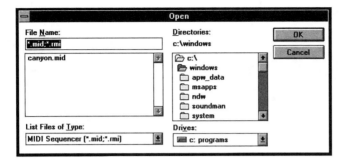

Figure 12.8:
Windows includes the CANYON.MID MIDI song.

Listen Up!

If your Media Player doesn't work, consider these cures:

♪ Make sure the correct MIDI driver is installed. Check the Control Panel.

♪ Make sure you selected **M**IDI Sequencer from the **D**evice menu.

♪ Check to make sure you're using the right MIDI mapping setup. If you added MIDI hardware, check the MIDI Mapper settings in the Control Panel.

Sound Recorder

Besides the Media Player, Windows also provides the Sound Recorder. It too is located in the Accessories group. Sound Recorder plays, records, and edits sound files. These sound files are in Windows waveform, or WAV, audio files. As a file is played, you graphically see the sound waves (see fig. 12.9).

Chapter 12

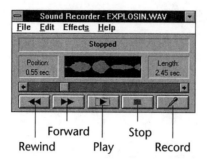

Rewind | Forward | Play | Stop | Record

Figure 12.9:

The Sound Recorder plays waveform (WAV) files.

Listen Up!

Before Sound Recorder can be used, you must have the sound hardware installed and its driver installed and configured. If you don't own a sound card, you can use the PC speaker driver included on the *Crank It Up!* bonus disk to play WAV files through Sound Recorder.

Start the Sound Recorder, which is in the Accessories group. Like Media Player, the Sound Recorder includes VCR buttons:

♪ Rewind

♪ Forward

♪ Play

♪ Stop

♪ Record

To play a sound file, choose File,Open. Windows includes four simple WAV files; select one and then press the play button. While playing a sound file, you can click on the scroll bar to move the scroll box to that position in the sound. Otherwise,

you can drag the scroll box to the position you want. You can enhance your sound by using special effects in the Effect**s** menu. You can increase or decrease volume or speed by 25 percent, add echo to a sound, or play it in reverse. (You'll probably find angelic messages!)

Sound Check

The far right button is used to record a WAV file using a microphone. A later section in this chapter discusses how to record a WAV file using the Sound Recorder and placing the recorded message in a Windows document.

Sound Recorder has other features, such as mixing and inserting sound files, but the editing utilities included with sound cards are often superior.

Listen Up!

Windows Media Player also plays WAV files. Select **D**evice, **S**ound then load a WAV file and press the play button.

Ta-Daaa! Ding?

One new feature in Windows 3.1 is the capability to add sound effects to certain Windows actions, or *system events*. The Sound icon in the Control Panel lets you replace Windows' error beep and other sounds with pre-recorded WAV files. For example, you can start Windows with a loud "ta-daaa" or have an error message announced with a "ding."

Chapter 12

Sound Check

Windows only comes with four WAV files, so New Riders has included some extras on the enclosed *Crank It Up!* bonus disk. We hope you enjoy them.

To set up sounds for your system events, you first must turn on the Sound feature. Access Control Panel and click on the Sound icon. On the left-hand side of the Sound dialog box (see fig. 12.10) are various system events; on the right are WAV files you can assign to these events. Before you assign any sounds, you first must turn on the sound. Click on the Enable System Sounds box until an X appears in it. Each system event already is assigned a default sound. To see which sounds are preset, highlight a system event on the left and note which WAV file is associated with it. To assign a different sound to a system event, highlight an event, and then select which WAV file you want for that event. If you don't want a sound for that system event, select <none>. If you want to hear the sound before assigning it, select a sound and press the Test button.

Sound Check

Where is sound information kept? In your Windows WIN.INI file. A [sounds] section for the current events looks like this:

```
[sounds]
SystemAsterisk=chord.wav,Asterisk
SystemHand=chord.wav,Critical Stop
SystemDefault=ding.wav,Default Beep
SystemExclamation=chord.wav,Exclamation
SystemQuestion=chord.wav,Question
SystemExit=chimes.wav,Windows Exit
SystemStart=tada.wav,Windows Start
```

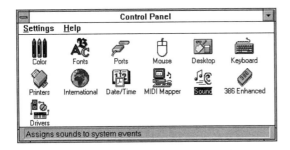

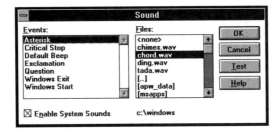

Figure 12.10:
You can assign sounds to various Windows actions.

You can add more system events to your system with the use of special software utilities. SoundWAV PRO, for example, from Window Ware adds four new sound events (Minimize, Maximize, Restore, and Move/Size). The program includes hundreds of sounds from popular movies and TV shows. Some of these sounds are on the bonus disk included with this book.

Windows Mixes It Up

Sound cards typically include mixer software. As mentioned in the last chapter, a *mixer* allows you to control the volume, gain, and tone of various audio sources. With a mixer, you can set recording levels and sources, such as record from a CD at one volume level and play on your stereo system at another level. One use for mixers is setting the recording levels of your microphone different from the CD player for a voice-over. If you don't have a mixer, you cannot change the recording levels for the different audio sources.

You can often access your Windows mixer from your sound card's recording software. Typically, a little picture of a mixer (with little levers) is displayed in the right-hand corner.

Sound Blaster 16's Goodies

Sound Blaster 16 ASP includes the Windows Mixer shown in figure 12.11. You can set the volume for WAV files, MIDI, CD audio, microphone, and more. Simply use your mouse to grab and move a pair of slide controls.

Figure 12.11:
The Sound Blaster 16 ASP Windows Mixer.

Sound Check

The Voc choice on the Windows Mixer stands for digitized voice, or waveform audio. This choice affects the volume of WAV files.

Each slide control is for each channel. If you want to set the volume/recording level for the left channel separately from the

right, remove the checkmark from the choice Lock L/R Vol in the Options menu. You can then move each slider individually.

In the right-hand side of the mixer, you can set the master volume and the bass and treble. The Gain controls allow you to increase or decrease the amplification of an audio source so that the sound can be adjusted during recording and playing. The gain can be increased two, four, or eight times.

The Output section of the Windows Mixer allows you to set the sound sources you will hear through the sound card and your speakers. If you place a dot in the Mic (microphone) box, for example, you can hear your voice through the speakers as you are recording. (Typically, you wouldn't want to do this, unless you were using a pair of headphones.)

The **Settings,Recording** command provides a number of recording options (see fig. 12.12). You can, for example, select Automatic Gain Control (AGC) to have the microphone recording level change automatically to suitable levels. (You wouldn't want AGC on if you are surrounded by sudden extraneous noises.) To get stereo recording, make sure the left signal from the audio source is directed to the Left In channel and the right signal to the Right In channel.

Figure 12.12:
You can fine-tune your recording options.

If you change any of the settings in SoundBlaster's Windows Mixer, select **Settings,Save** to make the changes permanent.

Pro AudioStudio's Mixers

Pro AudioStudio 16 from Media Vision provides two mixers: Pocket Mixer and Pro Mixer. The easy-to-use Pocket Mixer allows you to save mixer files; you most likely will only need to use this mixer.

Pocket Mixer

Pocket Mixer is very similar to the Sound Blaster Windows Mixer and easier to use since it resembles the knobs, buttons, and levers found on a stereo system.

To start the Pocket Mixer, double-click on its icon in the Multimedia Tools group (see fig. 12.13).

Figure 12.13:

Pocket Mixer provides simple, powerful controls.

From left to right, the recording levels are as follows:

Monitor level allows you to hear what you are currently recording.

FM channel allows you to set the level for music that uses your sound card's FM synthesizer.

Microphone sets the level of your microphone.

Digital audio sets the level for digital waveform (WAV) files.

CD sets the level for internal or external CD-ROM drives connected to your sound card.

PC speaker sets the volume for sounds normally generated by your PC's speaker.

Listen Up!

The PC speaker volume only works if your PC speaker sound is played across your computer's bus and not through a speaker connector on your computer's motherboard. Newer PCs play PC speaker sounds across the bus, which allows the sound card to intercept and play it through its speakers.

Auxiliary sets the level for CD players, tape players, stereo systems, and other devices that are plugged into your sound card's line-in jack.

To set the level for recording or playback, you can click on the Record/Play buttons underneath each meter. (Green bars indicate Play mode; red indicates Record mode.)

The Pocket Mixer includes four round knobs for controlling volume, balance, treble, and bass. To adjust the volume, either click on the knob at the position you want the volume or click on the plus or minus keys below the knob. To save your settings, choose **File,Save**. The three buttons underneath these controls are, from left to right:

Stereo Enhance modifies audio so that it sounds richer and fuller. This choice makes the left and right channels a little out of synch to enhance the stereo effect or make mono sounds imitate stereo.

Loudness boosts the lower bass frequencies.

Mute turns off all audio output.

When would you use these controls? Turn on Stereo Enhance if your speakers are very close together or if you are using monophonic sounds. The phase shift used to separate the two signals enhances the stereo sound or makes monophonic sounds appear to be stereo. If your speakers are further apart or you are wearing headphones, turn this control off. Most likely, you will want to turn on the Loudness control. It mostly enhances the bass, improving the motor sounds and explosions of computer games. If you want to avoid disturbing family members or neighbors with the deeper bass, leave this control off. The Mute button immediately turns off all sounds. Experiment with each control.

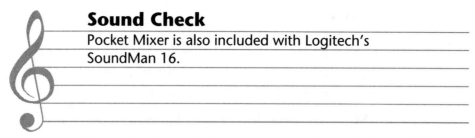

Sound Check
Pocket Mixer is also included with Logitech's SoundMan 16.

You can optimize the mixer for playing WAV files. To do so, turn up the volume on the waveform meter and monitor. You may want to turn down the master volume. When finished, save your settings as PLAYWAV.MIX (see fig. 12.14) or some other descriptive name.

Listen Up!
When the Pocket Mixer is minimized, you can select Volume Control Only to change the volume quickly (see fig. 12.15).

Figure 12.14:
You can save mixer settings to a MIX file for later use.

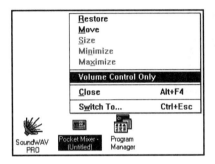

Figure 12.15:
You can quickly adjust the volume when Pocket Mixer is minimized.

Pro Mixer

Pro Mixer includes plenty of controls for your unique recording and playback needs. Like the Pocket Mixer, Pro Mixer allows you to change the recording and playback levels of different audio sources. Pro Mixer includes some special features, such as a volume meter, timed fade-ins and fade-outs, and more. Most likely, you will only need Pocket Mixer, whose controls are much more accessible than those of Pro Mixer.

The Multimedia Mixer dialog box (see fig. 12.16) enables you to set the volume for each of your audio sources. Although similar to Pocket Mixer, Pro Mixer has one choice not found with Pocket Mixer: BLSTR. The BLSTR setting controls the volume of the Sound Blaster-compatible portion of the sound card. For example, you can set the volume of a Sound Blaster-compatible game.

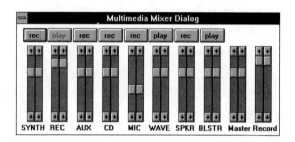

Figure 12.16:

Pro Mixer provides extensive mixing controls.

When Pro Mixer is minimized on your Windows desktop, you have more choices available from its menu (see fig. 12.18). You can select Equalizer to set the treble, bass, stereo enhance, and loudness (just like Pocket Mixer). Pro Mixer also includes a timed fade so that a sound either fades to nothing or rises to a climax. Once you start the fade, you can start Sound Recorder to begin a recording from an audio source. The recording will then fade in or fade out as you've chosen. After you set the levels for Pro Mixer, you can save these values to a file called a *state*. Simply select Save State from its minimized menu. To load a saved state, select Load State.

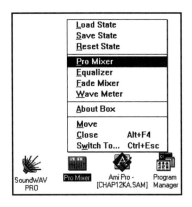

Figure 12.17:
You have more settings available when Pro Mixer is minimized.

Listen Up!

Avoid having both Pocket Mixer and Pro Mixer open at the same time. Occasionally, my PC would "lock up." Most likely, all of your mixing needs will be met by Pocket Mixer.

No Mixed Drinks

Windows Sound System does not provide any real mixing controls. Instead, you select either Volume Control or Recording Control from the Windows Sound System group. To change the level, simply move the volume control up or down with your mouse. If you select Expanded View (Alt-E) from the upper left-hand corner of the volume control, you can fine tune your controls even further (see fig. 12.18). These controls can also be accessed from within several of the Windows Sound System utilities.

Chapter 12

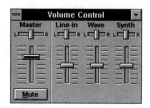

Figure 12.18:
The expanded view of the Windows Volume Control.

Riding the WAV

Although Windows Sound Recorder is fine for simple recording and playing of WAV files, almost all sound cards include advanced waveform utilities for creating and modifying WAV files.

WaveStudio

Sound Blaster 16 ASP comes with Creative WaveStudio, which is located in the Sound Blaster 16 group. WaveStudio can record, play, and edit WAV files. Once you open a file in WaveStudio, you can use VCR-like buttons to play it.

Figure 12.19 shows the TADA.WAV file. The bottom window displays the entire WAV file; the lower right-hand corner displays information about the waveform, such as playing time, whether the file was recorded in stereo or mono, resolution (8- or 16-bit), sampling rate, and file size.

Listen Up!
You can load more than one WAV file at a time in the Creative WaveStudio.

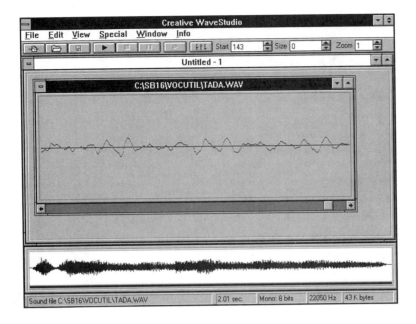

Figure 12.19:

WaveStudio shows the entire waveform in the bottom window.

The three boxes in the upper right-hand corner (Start, Size, and Zoom) provide the following information on the waveform file:

>   **Start Box** displays the numeric position of a selected portion of the WAV file.

>   **Size Box** displays the numeric size of the selected portion of the WAV file.

>   **Zoom Box** sets the ratio for viewing the WAV file. The higher the ratio, the more you'll see.

You can use your mouse to highlight a portion of the WAV file (see fig. 12.20), and then play the selected portion.

Chapter 12

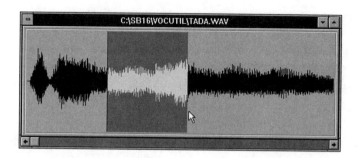

C:\SB16\VOCUTIL\TADA.WAV

Figure 12.20:

Highlight a part of the WAV file with your mouse, then press Play.

After highlighting a portion of the waveform, you can copy it by pressing Ctrl-C or selecting Edit,Copy. You can then either paste it into another waveform or another place in the current waveform. If you want to mix the copied sound with another sound (such as an announcer's voice with the sound of the crowd), select Edit,Paste Mix.

The Special pull-down menu contains several special sound effects (see fig. 12.21). You can reverse a section of sound, add an echo to it, or repeat (rap) it. You can also insert a silence, force a section to silence, fade in or out, and amplify the volume of a section.

Recording with Creative WaveStudio

If you attach a microphone to the Sound Blaster microphone jack, you can use WaveStudio to record a waveform file. To record a WAV file, press the record button along the button bar at the top. Then select how you want to record, such as mono or stereo, sampling resolution, and frequency (see fig. 12.22). Turn on your microphone and begin recording. When finished, click on stop and save your WAV file. Table 12.1 demonstrates the disk space required for various settings.

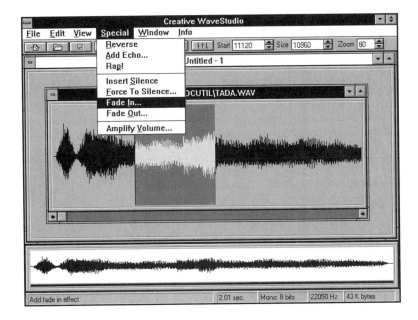

Figure 12.21:

You can add fades and silence to your sound file.

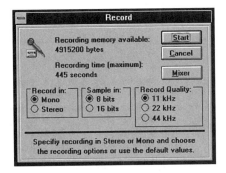

Figure 12.22:

You can select the quality of your recording.

Chapter 12

Table 12.1
Disk Space Required for Various Settings

Sampling Rate	Resolution	Megabytes consumed per Minute
11.025 KHz	8-bit	0.66M
11.025 KHz	16-bit	1.32M
22.05 KHz	8-bit	1.32M
22.05 KHz	16-bit	2.64M
44.1 KHz	8-bit	2.64M
44.1 KHz	16-bit	5.29M

NOTE: These file sizes are based on mono, not stereo recording. For stereo recording, double the size of the file.

Listen Up!
The higher the sampling resolution and frequency, the more disk space your recording will take. For adequate voice recording through a microphone, select mono, 8 bit, and 11KHz.

Soundo'LE

Soundo'LE is a down-and-dirty WAV file player and recorder (see fig. 12.23). Soundo'LE is very easy to use: you simply open an existing WAV file or begin recording your own. The default recording method is set to mono, 8 bit, and 11KHz.

Figure 12.23:

Soundo'LE provides simple WAV file recording and playback.

You can change these settings by selecting **O**ptions,**R**ecording Settings. In the dialog box, you can set the sampling resolution, frequency, and a compression scheme for saving disk space (see fig. 12.24). For the most compression (4:1), use Creative Labs' ADPCM compression format. You cannot share an ADPCM-compressed file with a friend who owns a different sound card, however. This compression format relies on Sound Blaster 16 ASP's circuitry for compression/decompression. The two CCITT-compressed formats may be shared with someone owning a different brand of sound card but only if that person's software supports these international formats. For example, an 8-bit compressed file created on a Sound Blaster 16 ASP may be shared with someone who owns a Sound Blaster Pro Deluxe sound card. (Soundo'LE cannot be used with other makes of sound cards.)

Listen Up!

To share a compressed WAV file with someone, load the compressed file, change compression to None, and then save the file as a regular WAV file.

Chapter 12

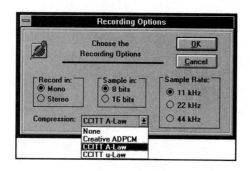

Figure 12.24:

To save disk space, select a compression method.

Pro AudioStudio's Pocket Recorder

Pro AudioStudio includes Pocket Recorder for easy recording and playback of WAV files. Pocket Recorder can record waveform data in 8- or 16-bit resolutions. It can also splice and blend files together for interesting audio effects.

After you select Pocket Recorder from the Multimedia Tools group, load a WAV file and become a sound recording engineer!

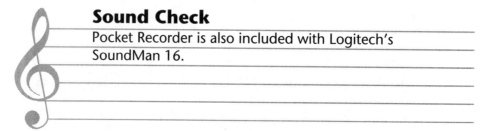

Sound Check

Pocket Recorder is also included with Logitech's SoundMan 16.

The total length of the file is displayed in the window. The remaining recording time (based on space left on the temporary directory) is also displayed. By default, the temporary directory is the drive and directory you've chosen for your Windows

temporary directory. To increase recording time, choose another drive that has more space available. To change the temporary directory, select <u>F</u>ile,Set Temp <u>D</u>irectory.

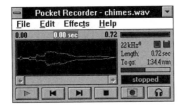

Figure 12.25:
Pocket Recorder lets you see the entire waveform.

Plenty of detailed information is provided on the right-hand
side of Pocket Recorder. A type of audio shorthand displays the
sampling frequency and resolution. If the sound is stereo, two
speaker boxes appear to the right. Mono is indicated by one
speaker. The beaker to the right of the stereo speakers indicates
if the file was compressed. Pocket Recorder can compress 16-bit
sound files at a ratio of 4:1 or 2:1.

Listen Up!

Pocket Recorder does not compress files
as you record them. It performs the
compression when you save the file to
disk. Therefore, the drive used by your
temporary directory must have ample space
for the uncompressed temporary recording.

If you select <u>F</u>ile,<u>N</u>ew, you will be asked at what resolution and
sampling rate you want to record (see fig. 12.26).

Chapter 12

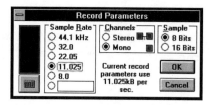

Figure 12.26:

Select your recording settings for a new file.

To edit a sound file, you highlight a portion of the sound file using your mouse. Then use the editing choices found in the Edit pull-down menu (see fig. 12.27). You can, for example, delete part of the waveform, and insert, paste, or blend another WAV file into the current waveform.

Figure 12.27:

You can copy, delete, or paste parts of the waveform.

If you select **P**aste, first use your mouse to select the insertion point in the waveform. You can only paste sound into the waveform if it has the same format. You cannot, for example, paste stereo sound into a mono waveform. What must match? All of the following:

♪ Sampling rate (such as 22.05 or 44.1KHz)

♪ Resolution (8 or 16 bits)

♪ Channels (stereo or mono)

Listen Up!
When you blend files, you may encounter a type of distortion called *clipping*. *Clipping* occurs when the amplitude, or loudness, of a blended file is excessive.

Pocket Recorder also includes special effects. You can make the entire—or highlighted portion—of a sound file louder, softer, faster, slower, higher, or lower (see fig. 12.28). You can also add a staggered echo, *reverb* (simultaneous echoes), or reverse the file as if you were playing a record backwards.

Figure 12.28:
You can add special effects to your WAV files, such as reverb.

Windows Sound System Quick Recorder

Quick Recorder included with the Windows Sound System is just that: quick. It can create, edit, and play back WAV files (see fig. 12.29). You can even add a picture, label, and description to each sound.

Chapter 12

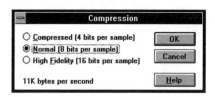

Figure 12.29:

Quick Recorder is the simplest of the recording utilities.

Quick Recorder is simple. Only a record, play, and stop button are provided. The length of the current file is displayed in the lower right-hand window. You have little control over the sampling rate. Depending on what resolution you pick (8- or 16-bit), the sampling rate is set accordingly (see fig. 12.30). One plus for Quick Recorder is the capability to have several sound files open simultaneously.

Figure 12.30:

Recording options are somewhat limited in Quick Recorder.

You can turn on compression from the **O**ptions menu or set the volume or recording levels. If you want, you can change your recording method so that sound is only recorded when you hold down the record button, not when you click it on or off (the default). When Quick Recorder is minimized, you can drag sound objects to it to open them.

OLE without Learning Spanish

Many Windows programs allow you to transfer and share information between them. Several of the utilities included with Windows, such as Write, Cardfile, and Sound Recorder, have this capability. *Object linking and embedding*, or OLE, lets you place a file created in one Windows application into another. Once in another file, you can either open that file or use it.

Linking and embedding are two different facilities. *Embedding* is when you copy information (an object) created in one application into another. For example, you can embed a voice message created with Sound Recorder into your Ami Pro word processing document. This is called embedding an object.

Linking is when you create a reference in a file to another file; you are not copying the information. When you edit a linked object, you are actually editing the information in the original file.

Linking and embedding are made possible through clients and servers. The linked or embedded object is created in one application (the server), and connected to a second application (the client).

Servers and Clients

OLE-capable applications fall into two categories:

♪ Servers

♪ Clients

Servers are applications whose objects can be embedded or linked into other documents. For example, Sound Recorder is a server application: its WAV files can be inserted into other Windows applications. *Clients* are applications that accept embedded or linked objects. Some applications may be servers; others may be only clients; some may be both.

Embedded or linked information can easily be edited. You simply open the object from your current application. Windows recognizes the program that created the object and starts it. You can then make your changes and exit. For example, you may have a Windows Paintbrush drawing inserted in your Windows word processor. To change the drawing, double-click on it. This action opens the Paintbrush program without forcing you to leave your document.

Sound Check

OLE is similar to copying information to the Windows Clipboard with one major difference: when you update the original drawing or other OLE-server file, your OLE-client document or other type of file is automatically updated to reflect the changes.

In some ways, OLE is a blessing and a curse. Although OLE reduces the work required to update several documents, you may be surprised when your document has changed because you modified its OLE-client file.

Adding a Sound File

OLE becomes especially powerful when you can add a sound file to a document. This message is called a *voice annotation*, but I like to call this a verbal Post-It note. Another name for voice annotation is *business audio*.

With voice annotation, you can record a short message to a WAV file and insert it in your document or spreadsheet. A business executive, for example, can pick up a microphone and embed a message in a contract that gives his or her secretary explicit instructions. Many Windows applications can accept a voice annotation. In other words, several Windows applications are OLE clients.

To add a voice annotation, simply place the cursor where you want the note to appear. Select the Insert Object option from your software's menu. (Where this choice is located varies by software program.) In Ami Pro, for example, this choice is available in the Edit menu (see fig. 12.31).

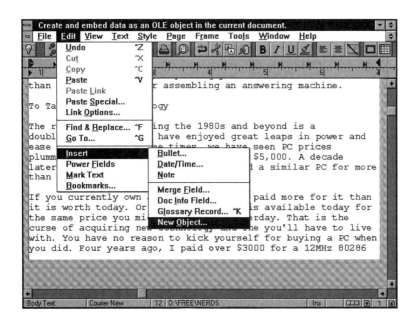

Figure 12.31:

For OLE to work, you must insert an object in your Windows file.

You must select the OLE server for your recording device. In figure 12.32, Windows Sound Recorder has been selected. Notice the other choices, such as Pocket Recorder included with Pro AudioStudio 16, Soundo'LE included with Sound Blaster 16 ASP, and Quick Recorder included with Windows Sound System.

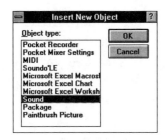

Figure 12.32:
You can select any recorder utility for your audio message.

After the OLE server is selected, you can record your verbal Post-It note. Click on the record button of your OLE server and begin speaking. Don't make your message too long; even at 8-bit resolution and 11.025KHz sampling, a one-minute mono message requires over 600K of disk space. At CD quality (44.1 KHz and 16-bit resolution), the same message requires over 5M!

Listen Up!
The Windows Sound Recorder is limited to one minute of recording.

When finished recording, select **U**pdate from the **F**ile menu (see fig. 12.33). Then select E**x**it.

Listen Up!

Your command to return to your document varies with the recording software used. In Pocket Recorder, for example, the command is "Return to..."

Figure 12.33:

When finished recording, select Update and return to your document.

With the recording finished, your WAV file is embedded in the document. The WAV file is represented by an icon, such as that in figure 12.34. Depending on which recording software you use, the icon will look different. Most likely, you will want to resize it to a more-manageable size.

To play your sound file, simply double-click on the icon (see fig. 12.35). Your comments are played back. To delete an embedded sound file, simply click on it with the cursor and press Del. To move the embedded sound file or copy it elsewhere, use Ctrl-X or Ctrl-C or select the option from your software's Edit menu.

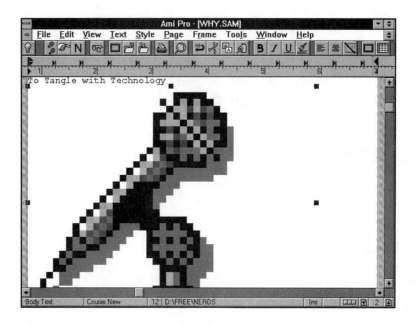

Figure 12.34:
Your embedded sound icon may be too large; resize it.

Listen Up!

Some OLE servers may not play back your file immediately. Instead, they will load the sound file and the recording software that created it. You then must select the play button to hear the file. To avoid this delay, use simpler recording software, such as Pocket Recorder or Soundo'LE.

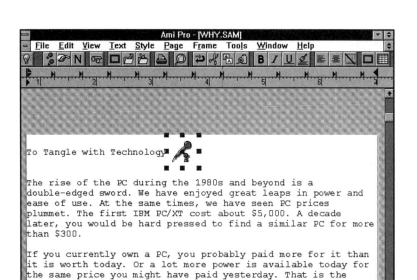

Figure 12.35:

To play back your message, double-click on the icon.

Recording Tips

To make the most of your recording, follow these tips:

♪ When recording, turn down to zero the volume levels of all audio sources not being used in the recording. This makes your recording as hiss-free as possible.

♪ For simple voice messages, select 8-bit mono sampling at 11.025 KHz. This keeps the WAV file from being too large.

♪ When not using your microphone, turn it off, and trim its recording level down to zero, especially if no microphone is connected to the jack. This reduces any possible noise.

♪   Avoid having any recording or playback settings at 100 percent (I recommend 90 percent or less). For example, never crank up the master volume to 100 percent; you may shorten the life of your speakers. Volume level moderation greatly increases the quality of your recordings.

♪   Avoid using too much bass or too much treble. If you reduce the treble the hiss is reduced, but the sound may be too muted. An increase of the bass may make your audio too muffled and "heavy."

Built-In Proofreader

Windows seems to be an ideal environment for proofreading text. Although spell checkers check for misspelled words, listening to the context of the text may find those correctly spelled words that are in the wrong place. For example, I often type "drives" instead of "driver." While my word processor's dictionary won't notice the wrong choice of words, my ears would.

Both Sound Blaster 16 ASP and Pro AudioStudio 16 include Monologue for Windows. As a Windows version of the DOS program, Monologue for Windows can act like a proofreader over your shoulder; it's there when you need it. Monologue for Windows allows you to change the pitch, volume, and speed of the spoken words. The built-in Dictionary Manager allows you to save your own preferred pronunciations of words and abbreviations. In addition, you can maintain several dictionaries and pick the one you currently want to use.

Listen Up!

You would use a text-to-speech utility to proofread a row or column of numbers against the master list from which you typed them. Another use is to have the utility read a memo or other document to you as you did other tasks, such as filing correspondence or opening mail.

You install Monologue separately from the Sound Blaster 16 ASP software (it's installed automatically with the Pro AudioStudio 16 software). Figure 12.36 shows the opening

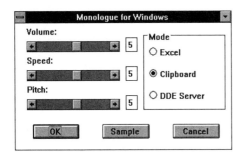

screen for Monologue for Windows.

Figure 12.36:

Monologue for Windows main screen.

Listen Up!

To read text and convert it into speech, Monologue requires a 386SX or faster computer with a hard disk. You will have trouble if you try using it over a network or from a floppy disk.

You can change Monologue's volume, speed, and pitch. You also can select which mode you want Monologue to use:

Excel mode is for spreadsheet numbers.

Clipboard mode is for text copied to the Windows Clipboard.

DDE Server mode allows Monologue to speak any words sent by another Windows application.

Listen Up!

Excel mode is provided as a convenience if you primarily work with Microsoft Excel spreadsheets. This mode doesn't require you to copy the selected text to the Clipboard. You simply highlight the numbers, place your mouse pointer over the Monologue icon, and press the right mouse button. Excel mode may be inconvenient if you plan to use Monologue for documents and other text applications; you'll have to switch modes frequently.

The most common method for using Monologue is through Windows Clipboard. After making your selections, choose OK. Monologue is then minimized and ready to use.

Need to proof some text or numbers? In your document or spreadsheet, simply highlight the text and copy it (press Ctrl-C or Ctrl-Ins) to the Clipboard. Finally, place your mouse pointer over the Monologue icon and press the right mouse button (see fig. 12.37). Monologue then reads back the text from the Clipboard. To stop Monologue's recitation, place the mouse cursor over the Monologue icon and press the left mouse button.

Listen Up!

If you can't see the Monologue for Windows icon, you can't use it. You must place your pointer over this icon. If your application is full screen, reduce its size until you can see the Monologue icon at the bottom of the screen.

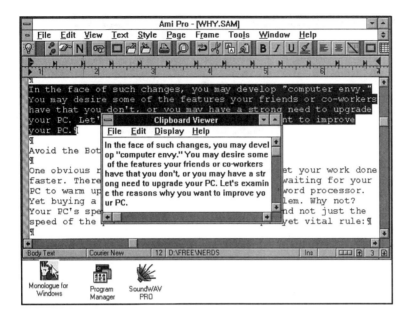

Figure 12.37:

To play back the copied text, place your mouse pointer over the Monologue icon and press the right button.

In actual use, Monologue does an excellent job. If it mispronounces a word, you can teach it the errors of its ways. Using the Dictionary Manager, you can manage the Monologue dictionary of exceptions. Type in the Sounds Like box how you feel the word should be pronounced (see fig. 12.38). After you add words to the dictionary, save the dictionary to a new name. To ensure your custom dictionary is used, click on the Active Dictionary button and specify the dictionary. Monologue will use it each time it starts, and your special words will be pronounced.

Chapter 12

Monologue Exception Dictionary - UNTITLED.DIC	

English Word: `megabyte`   Say **E**nglish Word

Sounds Like: `mega-bite`   Say Sounds **L**ike

Dictionary Contents

ABSENCE
ACCOMPANIED
ACCURACY
ACCURATE
ACRES
ACTIVE
ACTUAL
ACTUALLY

Entry Options

Insert Entry

Find Entry

Delete Entry

File Options

Open Dictionary

Save Dictionary

Active Dictionary

Figure 12.38:

You can teach Monologue new words and pronunciations.

Listen Up!

Think you'll be using Monologue often? Have it load automatically each time you start Windows by adding this line to your WIN.INI file:

```
LOAD=C:\MONOLOGW\MONOLOGW.EXE
```

Your PC's WIN.INI file may already have a LOAD= statement; if so, just add the text after the equal sign. The LOAD= command will then start Monologue and place it in the corner of your Windows desktop.

If you want to set the pitch, speed, and volume every time Windows starts, you can place the line to start in the RUN= line instead of LOAD= line. An alternative is to copy the Monologue icon to the Windows StartUp group. Any icon in the StartUp group is automatically started. To copy the icon, press Ctrl as you drag the icon to this group. To start Monologue in its minimized state, highlight the Monologue icon in the StartUp group and press Alt-Enter. Activate the **R**un Minimized check box (see fig. 12.39), and then exit.

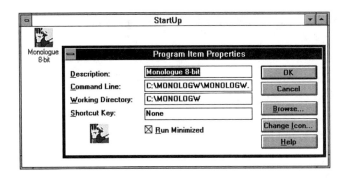

Figure 12.39:

From the StartUp group, you can automatically load a minimized Monologue.

Spreadsheets Only

Windows Sound System includes ProofReader for your
Microsoft Excel or Lotus 1-2-3 for Windows spreadsheets.
ProofReader modifies these programs so that you have a pull-
down menu of proofing options (see fig. 12.40). ProofReader
can read your spreadsheet data back to you as you enter new
numbers or read numbers you've highlighted either by rows or
by columns. You can create and add to custom voice dictionaries, and adjust the reading speed and length of pause between
items.

Sound Check

ProofReader is not as versatile as Monologue for Windows. Monologue works with the Windows Clipboard,
which allows you to even have Monologue read DOS
text from applications running in a DOS window (Windows 386 Enhanced mode only). ProofReader is strictly a
spreadsheet assistant.

	Microsoft Excel - COST.XLS						

File Edit Formula Format Data Options Macro Window Proof Help

Normal

On Entry

B17 | 0.06

	A	B	C	D	E	Selected Range	Ctrl+N
9	TOTAL		1229.09		1229.09	Stop	Ctrl+S
10						Resume	Ctrl+U
11	Response	5.00%		3.00%			
12	Orders	301		181		Set Volume...	
13	Book price	$14.95		$9.95		Options...	
14	Revenue	4501.45		1797.57	9002.89		113
15	Per book	$6.09		$0.73	$9.38		$
16							
17	Labels	0.06	18.07	0.06	10.84	0.06	36.13
18	Envelopes	0.08	24.09	0.08	14.45	0.08	48.18
19	Book	1.55	466.71	0.8	144.53	0	0.00
20	Postage	2.59	779.85	0.98	177.05	1.3	782.86
21	Royalties	0.5	150.55	0.5	90.33	0.5	301.10
22	TOTAL		1439.26		437.20		1168.27
23							
24	Total costs		2668.35		1666.29		3353.35
25	Total revenue		4501.45		1797.57		9002.89
26	Profit/loss		$1,833.10		$131.28		$5,649.54
27	% PROFIT		40.72%		7.30%		62.75%
28							

Proofread selected range | NUM

Figure 12.40:
ProofReader can read your Excel or 1-2-3 for Windows numbers.

"Computer, Do This"

A new trend in sound cards is to provide crude voice recognition software. By using a microphone, you can give your computer commands without touching the keyboard. Some sound cards, such as Microsoft Windows Sound System and Media Vision Pro AudioStudio 16, include voice recognition utilities, with varying levels of success.

Voice recognition is far from the ease of use of interacting with HAL in *2001: A Space Odyssey* or the Enterprise's computer in a "Star Trek" television episode. Typically, only a few hundred commands are supported. To make matters worse, the software often does not recognize your words. Here are some tips to improve your chances of recognition success:

♪ Relax while you speak; you want the voice recognition software to recognize your normal voice. You can always retrain your voice recognition software.

♪ Use the voice you'll use when you work, instead of trying to speak "perfectly."

♪ Do not pause between words in each command.

♪ Hold the microphone six to 12 inches from your mouth.

♪ If you are using a headset microphone, place it a thumb-width from the corner of your mouth rather than at the center.

♪ Keep the microphone at the same distance and location to your mouth each time you use your voice recognition software.

♪ Keep the microphone cable straight or the signal may be lost.

♪ Adjust the microphone volume to the best setting, according to the recording levels displayed by your voice recognition program.

ExecuVoice

Media Vision includes ExecuVoice with its sound card. This utility, developed by Dragon Systems, Inc., is installed separately from the other Pro AudioStudio 16 software.

You must "teach" ExecuVoice how you speak (see fig. 12.41). After a five-minute Quick Training, ExecuVoice was ready to respond to my voice. You won't be freed from typing keyboard commands; ExecuVoice only provides a few hundred commands, some of which are for specific applications, such as Windows Calendar or Media Player.

Figure 12.41:

You can quickly train ExecuVoice to recognize your voice.

To start ExecuVoice, double-click on the Voicebar icon placed in the ExecuVoice group. A bar appears across the top of the screen that provides options for the voice profile you want (see fig. 12.42).

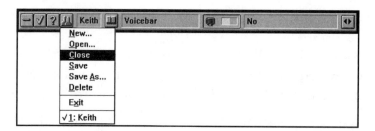

Figure 12.42:

ExecuVoice can store your specific voice information.

When the Voicebar and your microphone are turned on, you can give your PC commands. Which voice commands will ExecuVoice understand? A "cheat sheet" of the active commands can be displayed on-screen (see fig. 12.43). From this list, you can also train ExecuVoice to recognize or better recognize the way you pronounce words. In the right-hand side of the Voicebar, you can see if ExecuVoice correctly recognized your last command.

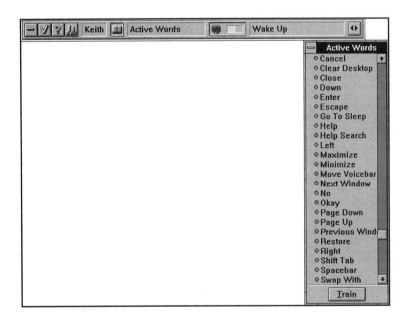

Figure 12.43:

A "cheat sheet" of words can be displayed at all times.

After using ExecuVoice for an evening, I was impressed but not dazzled. The program had about a 90 to 95 percent success rate in recognizing my voice. (The rate would probably increase if I fully trained the program.) Although I had a 40-MHz 80386 PC, the recognition speed was tardy but not unbearably so. Hopefully, this program will be zippier with an 80486 PC.

Voice Pilot

Windows Sound System includes Voice Pilot, also developed by Dragon Systems, Inc. Voice Pilot, like ExecuVoice, allows you to give your PC spoken commands. The Voice Pilot window (see fig. 12.44) includes a toolbar to control Voice Pilot. Active words Voice Pilot can recognize are listed in the window. You can hide this list by pressing the Active Words button (the third button from the left).

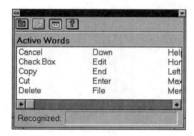

Figure 12.44:

Voice Pilot toolbar is very easy to use.

When you depress the microphone button, Voice Pilot becomes activated. Voice Pilot displays the words it recognizes in the Recognized box. If Voice Pilot cannot understand you, it displays question marks.

Voice Pilot relies on a hierarchy of commands. When you say a top-level command, such as "File," a list of words is displayed for the next level, such as New and Open. To train Voice Pilot on a word, click on the word and select Train (see fig. 45).

You can take the current Voice Pilot vocabulary and train it for a specific application, although Voice Pilot includes vocabularies for sixteen applications (see fig. 12.46). Most of these applications are understandably Microsoft products. You can delete

words you won't use in your application, and then save it to a
new name. You can then load this reduced vocabulary when
you use the application. Like ExecuVoice, you can save voice
models for different users.

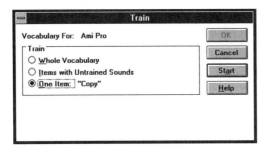

Figure 12.45:
You can train Voice Pilot on the fly.

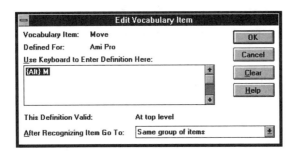

Figure 12.46:
You even can change the keystrokes assigned to a word.

A Built-In CD

Although Windows Media Player can play audio CDs in your
CD-ROM drive, you can use the more-sophisticated Pocket CD
included with Pro AudioStudio 16. With Pocket CD, you can
start an audio CD, minimize Pocket CD, and do other work on

your computer. Pocket CD lets you add play lists to a CD database so that you can play each track on your favorite CD in a certain order.

Listen Up!

Your CD-ROM drive must support the Microsoft CD extensions called MSCDEX.EXE.

Why use a separate CD utility in lieu of the Media Player? Most CD utilities are more powerful than Media Player. They may include the capability to:

♪ Skip tracks easily

♪ Repeat and shuffle the tracks to be played

♪ Assign names to CDs and their tracks for easy recognition

♪ Make custom playlists to play the songs you want in a specific order

Sound Check

To play an audio CD from DOS, Pro AudioStudio also includes the Music Box.

To start Pocket CD, double-click on its icon in the Multimedia Tools group. Pocket CD uses controls similar to those you find on a CD player, such as play, advance, pause, and stop (see fig. 12.47).

Figure 12.47:
Pocket CD lets you play your favorite audio CDs.

The four icons in the middle of the dialog box control several options:

Cue Device places Pocket CD in standby mode to be cued by Pocket Recorder.

Pocket Mixer activates Pocket Mixer so that you can change volume settings.

Shuffle randomly shuffles music selections.

Continuous Play turns on or off continuous play of the same CD.

Pocket CD gives a "fingerprint" to each CD so that it can quickly recognize it. This unique number is created by taking the total number of tracks and multiplying it by the total play-back time of the first track.

To create a playlist (the order in which you want a CD's tracks to play), select **E**dit,**A**dd Songs. If you select **E**dit,**M**odify, you can give the current CD a title and its artist's name. The next time you use this CD, Pocket CD recalls this information. You can also give each track a name, rather than seeing Song: [X] appear (see fig. 12.48). This allows you to see which of your favorite songs is currently playing.

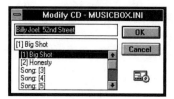

Figure 12.48:

You can give your CD and each of its tracks a title.

Sound System's Music Box

Windows Sound System includes Music Box as its audio CD player (see fig. 12.49). Like Pocket CD, you can assign names to CDs and individual tracks. You can also make playlists, which play specific tracks in a specific order. Like Pocket Recorder, you can shuffle and repeat playlists.

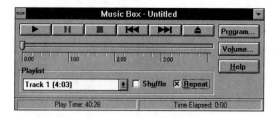

Figure 12.49:

Music Box is very simple but powerful.

Music Box uses CD-like controls, such as play, stop, and pause. If you click on the Program button, you can assign titles to the current CD and to its tracks (see fig. 12.50).

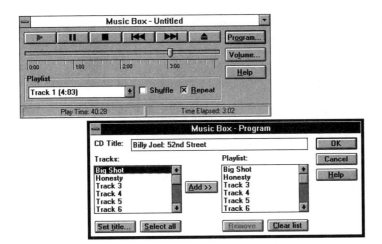

Figure 12.50:

You can quickly name and develop playlists of your favorite songs.

Finding the Sounds

Sound Finder, included with Microsoft Windows Sound System, lets you browse, edit, and preview sound files or convert sound files from one format to another (see fig. 12.51).

Sound Finder can find and play files stored in any of several sound formats, such as WAV (Windows waveform), MID (MIDI), VOC (Sound Blaster), RMI (Microsoft MIDI), SND (NeXT), and AIF (Apple) files. The conversion choices are limited; you can convert AIF, SND, or VOC files to the WAV format. MID and RMI files cannot be converted to the WAV format.

Sound Finder

File Name:
clunk.wav

b2fhome.wav
batdevil.wav
batshut.wav
clunk.wav
dh-punk2.wav
dnoquest.wav
down.wav
fltbothr.wav
fltknow.wav
fltwork.wav

Directories:
c:\soundwav\errors

c:\
soundwav
errors

Volume...
Convert...
Edit...
Play
Skip
Properties...

List Files of Type:
Sound files

Drives:
c: programs

Help

Label:
Bell sound

Picture:

Description:
A bell-sounding clunk.

Figure 12.51:

Sound Finder can play a variety of audio files.

Listen Up!

Why convert a sound file to the WAV format?
Speed. Sound files in these other formats
must be converted to the WAV format each
time they are played. Once in the WAV
format, you can add labels, descriptions,
and pictures to them. Another advantage to WAV
files is they can be used by your other Windows
applications.

To see the properties of a sound file, highlight its name in the
list of files and click on Properties. From the Properties dialog
box, you can add a description to the sound and assign a picture to it. This picture may come from either an ICO (Windows
icon) file or BMP (Windows bitmap) image.

A Quarter in the JukeBox

Sound Blaster 16 ASP includes JukeBox, which plays MIDI (MID) files (see fig. 12.52). With JukeBox, you can select several MIDI files and play them one at a time. Midi is discussed in detail in Chapter 13.

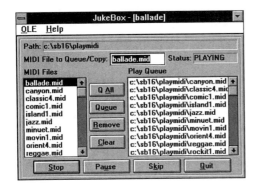

Figure 12.52:

With JukeBox, you can queue up and play several MIDI files.

You can queue up all MIDI files in the current directory by selecting Q All. Otherwise, you can highlight individual MIDI files in the left-hand window and select Queue. To remove a choice from the queue list, highlight the MIDI file in the right-hand window and select **R**emove. To clear the entire playlist, select **C**lear.

Once you've selected the files you want to play, select **P**lay from the row of buttons along the bottom. During play, you can skip over a selection or quit the JukeBox.

Listen Up!

With the JukeBox, you can make a MIDI file an OLE object. From the **O**LE menu, select **C**opy MIDI file as an object. Finally, paste the copied MIDI file into your other Windows application.

Sound Blaster Scheduler

Creative Labs includes a talking appointment scheduler with its Sound Blaster 16 ASP. The scheduler is like having an appointment secretary on disk. Talking Scheduler makes scheduling appointments easy. You first open the Talking Scheduler from the Sound Blaster 16 group (see fig. 12.53). This applet has a number of nifty features.

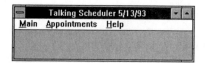

Figure 12.53:

Talking Scheduler is deceptively simple looking.

First, select **M**ain,**S**etUp. From the setup dialog box (see fig. 12.54), you can pick which animation character (Simon, Perkins, or Igor) will appear to warn you of impending appointments. Each character has a default pitch and speed, which you can change.

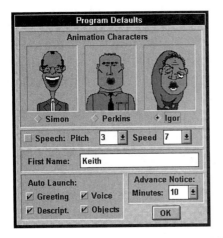

Figure 12.54:

You can pick your own "appointment secretary."

Listen Up!

For Talking Scheduler to work, it must be running and minimized; otherwise it won't remind you of appointments. Like Monologue for Windows, you can place Talking Scheduler in the LOAD= line in your WIN.INI file or in your Startup group to load it automatically each time you start Windows.

The Auto Launch settings in the lower left-hand corner refer to how an appointment is presented. For example, if you place a checkmark in the Objects box, any OLE objects will automatically be launched at appointment time. A checkmark in the Description box makes the animated character read the appointment's description.

To add or modify an appointment, select **A**dd/Modify from the **A**ppointments pull-down menu (see fig. 12.55). You select a date for the appointment, and then highlight the portion of the

Chapter 12

day for the appointment from the 24-hour clock. You enter a description, and then record a voice message to yourself for appointment (this part's optional). You can then change the animation character that will remind you of your appointment. When the appointment time arrives, your character will speak to you (see fig. 12.56).

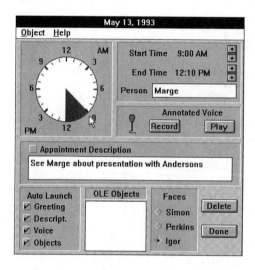

Figure 12.55:
You can use the 24-hour clock to set the appointment time.

Overall, Talking Scheduler is an exceptional value compared to other gimmicky schedulers. It can warn you of upcoming appointments and show you how hectic your day is (or will be) at a glance.

Listen Up!

Talking Scheduler is an OLE client, meaning it can accept objects or files from your other Windows applications. For example, you can place an Excel spreadsheet in your appointment calendar to be opened at 4pm on Friday.

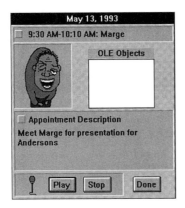

Figure 12.56:
Your animation character appears when your appointment is due.

Sound Games

Sound Blaster 16 ASP includes the game Creative Mosaic. The goal is to arrange the tiles in numerical order in the least number of moves. If you succeed, you will hear the roar of applause. (As you can see in Figure 12.57, I didn't do very well.)

You first choose a skill level from the Skill pull-down menu. You can also pick the size of the grid up to eight by eight tiles. Creative Mosaic relies heavily on sound. You start the game by clicking on the key in the upper left-hand corner; a car engine starts. With each move, you hear a click. If you make a mistake by trying to drag a tile to an ineligible spot, you'll hear a shriek. If you exceed 100 moves, you'll hear a sudden gasp. To turn the sounds off, click on the box containing the ear.

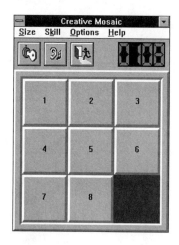

Figure 12.57:

Mosaic is a very challenging and entertaining game.

You can also use a bitmap image, or picture, for your tiles. Instead of rearranging numbered tiles, you can form the original picture. First, select **P**icture from the **O**ptions pull-down menu, and then select which bitmap image (BMP) to use for the picture. In Figure 12.58, I've successfully rearranged the Windows logo file (WINLOGO.BMP).

Talking Screen Saver

Windows Sound System includes SoundScapes as a Windows screen saver. Instead of displaying a moving picture, SoundScapes blanks your screen and plays soothing sounds.

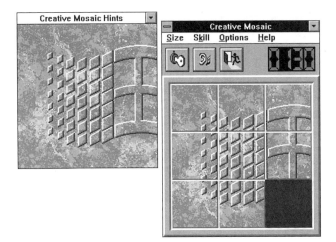

Figure 12.58:

You can also reassemble a bitmap (BMP) picture in Creative Mosaic.

Listen Up!

A *screen saver* is a software program that either blanks your screen or replaces it with moving images after a preset amount of time. Why? If you leave your current work, such as a document, visible on the screen, the monitor's electron beams may permanently etch the static image into the screen's surface.

Screen savers often include passwords to protect your work from being seen by prying eyes. For example, Microsoft Windows 3.1 has a built-in screen saver with password protection.

In Control Panel's Desktop utility (see fig. 12.59), select SoundScapes. If you select Set**u**p, you can select which sounds you want to hear and how soon you want the screen to blank.

Figure showing a Windows "Desktop" control panel dialog box with the following elements:

Desktop

Pattern
Name: [None]
Edit Pattern...

Applications
☒ Fast "Alt+Tab" Switching

Screen Saver
Name: SoundScapes
Delay: 1 Minutes

Wallpaper
File: [None]
○ Center ◉ Tile

Icons
Spacing: 75 Pixels
☒ Wrap Title

Sizing Grid
Granularity: 0
Border Width: 3

Cursor Blink Rate
Slow   Fast

OK
Cancel
Help

Test
Setup...

Figure 12.59:
You select SoundScapes like any other Windows screen saver.

The Future Is Windows

The overall quality of the Windows utilities included with manufacturer's sound cards indicates that the future is with Microsoft Windows.

Sound under Windows has both practical and playful sides. Business users can use object linking and embedding (OLE) to place a voice note into a file. Home users can play an audio CD while writing the Great American Novel. By appealing to both markets, sound is being adopted more quickly than anyone anticipated. With improving voice recognition technology, perhaps Windows someday will be heard and not just seen.

Making the Most of MIDI

The right equipment can turn your PC into a home recording studio. With a sound card, a keyboard, a stereo system, and the right software, the musical hobbyist can learn about music by hearing and playing it. Musicians, on the other hand, can record, edit, arrange, print, and play their compositions. This is all possible through a standard called *Musical Instrument Digital Interface* (MIDI).

In this chapter, you learn:

- ♪ What the definition and history of MIDI is
- ♪ How MIDI songs are constructed
- ♪ How MIDI works with Windows
- ♪ What the requirements for MIDI work are
- ♪ What MIDI utilities are included with sound cards

Chapter 13

Why All the Hype about MIDI

The Musical Instrument Digital Interface, or MIDI, is two-faced. It is both a digital communication language for making music and a hardware specification for using equipment for that purpose. MIDI allows multiple electronic instruments, such as keyboard synthesizers, and computers to work together. With MIDI, a musician becomes a techno-conductor, creating and developing a composition in a flexible and affordable computer environment. The result is that a person can become the proverbial one-man band.

Sound Check

In a way, a MIDI system is like a small musical network. MIDI equipment is interconnected and then connected to your PC through a MIDI interface. Each MIDI device can be independently controlled through a single MIDI line. Just as a public speaker can single out and communicate a message to one individual in the crowd, MIDI messages can be directed to a specific MIDI device.

To connect MIDI instruments to your PC, you need a sound card with a MIDI input port and a MIDI output port. Often, the joystick port on the sound card doubles as this MIDI interface. With a MIDI connector box, which is often sold separately, you can connect your MIDI devices to your sound card and, therefore, to your PC. Media Vision, for example, sells the MIDI Mate for its line of MIDI-capable sound cards.

Adding to your MIDI network is simple. To connect MIDI devices in a network, simply plug in a cable from the MIDI out port to the MIDI in port of the new device. What MIDI devices can be connected together? A professional musician can have a drum machine for developing percussion sounds, a synthesizer for entering musical notes, and an audio mixer to blend the

sounds. At home, you can do everything from your own computer and perhaps an attached CD player or stereo system. What would have cost an artist a fortune a decade ago is now within the reach of every aspiring musician.

The MIDI specification is used to transmit digital messages to other MIDI devices on this network. The signals are then used to control the sounds generated by the instruments, such as *timbre* (sound and tonal quality) and *blend* (recording level and panning).

This MIDI data can be sent to a sequencer. A *sequencer* allows you to record, play, and edit MIDI musical scores. Often, a sequencer is a software program running on your PC.

The sequencer allows you to select from 128 instruments and assign them to any of 16 channels. This is called *mapping*. Each specific MIDI instrument, such as a guitar or piano, is called a *patch*. After the patches are chosen, the channels are funnelled together and manipulated. You then have the ability to create and orchestrate your own band. With a sequencer, you can modify things like tempo, sound, and volume, or cut and paste various prerecorded music sequences together. After you complete your editing, the sequencer can print a neatly penned copy of your musical piece to paper.

How do you reliably play a MIDI score that was created on a different computer system? If the mapping isn't exactly the same, a MIDI file originally composed with a piano and a clarinet may be played back with a rock organ and a whistle. To solve this mapping dilemma, the General MIDI numbering system was developed. Each instrument is given a unique number from 0 to 127. A flute, for example, is number 73; a glockenspiel is number 9. The General MIDI system offers standard mapping of the most common musical instruments, as well as mapping of percussion instruments.

Listen Up!
The Windows MIDI Mapper utility found in the Control Panel allows you to remap your sounds to non-standard instruments, such as a Peruvian pipe flute.

The History of MIDI

MIDI is an outgrowth of the development of electronic synthesizers. The first keyboard synthesizers were *monophonic*, capable of playing one note at a time. The development of *polyphonic* synthesizers allowed musicians to generate multiple sounds at the same time. With such emerging capabilities, the industry sought a standard to connect and control these devices. Otherwise, one manufacturer's devices would not work with that of another.

Dave Smith and Chet Word began creating an electronic instrument protocol that allowed equipment from different manufacturers to communicate with each other. In 1981, their *Universal Synthesizer Interface* (USI) was proposed to the Audio Engineering Society as an audio standard. A panel created from members of that group and representatives from the major electronic instrument manufacturers, modified this standard. Two years later, it was adopted under the name of Musical Instrument Digital Interface or MIDI.

With the adoption of this industry-wide standard, any device providing MIDI ports was capable of transmitting or responding to MIDI data. Musicians could finally join computers with musical instruments.

MIDI versus Digital Audio

Unlike waveform (or digital) audio or the audio supported by CDs, MIDI songs take up very little disk space. For example, a 500K MIDI file can store an hour of stereo sound. A similar WAV file requires over 600M. The reason for this discrepancy is that a MIDI file contains the commands for a recording (hold down this piano key for so long), whereas a WAV file contains the actual sound. This reduction in space alone should convince you that MIDI is the best format for adding music to your business presentations or other software you author.

MIDI does have other advantages besides hard disk conservation. First, MIDI files can be edited. A file can be slowed down or sped up without changing its pitch. You can, for example, slow down your MIDI background music to match the length of your presentation or animation. Second, MIDI doesn't push your sound card to its limit. In other words, a MIDI file on an 8-bit sound card doesn't contain a distracting hiss.

Finally, MIDI's flexibility makes it easy to work with clip music and clip instrument patches. Software companies like Passport Designs, Voyetra, and Twelve Tone Systems provide such music files that can be used in presentations freely without paying royalties. Also, patches for other instruments can be imported from other synthesizers, computer bulletin boards, or MIDI chip libraries. E-mu Systems of Scotts Valley sells MIDI patches from around the world including samples of Australian Digeridus, Pacific Rim Hula Sticks, and African Udu Drums.

Sound Check

Despite the space required, a digital audio file does have one up on MIDI. It provides more-reliable, hassle-free playback because it doesn't require any special MIDI hardware. Also, a WAV file can contain spoken dialog and singing voices; a MIDI file can't.

Chapter 13

What You Need for MIDI

The MPC Level 2 specifications call for a MIDI interface if you want your humdrum PC to become a multimedia PC (MPC). To comply with this standard, many sound cards contain an FM MIDI synthesizer chip. Most sound cards use synthesizer chips developed by Yamaha. The least expensive sound cards use the monophonic 11-voice YM3812 or OPL2 chip. Better sound cards use the stereophonic 20-voice YMF262 or OPL3 chip.

The FM synthesizer chip acts like a minisynthesizer and can imitate the sounds of many instruments. To be MPC-compatible, the sound card must be able to play six simultaneous melody notes and two simultaneous percussive notes.

Imitated musical instruments are not as impressive as the real thing. High-end sound cards use digital recordings of real instruments and sound effects. These sounds are embedded in memory chips on the card. If you intend to record soundtracks and the like, you'll want a card with this serious MIDI capability, such as Roland Corporation's SCC-1 GS for $400. This card contains 16-bit samples of real instrument recordings in ROM (read-only memory), which result in far more realistic musical tones.

Listen Up!

If you own the Sound Blaster 16 ASP sound card, a cheaper alternative to purchasing a high-end sound card is to buy its companion Wave Blaster for $249.95. When MIDI music is played, it looks to Wave Blaster for any of 213 CD-quality, digitally recorded musical instrument sounds. Without Wave Blaster, Sound Blaster 16 ASP imitates these sounds through FM synthesis.

Besides FM synthesis, you'll need sequencer software, such as Midisoft Recording Session, which is included with Pro AudioStudio 16. You also need a sound synthesizer. You probably already own a synthesizer if you own a sound card. A MIDI capability is typically built into the sound card.

The addition of a MIDI keyboard can be helpful but not necessary. By using the keyboard, you can enter the notes for various instruments. Several MIDI keyboards are available, such as Roland's A-30 or PC-200 MK2. These keyboards cost from $395 to over $7,000. MIDI is not cheap.

Where's the Beef?

Your PC may have to be beefed up to handle MIDI music-making. To have the most speed for your MIDI music, I recommend *at least* the following configuration:

- ♪ 33-MHz 80486DX PC (although the math coprocessor isn't used)

- ♪ 16M RAM

- ♪ A large, permanent (not temporary) swap file on your PC

- ♪ Ample disk space to save your compositions

Sound Check

What's a swap file? In Windows' 386 Enhanced mode, a *swap file* is a hidden file that turns your hard disk into overflow memory when actual memory is low. Of course, using a physical hard disk is slower than real-life memory, but it certainly is better than getting an Out of memory error message. There are two types of swap files: permanent and temporary. A *permanent* swap file is

continues

continued

permanently set aside for Windows, whereas a *temporary*
swap file is carved out of your remaining hard disk space
each time Windows starts.

MIDI under Windows

Microsoft Windows 3.1 supports two different standards for
playing MIDI music: the general MIDI guidelines and the
Microsoft authoring guidelines. Both are similar, yet they differ
in the channel settings they require.

To work with low-cost synthesizers, Windows defines two
types of synthesizers: base-level and extended.

A *base-level* MIDI device can play back at least three melodic
instrument parts with at least six notes playing simultaneously.
A percussion track also can be played with at least three notes
playing simultaneously. Most sound cards are considered base-
level devices.

An *extended-level* MIDI device can play back at least nine melodic instrument parts with at least 16 notes playing simultaneously. A percussion track can be played alongside the
melody with at least 16 notes playing at one time. Most sound
cards that contain ROM samples of instruments, such as Turtle
Beach's MultiSound card, are extended-level devices.

MIDI channels 1 through 10 are used for extended synthesizers;
channels 13 through 16 are for base-level synthesizers. For a
MIDI file to play on both base-level and extended synthesizers,
a MIDI file must contain two complete renditions of the same
composition—one using channels 1 through 10, and the other
using channels 13 through 16.

When you install Windows, the Setup program installs MIDI settings that support both standards for playing MIDI information on common sound-card and synthesizer combinations. This setup information is contained in the MIDI Mapper, which is found in the Control Panel (see fig. 13.1).

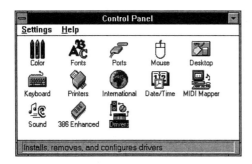

Figure 13.1:

The MIDI Mapper is found in the Control Panel.

The MIDI Mapper allows you to select and modify your setup for your MIDI-capable sound card. If you double-click on the MIDI Mapper, you can change and modify your settings (see fig. 13.2). These settings include:

♪ Setups

♪ Key Maps

♪ Patch Maps

Listen Up!

The current MIDI Mapper information is stored in the file MIDIMAP.CFG, which is found in your \WINDOWS\SYSTEM directory. Some sound-card manufacturers provide updated MIDIMAP.CFG files for your model of sound card.

Figure 13.2:
The MIDI Mapper controls three MIDI aspects.

Set Up the Setups

With the Setups button highlighted, click on the Name list drop box. A list of possible setups displays. Each corresponds to a specific MIDI-capable sound card. Some setups are included with the basic Windows installation; others are added when you install your sound-card software. In figure 13.3, note that the Media Vision installation software has added some Media Vision (MVI) setups to the list.

Figure 13.3:
Your sound-card software may modify the MIDI Mapper.

When you select Edit, you can edit the chosen setup (see fig. 13.4). The leftmost column lists the 16 source channels available in a MIDI setup. The second column lists the destination channel. For synthesizers that support general MIDI, this number is the same as the source channel.

Src Chan	Dest Chan	Port Name	Patch Map Name	Active
1	1	Pro Audio/CDPC MIDI O	[None]	☒
2	2	Pro Audio/CDPC MIDI Output	[None]	☒
3	3	Pro Audio/CDPC MIDI Output	[None]	☒
4	4	Pro Audio/CDPC MIDI Output	[None]	☒
5	5	Pro Audio/CDPC MIDI Output	[None]	☒
6	6	Pro Audio/CDPC MIDI Output	[None]	☒
7	7	Pro Audio/CDPC MIDI Output	[None]	☒
8	8	Pro Audio/CDPC MIDI Output	[None]	☒
9	9	Pro Audio/CDPC MIDI Output	[None]	☒
10	10	Pro Audio/CDPC MIDI Output	[None]	☒
11	11	[None]	[None]	■
12	12	[None]	[None]	■
13	13	Voyetra OPL-3 FM Synth	[None]	☒
14	14	Voyetra OPL-3 FM Synth	[None]	☒
15	15	Voyetra OPL-3 FM Synth	[None]	☒
16	16	Voyetra OPL-3 FM Synth	[None]	☒

MIDI Setup: 'MVI Pro Audio'

[OK]   [Cancel]   [Help]

Figure 13.4:
You can map source channels to different destination channels.

Listen Up!
It is highly unlikely that you would edit the MIDI Mapper setup. Most sound-card makers include a MIDIMAP.CFG file. Otherwise, Windows may include a MIDIMAP.CFG file for your sound card. You might need to create a MIDI setup if you connect your PC to a MIDI synthesizer that does not support General MIDI, which is unlikely, and you want to play MIDI files authored according to general MIDI guidelines. In general, the standard MIDI Mapper setups provided should work fine.

The port name in the third column lists the available ports where sounds on the source channel are sent. You can, for example, have two synthesizers, such as an Ad Lib and a synthesizer connected to the MIDI output port on your computer. You could send some sounds on certain channels to the Ad Lib

port, and others to the MIDI output port. To see the list of choices, click on the drop box arrow. From the far right column, you can select the patch map name to use with that source channel. The far right box enables you to turn the source channel on or off. If you select a port name, this box is selected automatically.

Patch Time

If you select **P**atch Maps,**E**dit, you can change the patch map. As defined earlier, a patch is MIDI jargon for a particular instrument, such as a harpsichord. A *patch map* links the individual instruments to destination patches and sets their volume (see fig. 13.5). If your synthesizer supports General MIDI guidelines, the source patch number must match the destination patch number. The key map name in the far right column specifies the key map to use with that instrument.

MIDI Patch Map: 'MT32'

1 based patches

Src Patch	Src Patch Name	Dest Patch	Volume %	Key Map Name
0	Acoustic Grand Piano	0	100	[None]
1	Bright Acoustic Piano	1	100	[None]
2	Electric Grand Piano	3	100	[None]
3	Honky-tonk Piano	7	100	[None]
4	Rhodes Piano	5	100	[None]
5	Chorused Piano	6	100	[None]
6	Harpsichord	17	100	[None]
7	Clavinet	21	100	[None]
8	Celesta	22	100	[None]
9	Glockenspiel	101	100	[None]
10	Music Box	101	100	[None]
11	Vibraphone	98	100	[None]
12	Marimba	104	100	[None]
13	Xylophone	103	100	[None]
14	Tubular Bells	102	100	[None]
15	Dulcimer	105	100	[None]

OK   Cancel   Help

Figure 13.5:
You can change which instruments play to which patches.

Changing Your Keys

If you select **K**ey Maps,**E**dit, you can change the key map. The *key map* allows you to raise or lower the pitch of an instrument by an octave. For percussion patches, you can remap keys so that a different percussion instrument plays when a source key is used (see fig. 13.6). To do this, simply place a different destination key that maps to the source key listed in the first column.

```
┌─────────────────────────────────────────┐
│  ─           MIDI Key Map: '+1 octave'    │
├─────────────────────────────────────────┤
│  Src Key    Src Key Name        Dest Key  │
│  ┌──────┬───────────────────┬──────┐  ▲ ▲ │
│  │ 35   │ Acoustic Bass Drum │ 47  │  ▼ ▼ │
│  │ 36   │ Bass Drum 1        │ 48  │      │
│  │ 37   │ Side Stick         │ 49  │      │
│  │ 38   │ Acoustic Snare     │ 50  │      │
│  │ 39   │ Hand Clap          │ 51  │      │
│  │ 40   │ Electric Snare     │ 52  │ ░    │
│  │ 41   │ Low Floor Tom      │ 53  │      │
│  │ 42   │ Closed Hi Hat      │ 54  │      │
│  │ 43   │ High Floor Tom     │ 55  │      │
│  │ 44   │ Pedal Hi Hat       │ 56  │      │
│  │ 45   │ Low Tom            │ 57  │      │
│  │ 46   │ Open Hi Hat        │ 58  │      │
│  │ 47   │ Low-Mid Tom        │ 59  │      │
│  │ 48   │ High-Mid Tom       │ 60  │      │
│  │ 49   │ Crash Cymbal 1     │ 61  │      │
│  │ 50   │ High Tom           │ 62  │  ▼   │
│  └──────┴───────────────────┴──────┘      │
│    [  OK  ]   [ Cancel ]   [  Help  ]     │
└─────────────────────────────────────────┘
```

Figure 13.6:

The key map adjusts an instrument's pitch.

Free Sequencers

Few of the sound cards reviewed in this book include MIDI software. The only MIDI sequencing software I found included with a sound card was the Recording Session from MidiSoft, which is included with the Pro AudioStudio 16 card from Media Vision.

You can buy separate sequencing software. One favorite is Midi-Soft Studio for $249.95. It offers a full complement of prerecorded music tracks in classical, jazz, and blues. You can select tracks from one prerecorded sample, and cut and paste them onto other music sequences. An interface at the bottom of the screen that resembles a tape deck lets you press buttons to stop, re-wind, fast forward, play, and record one step at a time.

A Session with Recording Session

To start Recording Session, double-click on the MidiSoft Re-cording Session icon in the Multimedia Tools group. The first time you start Recording Session, you must provide some setup information (see fig. 13.7). For example, pick a base-level setup if you have a low-end sound card, such as a Pro AudioSpectrum Plus or Sound Blaster Deluxe.

```
                   MIDI Drivers Setup
            Please select the appropriate MIDI drivers.

  ● Multimedia Drivers for Windows 3.1
     - For a sound card (Ad Lib, Pro Audio Spectrum, Sound Blaster, or compatibles),
     - Or, Roland/compatible to use the MIDI Mapper or other Windows MIDI software.

        ┌Choose MIDI Mapper Status──────────────────┐
        │  ● Base-level Setup (channels 13-16).     │
        │  ○ Extended-level Setup (channels 1-10).  │ ┌──────────────────┐
        │  ○ General MIDI Setup (channels 1-16).    │ │ Help and Examples│
        │  ○ Do not use MIDI Mapper.                │ └──────────────────┘
        └───────────────────────────────────────────┘

  ○ Midisoft Drivers for Windows 3.0/3.1
     - Optimized drivers for Roland/compatible or Midiface MIDI cards.

  ○ No Drivers
     - For using software without sound.

            [  OK  ]         [ Cancel ]
```

Figure 13.7:
Tell Recording Session which level MIDI device you have.

Listen Up!

If your MIDI song doesn't play with your sequencer, try playing CANYON.MID with Windows Media Player, which is found in the Accessories group. If you can't play CANYON.MID, then you may have a problem with your MIDI mapping. Until the Media Player works, your sequencer software won't work either. You may have to reinstall your sound card's Windows drivers.

At first glance, the Recording Session looks intimidating (see fig. 13.8). Several dozen knobs, sliders, and buttons are provided. (Probably more controls than the space shuttle!) Actually, this screen is two windows: the upper-half Score View and the lower-half Mixer View.

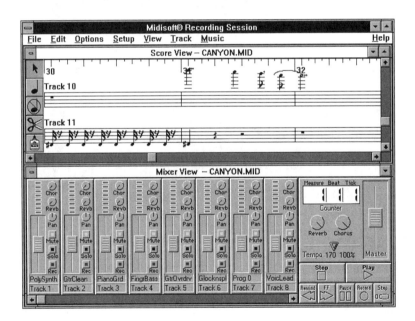

Figure 13.8:

The Recording Session looks intimidating, but isn't.

The *Score View* shows the musical score—the actual notes. When you play back a song in Recording Session, you see the notes highlighted as they play. You also can add, delete, and edit notes and phrases from this window.

The *Mixer View* allows you to record, play, name, and adjust music tracks. As your song plays, you can adjust the characteristics of each track. You also have controls to control master volume and tempo.

In figure 13.9, the CANYON.MID MIDI song included with Microsoft Windows is loaded. Press the right-hand Play button to play it. Each note briefly turns green as it is played. The mixer section displays the volume level of each track.

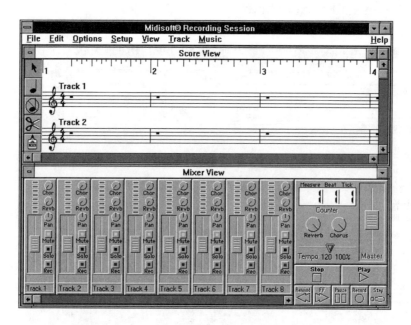

Figure 13.9:
The Windows CANYON.MID song displayed in Recording Session.

If making a new song, click on the note tool in the upper-left corner. You can then place notes in each bar to compose your own song (see fig. 13.10). You can also edit the notes of an existing song, such as CANYON.MID. For example, click on the scissors tool to remove some notes, and click-on the glue bottle to paste them.

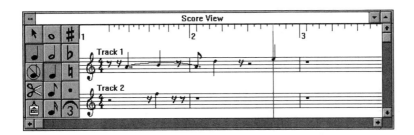

Figure 13.10:
With a sequencer, you can add, copy, and delete musical notes.

If you click on a specific track, you can give it a descriptive name and change patches, or instruments. For instance, you can change music currently played by a flute to be played by a trombone. In figure 13.11, I've changed the instrument to an electric piano and named it "Melody."

While playing a song, you can manipulate the features of each track. You can mute a track, for example, or press the Solo button to hear only that track. You also can adjust the amount of volume, reverb, and so on.

When finished with your editing or composing, you can save your song to a MIDI file.

The Recording Studio has too many features to be covered in this chapter. For instance, you can change from the treble to the bass clef, combine tracks, change your song's key, modify scale velocity, and more. Recording Session is an amazing product with ample capabilities.

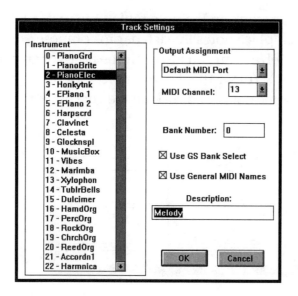

Figure 13.11:

You can pick a different instrument for each track.

Learning Music

You don't have to be a music major to play with MIDI. To learn about music history, theory, and styles while you learn to compose, try Midisoft's Music Mentor ($149.95). Music Mentor combines an interactive music tutorial with recording and editing software. The Windows-based tutorial covers five major musical styles in Western music history, describing and illustrating the basic attributes of each: melody, rhythm, harmony, timbre, texture, and form. You can view each piece of music as it plays, and then play, record, or edit by using Recording Session, the sequencing software that comes with the package.

If your sound card has MIDI capabilities and you want to explore the world of music, don't hesitate to use it. Although you don't have to buy a MIDI keyboard, consider doing so. Without a MIDI keyboard, you'll be a MIDI dabbler; with one, you can become a MIDI maestro.

 # Lights, Camera... Sound!

14

Describing multimedia is difficult. Like pornography, you know it when you see it. (In our case, hear it.) The preceding chapters all have talked of multimedia, but this chapter focuses on this evolutionary technology.

In this chapter, you learn:

- ♪ What multimedia is
- ♪ How to create a multimedia-ready PC
- ♪ What multimedia presentation software is available
- ♪ What multimedia utilities are provided with sound cards

Vaporware?

For the last few years, the word "multimedia" smelled of "vaporware." There was a lot of talk about it, but not much action. Some people called multimedia a buzzword in search of a technology. Today, multimedia products are everywhere.

The Multimedia PC Marketing Council has given "multimedia" some substance with the following specifications that define a multimedia PC (MPC). That group defines an MPC as a computer system having at least the following configuration:

♪ Multimedia Windows (either Windows 3.0 with Multimedia Extensions for Windows or Windows 3.1)

♪ 80486SX computer operating at 25 MHz

♪ 4M of memory

♪ 160M hard disk

♪ VGA monitor and video card

♪ 400-millisecond or faster CD-ROM XA-ready drive that can sustain 300 KBps to your PC without requiring more than 60 percent of your PC's thinking power

♪ 16-bit digital sound card capable of CD-quality sound at 44.1 KHz

♪ 3 ½-inch high-density disk drive (1.44M)

♪ 101-key keyboard and two- or three-button mouse

♪ MIDI interface and joystick ports

♪ Standard 9- or 25-pin serial port and a 25-pin bi-directional parallel port

♪ A pair of speakers or headphones

These specifications are based on the Level 2 specifications announced by the MPC Marketing Council in June 1993. The prior Level 1 specifications were more modest, requiring only an 80386SX PC. Eventually, every PC will be an MPC, requiring no distinction between the two.

But What IS Multimedia?

Despite the definition of what equipment you need to perform multimedia, no one has really defined what multimedia is. Basically, multimedia is just what its name implies—multiple media. *Multimedia* is the dissemination of information in more than one form. Whereas an audio CD is *unimedia*, multimedia provides more. For example, a multimedia encyclopedia on CD-ROM contains text, digitized photographs, bar charts, audio clips of famous speeches, animation, and more. Multimedia also can be quite simple. Combining a MIDI song with a WAV file of a presentation can be considered multimedia.

By appealing to more of our senses, multimedia can greatly enhance our learning experience. You can, for example, simultaneously view windows containing text, photographic images, and animation while a narrator's voice describes in detail what you are seeing. By having your senses flooded with so much information, how can you not learn?

Multimedia becomes even more potent when it is interactive. *Interactive multimedia* is when the user can control what and when multimedia information is delivered. The user can point with a mouse and click on certain screen objects, such as a button or highlighted text. For example, Compton's Encyclopedia allows the user to pick any historical event along a timeline and begin a self-directed path of learning and discovery. You can pick the start of the American Revolution.

While reading about the revolution, you can choose the Thomas Paine cross-reference and read his biography. From there, you can view a digitized painting of him. Unlike a book that is read in a linear fashion, interactive multimedia allows you to jump around and learn what you are curious about. Appeasing this curiosity is a great motivator.

Sound Check

For more information about multimedia, pick up a copy of *Technology Edge: A Guide to Multimedia* (New Riders Publishing).

Putting Multimedia To Work

Where can multimedia be used? Several areas can benefit from this technology. In education, multimedia can help students understand new ideas and concepts. By grabbing and holding the student's attention, the student learns faster. Instead of waiting to get to the chapter's end or a section that gives more details, the user can immediately access more information. Multimedia is an excellent tool for learning a foreign language. Whereas a book doesn't pronounce the words and a language tape must be searched, a multimedia CD-ROM offers flexibility. The student sees words and phrases on the screen as they are pronounced by the program. Students can point to an unfamiliar word for a quick translation to the student's native language.

Multimedia can reduce training costs. Some companies even have multimedia programs that train new employees about personnel policies, company procedures, and other aspects of company business. Sometimes this training is called *computer-based training,* or *CBT.* Such training allows employees to learn

when they are available and free from distractions. For night-shift workers, routines don't have to be altered to attend day classes.

Sound Check

Multimedia can also be a good salesperson. Because multimedia can stir the senses, it has become a powerful marketing tool. For instance, some companies use multimedia to show homes to prospective buyers. A database guides the buyer to a range of homes for sale and then displays digitized photographs of each. Multimedia also can be used for the stand-alone sales booth, or *kiosk*. In an airport, a kiosk might provide information about tourist attractions, hotels, and restaurants. Voice instructions and maps show you how to get there.

Multimedia is ideal for gaining access to reams of information. On a single CD-ROM disc, you can have access to about 300,000 pages of text, all U.S. addresses and their nine-digit zip codes, a year's worth of magazine articles, and more. For example, I subscribe to *Computer Select*, a Ziff-Davis service. *Computer Select* provides either abstracts or the full text of 170 computer magazines for the past year. I own four years of computer history on four discs. The price: $995 per year.

Finally, multimedia provides plenty of entertainment, rivaling the plug-in cartridges of Super Nintendo. A CD-ROM disc provides digitized sounds, enthralling musical scores, plenty of animation, and more. For more information about CD-ROM games, see Chapter 10.

Author, Author!

Multimedia applications can play sound from digitized files and display bit-mapped computer graphics, animation

sequences, and video captured from external sources, such as laser disc players and video cameras.

These many facets of multimedia are brought together through *multimedia authoring tools.* These software programs are designed to manage multimedia elements and allow the user to interact with the final product. Such software enables you to create and edit text and images from videodisc players, videotape players, and other hardware tools.

Listen Up!

You'll need to settle on a specific authoring tool before you begin. Just as WordPerfect and Microsoft Word once could not read each other's file formats, multimedia applications generally don't work together.

On the Cheap

If you are new to multimedia, don't expect to go on the cheap. As you can see from the preceding specifications, even bare bones multimedia requires a significant investment.

To create multimedia, you need to invest a bit more. To play or record video on your MPC, you'll need the following:

♪ Video system software, such as Microsoft's Video for Windows

♪ A compression/digitization video card

♪ An NTSC-to-VGA adapter that combines TV signals with computer video signals for output to a VCR

Sound Check

NTSC stands for National Television Standards Commit-tee. The initials are used to describe the method of television transmission in North America. This standard is used also in Central America, a number of South Ameri-can countries, and some Asian countries, including Japan. PAL is the name of the format for color TV signals used in western Germany, England, Holland, Australia and several other countries. The two systems are not compatible. For example, you cannot view an Australian videotape on a U.S. TV.

Microsoft's Video for Windows includes tools for capturing, editing, and playing back video. It retails for $199, which includes hundreds of sample video clips on a CD-ROM disc.

You may require a video capture, or NTSC-to-VGA, card to capture a graphic image and save it as a file. More sophisticated cards enable you to capture several frames, simulating movement. The source for the image can be a VCR or a video camera. The 8-bit, 256-color Bravado from Truevision, Inc. costs $1,295. It allows you to play video in a window on Microsoft Windows. To edit the image, you'll need even more hardware and software. The Video Toaster from NewTek provides affordable video editing. At $4,995 (compared to $250,000 for other systems), the Video Toaster creates special effects, such as digital wipes.

Sound Check

A *wipe* is a transition between two video sources. Instead of fading out one image to the other, a wipe may have one image, such as a weight lifter doing squats. When the weight lifter lowers the weight, a new image appears in place of the area he covered up.

Capturing a video image requires large amounts of disk space. A single, full-screen color image requires almost 2M of disk space. A one-second moving video requires 45M. To conserve space, you can buy a video compression card. Intel's ActionMedia 750 Delivery expansion card costs $1,895. This card uses the company's Digital Video Interactive (DVI) compression algorithm. The companion $695 ActionMedia 750 Capture card lets you capture video from a VCR.

Show on the Road

For simpler presentations, you don't need to spend thousands of dollars. In fact, software included with your sound card may be sufficient.

Eclipse Technologies' Madison Avenue ($169.95) is a low-cost, easy-to-use multimedia software package for DOS. It supports a number of sound and graphics cards, and the installation includes instructions for setting card switches.

Madison Avenue contains three modules: a screen capture facility called Camera, a slide-show organizer called Carousel, and a sound processor called Recorder that allows you to add music or narration. Camera runs as a 256K *terminate-and-stay-resident* (TSR) program that can be loaded into high memory in MS-DOS 5 or greater. Camera captures CGA, EGA, or VGA screens. To capture a screen, just load the application you want a picture from and press both Shift keys simultaneously. If you have a sound card, you'll hear a Nikon shutter sound effect.

After you've completed your screen capture session, you can edit the flow of images in Carousel, the slide-show organizer. Carousel uses an intuitive *graphical user interface* (GUI) that shows not only the slide being processed but also any visual

effects, voice files, or sound effects associated with it. Madison Avenue provides 14 visual transition effects, including color dissolves, fades, and wipes. Unfortunately, each slide must have effects attached to it individually.

The Recorder module lets you add your own narration blended with digitized audio. Madison Avenue comes loaded with 20 public-domain music clip files, and you can get sounds from other sources through your sound card.

Madison Avenue includes a free runtime version, which enables you to inexpensively distribute your presentations on floppy disks. A 1.44M floppy can accommodate the program and about 60 slides—fewer when sound files are attached.

Other choices for presentation software include Curtain Call from Zuma Group ($199.95), Action from MacroMedia ($495), and Animation Works Interactive from Gold Disk, Inc. ($495).

Free Multimedia Utilities

Some sound cards include both crude and sophisticated multimedia utilities. You may not even have to buy multimedia presentation software.

Simple SBSIM

Sound Blaster 16 ASP includes a crude utility called *Sound Blaster Standard Interface Module* (SBSIM). SBSIM is a large (111K) memory-resident program that lets you add sound and music to your multimedia presentation by using a set of commands.

Various voice and music files then are placed in memory where they can be called upon by a handle or name. Sound Blaster 16 ASP includes three utilities that work with SBSIM:

Chapter 14

♪ **Voice.** Plays Sound Blaster VOC files

♪ **Music.** Plays MID and CMF files

♪ **SoundFX.** Adds fading, panning, and repeating sound effects

Sound Check

What is fading? *Fading* is the process of increasing or decreasing volume until a certain level is reached. *Panning* is the process of moving sound from one channel or speaker to the other.

MMPlay

Sound Blaster 16 ASP also includes MMplay, a DOS-based multimedia program. MMPlay enables you to combine and orchestrate images, animation, voice, music, video images, and sound effects.

Listen Up!

MMPlay requires a super-VGA card compatible with the standards set up by the *Video Electronics Standards Association* (VESA).

This utility is similar to a programming language. The following is an excerpt from MMPlay:

```
.play TheCloud
.delay 350
.Aplay1 Creative
.delay 200
.Aplay1 sndblst
.delay 250
```

These three steps play a musical song called "The Cloud" followed by displaying two animation files. A delay is inserted between each step.

HSC InterActive SE

The most sophisticated utility included with Sound Blaster 16 ASP is HSC InterActive SE (special edition). HSC InterActive SE is a Microsoft Windows authoring system for creating interactive multimedia. The full-scale HSC InterActive retails for $495.

To create a multimedia application, you should have a plan. Before using InterActive SE, plan how you want your multimedia presentation to look.

InterActive SE relies on icons as its multimedia building blocks (see fig. 14.1). Each icon represents a function to be performed.

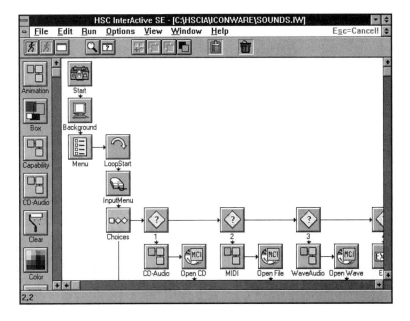

Figure 14.1:
HSC InterActive SE relies on linked icons.

You select icons from the vertical toolbar on the left to add to your structure. You drag the icon to where you want it to be located. You can later click on an icon to edit it (see fig. 14.2).

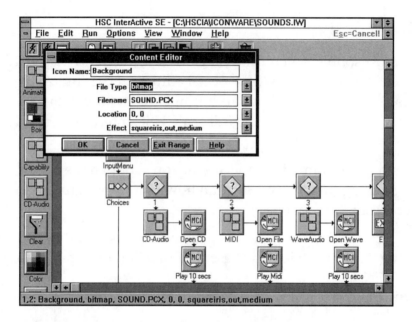

Figure 14.2:

Double-click on an icon to edit it.

You can run your existing structure at any time. You can copy working portions of the presentation for use in other places. To see the big picture, click on the zoom icon to pick any of four views (see fig. 14.3).

When you are finished creating a presentation, save your work to a file ending in an IW extension.

InterActive SE includes two multimedia sidekicks: RezSolution and IconAnimate. RezSolution is a conversion program that

turns graphics into the correct size and number of colors for use by HSC InterActive SE. It is not a drawing program; you cannot draw or merge graphic images. You can, however, capture and view images (see fig. 14.4). RezSolution works with BMP, PCX, and RLE graphics files.

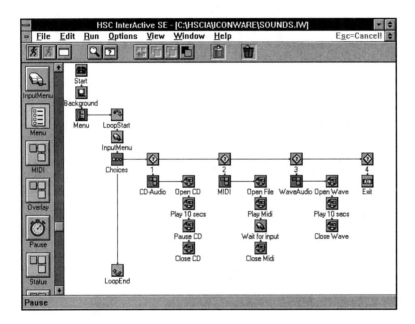

Figure 14.3:
You can select a reduced view to see the bigger picture and flow.

Icon Animate enables you to create animation files from a series of graphic screen displays. You can start it either from HSC or by double-clicking on its icon in the HSC Interactive SE group. In IconAnimate, add items in sequential order (see fig. 14.5).

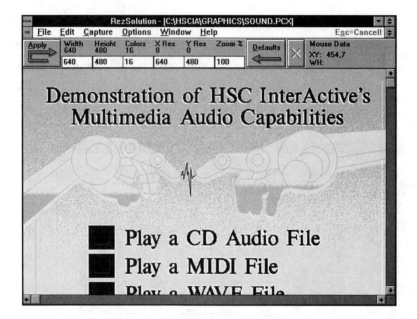

Figure 14.4:
RezSolution allows you to view and convert graphical images.

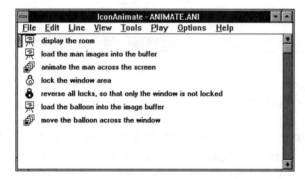

Figure 14.5:
With IconAnimate, you can create an animation one line at a time.

To edit a part of your animation, double-click on the icon representing it (see fig. 14.6).

Animate - Animates buffer graphics	
Comment: move the balloon across th	Move Increments: 5
Width,Height: FullW,FullH	Time Between (ms): 0
	Total Time (sec):
Buffer Locations	Mask Location:
0,0	Display Locations
	36,174
	575,-173

Figure 14.6:
You can edit or enhance each animation icon.

When you run an IconAnimate script, you can see it in action. Select **P**lay,**R**un Script. In figure 14.7, the ANIMATE.ANI animation file included with IconAnimate is running.

Figure 14.7:
Playing the demo script included with IconAnimate.

Chapter 14

Sound Impression

The Pro AudioStudio 16 card does not include animation software; rather, the company provides Sound Impression. Sound Impression allows you to load sounds from several audio sources. You can then play, record, edit, modify, mix, compose, and combine these sounds.

You start Sound Impression by double-clicking on the Sound Impression icon in the Sound Impression group. After the program loads, you can load WAV, MIDI, or RMI files. You can also queue CD tracks. Sound Impression uses the visual analogy of a rack stereo system (see fig. 14.8).

Figure 14.8:
Sound Impression looks like a rack stereo system.

You load each type of sound file into each part of the stereo system. Figure 14.9 shows the TADA.WAV wave file and the CANYON.MID MIDI file loaded.

Figure 14.9:
You load a different audio file in each part of the rack.

You can play each file. You can also record WAV files by clicking on the red record button, and you can edit a WAV file by clicking on the button to the left of Record. The editing tools are quite powerful, as shown in figure 14.10.

Figure 14.10:
You can edit a WAV file by using several controls.

Waveform Editor allows you to cut or copy entire WAV files or their portions. You can quickly clean up a file by removing silence or filtering out extraneous noises. You also can add special effects, such as echo, fade, pan, or crossfade. (A *crossfade* allows you to slowly switch the left and right channels so that the right stereo signal plays on the left speaker and vice versa.)

If you click on the button to the right of the information window, you can start Wave Composer (see fig. 14.11). Wave Composer allows you to mix as many as four WAV files into a single composition.

Figure 14.11:
You can combine WAV files with Wave Composer.

You'll Know It When You Hear It

Whatever utilities you use for multimedia, you'll know multimedia when you hear it. With a sound card and any of the utilities discussed in this chapter, you can enrich your life and perhaps the lives of those with whom you share your work.

Sound Investments

15

The Multimedia PC specifications may tell you what you *need* for multimedia and digitized sound, but this chapter lists the items you may *want* for audio variety and just simple entertainment.

In this chapter, you learn about:

- ♪ Audible screen savers
- ♪ Editing software
- ♪ Audio clip art
- ♪ Sound file organizers

Basic Needs

Your life can be enriched by surrounding yourself with different sounds. The four WAV files included with Microsoft Windows quickly become monotonous and limiting. You can extend your aural horizons by acquiring sound files and editing tools.

Your Screen Talks Back

If you want to add sound to your screen saver, look to the latest screen savers. Screen savers prevent the constant image displayed on your screen from permanently embedding itself in your monitor. When away for an extended period, the screen saver either blanks your screen or displays a constantly moving image.

After Dark for Windows

After Dark from Berkeley Systems started the screen saver craze. Whereas After Dark 1.0 is best known for its flying toasters, After Dark 2.0 ($49.95) lets you run multiple savers on the same screen. You could create, for instance, a rotating Earth hovering over an eerie moonscape. After Dark 2.0 delivers digital sound without requiring additional hardware. However, After Dark sounds better with a sound card.

After Dark includes the Randomizer and Slide Show. The Randomizer lets you select an unlimited number of After Dark modules to appear in the sequence of your choice. With the Slide Show module, you can create presentations that display a sequence of picture files.

Star Trek: The Screen Saver

True Trekkies will want to buy Star Trek: The Screen Saver. A $59.95 program from Berkeley Systems Inc., Star Trek: The Screen Saver adds 15 new modules to the original After Dark interface. Each screen saver pays tribute to a popular Star Trek feature, such as *The Final Frontier* opening sequence, Scotty's Files, Spock, Tholian Web, and everyone's favorite furballs, the Tribbles.

For Trekkie trivia fans, there's a final exam with hundreds of multiple-choice questions. By pressing the Num Lock key, you can disable keyboard reset and enter answers without actually disrupting the screen saver.

Besides great graphics, some of the modules have audio clips from the original "Star Trek" television series. Along with the voices of Captain Kirk, Mr. Spock, "Bones," and Scotty, you can hear the trilling of the Tribbles and the sucking of the Brain Cells. You can hear the sounds through a PC speaker, but a sound card provides much better results.

Energizer Bunny

For $24.95, it keeps going and going and going. The Energizer Bunny Screen Saver from PC Dynamics has several modes. When you run the program in guest-appearance mode, the Energizer Bunny randomly appears on your screen—right on top of your Microsoft Windows spreadsheet, word processor, Solitaire game, or other application. When your computer is idle for five minutes, the bunny makes a guest appearance. When you begin work, the bunny vanishes.

The Energizer Bunny strolls across the screen with half a dozen drum-beating variations, which include a masked bunny, a parachuting bunny, and an underwater bunny. Each has appropriate sound effects and recorded lines from the advertisement ("It keeps going and going…"). These same scenes also appear in a true screen-saver mode and in wallpaper mode.

Johnny Castaway

Screen Antics: The Adventures of Johnny Castaway is an entertaining Windows screen saver from Dynamix/Sierra On-Line. Billed as "the world's first story-telling screen-saver cartoon," the $34.95 Johnny Castaway weaves a month-long tale of desert island desertion. Each time you take a break, you'll spend it with the Robinson Crusoe of the desktop—performing rain dances, keeping in shape by jogging the perimeter of his 8-foot island home, high-diving from the coconut tree (the island's sole piece of vegetation), fishing for dinner, or frolicking with the local octopi and squid. There are also special events for holidays. On Halloween, Johnny carves up a pumpkin, and on December 25, he puts up a Christmas tree. It takes about 120 days—that's 120 days once you start Windows—to complete the tale. Johnny slowly builds a raft, he corresponds with a woman in New York by means of a glass bottle, and he eventually tries to escape. Does he succeed? You'll have to bring up Windows every day to advance the story.

Johnny Castaway includes simple sound effects. Johnny's vocabulary is limited to guttural grunts, moans, and squeals. You'll hear Johnny banging a coconut against the tree, accompanied by exclamations of physical exertion.

Matinee

Matinee from Access Softek is the first screen saver that uses full-motion video clips and lets you combine them in any order to create your own minimovies. The $49.95 program squeezes 38 2- to 5-second clips—roughly 2 minutes of video—into a 3.6M program, using a proprietary compression scheme. How you combine those shots is up to you. You can, for example, make a breakfast screen saver by combining a clip of eggs hitting a sizzling pan and two slices of perfectly browned bread shooting out of a toaster. You can follow up with a pair of smacking red lips.

The frame rate is adjustable from 5 to 30 frames per second. The higher the rate, the smoother the appearance of the clip; consider 30 frames per second full-motion video. Matinee's film clips come from public-domain movies and cartoons; only a few of them feature familiar scenes, such as Neil Armstrong walking on the moon. Additional film-clip packages are available for $19.95 each.

SoundWAV Pro 1 and 2

Although not a screen saver, SoundWAV Pro 1 and 2 from Window Ware allow you to have additional sound effects when you are performing certain Windows actions, such as minimizing a group. These sound effects can be made random so that the next time you start Windows, different sound effects are chosen. For $29.95, SoundWAV Pro not only changes the sound effects, but also changes your Windows background wallpaper.

SoundWAV Pro 1 contains 78 cartoon, movie, and television bits, including clips of Bugs Bunny, the Jetsons, Yosemite Sam, Popeye, Bullwinkle, the Simpsons, Dirty Harry, and Crocodile Dundee, and the movies *Star Wars* and *The Wizard of Oz*. A small manual suggests where the clips might be appropriate.

SoundWAV Pro 2 features 54 sound clips for the politically savvy. Among them are clips of Spiro Agnew, Richard Nixon, Harry Truman, George Bush, and Winston Churchill. The package also features sound effects, such as thunder and lightning, a flushing toilet, breaking glass, screeching tires, and a lawn mower. The collection includes a few TV and movie clips, such as Alfred Hitchcock's famous greeting, "Good evening. . . ."

Wired for Sound Pro

Wired for Sound Pro from Aristosoft, Inc. lets you change almost everything about the way Windows sounds and looks, from icons to cursors. Hundreds of colorful little pictures can be substituted for applications' standard icons. If you are unhappy with the standard Windows pointer, you can change that cursor; you can also adjust the wait, I-beam, crosshair, and other cursors. Among the 100 choices are fingers, stars, and happy faces.

The $79 program has hundreds of sound and voice clips that can be attached to Windows events. When you close an application, for example, you can hear a round of applause or a cow

mooing. My own favorite is the frail voice saying, "I've fallen, and I can't get up," when a Windows error occurs.

Wired For Sound Pro includes utilities, such as a talking clock, talking calculator, talking calendar, talking Solitaire, and an odd little feature called JobSaver. This soundtrack features keyboard clicks, throat clearing, and an occasional cough; the idea is that you can take a nap in your office, and no one will notice.

Text to Speech Programs

If your sound card didn't include a text-to-speech conversion program, consider Monologue for Windows from First Byte. This $149 program can read text that has been copied into the Windows Clipboard, as well as the contents of spreadsheet cells or text from other Windows applications. Monologue for Windows is included with both Pro AudioStudio 16 and Sound Blaster 16 ASP sound cards.

Monologue for Windows uses a rule-based paradigm to sound out words instead of relying entirely on a database of instructions for specific words. Therefore, some words will be mispronounced when the software is first installed. You can add to an exceptions dictionary to improve pronunciation or to create your own dictionary using the phonetic code displayed in Monologue for Windows' manual.

Monologue is also available for use with DOS. It acts as a 140K to 220K memory-resident program. It will attempt to read information from any text-based application or will read an ASCII file you provide it. Monologue for DOS also sells for $149. For more information on Monologue for Windows, see Chapter 12.

Waveform Editing

Waveform editors let you modify sound files. You can stick with the Sound Recorder bundled with Windows, or you can select a more-sophisticated product as described in the following sections.

Digital Soup

For $99, you can get Digital Soup Sound Professional from the company of the same name. If you own a sound card and a CD-ROM drive, you can go beyond canned sound clips to create audio backgrounds for your presentations. Digital Soup allows you to cut and paste sound segments from one or more recording sessions. You also can weave multiple recordings in a single mix. It also supports OLE (object linking and embedding) as a server, letting you insert a Digital Soup recording as an object in a document created by an OLE client, such as Excel or Ami Pro.

The Digital Soup track editor shows graphical representations of one or two recording tracks at a time, from the total of 16 input tracks and 2 output tracks available. You can edit tracks individually and then mix the input tracks to create output. You can work in mono or stereo at sampling rates up to 44 KHz (CD quality).

Wave for Windows

Wave for Windows from Turtle Beach Systems lets you record and edit professional music. The $149 digital audio editor provides many means of altering data and excellent control, though this capability can make large tasks difficult and slow. Wave's time compress/expand feature can decrease or increase a sound clip's playing time while keeping pitch, dynamics, and other characteristics the same. The package uses an interface that simplifies transforming WAV files. Wave for Windows also sports good dialog boxes. The software's more advanced features may take some time to learn and to perform, but the result is worth the effort.

AudioView

AudioView from Voyetra technologies records, edits, and plays VOC (Sound Blaster) and WAV files. It supports echo and other effects, conversion to other resolutions and sampling rates, and data compression. The Windows-based program sells for $79.95.

Sound on File

You can order various collections of audio files to enhance your presentations or Windows sounds. These audio files might include WAV files, CD audio tracks, or MIDI songs. Some of the files come in Sound Blaster VOC format, which may be played by or converted to WAV format by other sound cards. The entire group may be called "clip notes," the audio equivalent of clip art. All of these collections do not require you to pay royalties for their use.

MusicBytes

MusicBytes from Prosonus is a 634M collection of musical clips, MIDI song files, sound effects, and sampled instruments shipped on CD-ROM. The collection includes 108 sound effects and 28 songs. Songs are recorded in both audio CD and WAV formats. MIDI-compatible files are transcribed from the original recordings. MusicBytes lists for $100.

Mr. Sound FX

Mr. Sound FX includes over 150 sound effects from Michael Winslow, the sound-effects genius of *Police Academy*-movie fame. These sound effects include planes, trains, explosions, sirens, and automobiles. Mr. Sound FX retails for $29.95.

MusicClips and MusicClips Digital Audio

MusicClips from Voyetra Technologies are MIDI song files that ship on floppies. The series includes the Collectors Edition Volumes 1, 2, and 3; Classics Edition Volumes 1 and 2; or Signature Edition Volumes 1 and 2. MusicClips Digital is a CD-ROM set of sound effects and music in audio CD, WAV, and VOC formats. You can buy each for $70 or all three for $150.

Audio Tracks

HSC Software offers Audio Tracks for $49.95. Audio Tracks provides digitally mastered special effects and music. Audio

Tracks supports the Sound Blaster, Media Vision, and ATI sound cards. These files are in the VOC (Sound Blaster) format, which can be played on these sound cards.

Killer Tracks Multimedia Library

The Killer Tracks Multimedia Library offers three separate audio CDs: Sales Collection, Training Collection, and Education Collection. Each disc contains more than 60 minutes of music in a wide range of categories. You can buy each for $300, or for $800, you can buy the entire set.

Mediasource Library

The Mediasource Library from Applied Optical Media Corp. is extensive: 14 volumes containing historical topics, business graphics, medicine, and others. Each title includes at least 1,500 images and more than 90 minutes of music and sound effects. Shipped on a CD-ROM disc, the library costs $395.

Microsoft Soundbits

Microsoft itself offers Soundbits, a collection of three different sound-clip packages: Musical Sounds, Hanna-Barbera Cartoons, and Hollywood Movies. The first features 50 brief musical creations played on banjo, guitar, oboe, sax, steel drum, and violin. With the Hanna-Barbera Cartoons collection, you can choose from 50 sound clips of some of Toondom's greatest characters, such as Yogi Bear and Scooby-Doo.

The Hollywood Movies collection includes such classic lines as "I'll get you, my pretty! And your little dog, too!" Each Microsoft Soundbits costs $39.95.

For Space Cadets

Sound Source Unlimited provides three sci-fi choices: both the original and Next Generation versions of Star Trek and *2001: A Space Odyssey*. The packages contain between 70 and 77 clips from each and range in price from $59.95 to $69.95.

2001 features 77 clips from the classic movie, such as "I'm sorry Dave; I'm afraid I can't do that." There are also a number of sound effects, such as lasers and alarms.

Star Trek: The Original Television Series contains 70 clips, including authorized digital sound effects, phasers, photons, musical cues, and the voices of Spock, Captain Kirk, and "Bones" McCoy. Fans of "Star Trek: The Next Generation" will be interested in the third package, which contains 74 clips of dialogue, sound effects, and music from the pilot episode of the show.

Get Organized

Once you have collected several sound files, how do you organize them? One solution is the MediaOrganizer

A multimedia database that manages different types of Windows objects, MediaOrganizer is perfect for keeping track of audio. With additional hardware, MediaOrganizer will catalog audio from compact disc players, CD-ROM drives, digital audio tapes, videotapes, or a hard disk. MediaOrganizer sells for $795 from Lenel Systems International.

By acquiring and using various sound files, you can liven up your Windows desktop and digital editing. You can, for example, compose motivational music and record it to a cassette tape. Your only limits are your imagination.

Table 15.1
Sound Utilities

Product	Price	Comments
Audible Screen Savers		
After Dark for Windows	$49.95	The screen saver that started it all.
Star Trek: The Screen Saver	$59.95	For Trekkies only.
Energizer Bunny	$24.95	It keeps going and going…
Screen Antics: Johnny Castaway	$34.95	An ongoing saga.
Matinee	$49.95	Make your own moving screen saver.
SoundWAV Pro	$29.95	Add audio variety to Windows events.
Wired for Sound Pro	$79.00	Adds sound and changes icon and cursor sizes.
Text to Speech		
Monologue for Windows	$149.00	Included with Sound Blaster 16 ASP and Pro AudioStudio 16.
Monologue for DOS	$149.00	Available with some low-end sound cards.
Waveform Editing		
Digital Soup Sound Professional	$99.00	OLE-ready.
Wave for Windows	$149.00	Many controls for audio junkies.
AudioView	$79.95	Works with VOC (Sound Blaster) and WAV (Windows waveform) files.

continues

Table 15.1
Continued

Product	Price	Comments
Sound and Music Libraries		
MusicBytes	$100.00	634M of MIDI and WAV files.
Mr. Sound FX	$29.95	From the sound effects hero in *Police Academy*.
MusicClips	$70.00	Plenty of MIDI songs.
Audio Tracks	$49.95	VOC (Sound Blaster) format songs.
Killer Tracks Multimedia Library	$300.00	60 minutes of music on a CD.
Mediasource Library	$395.00	1,500 images and more than 90 minutes of music and sound effects.
Microsoft Soundbits	$39.95	WAV files from Microsoft.
Star Trek: The Original Television Series	$59.95	WAV files for fans of the original.
Star Trek: The Next Generation	$69.95	74 files of dialogue, sound effects and music.
2001: A Space Odyssey	$69.95	77 clips, including "I'm sorry Dave; I'm afraid I can't do that."
File Organizers		
MediaOrganizer	$795.00	Expensive, but organizes WAV files, CD-ROMs, DAT tapes, videotapes, and more.

Part six

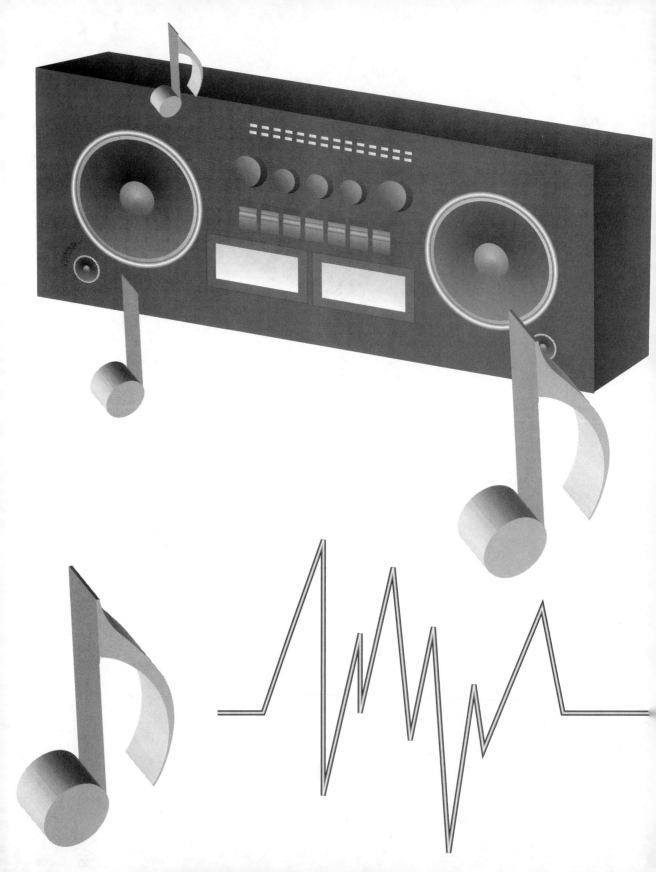

A The Crank It Up! Disk

The enclosed bonus disk includes the following software programs and sound files that can improve your sound system:

- ♪ **Wave After Wave.** From Ben Saladino, this Windows shareware utility triples as a WAV file, MIDI file, and audio CD player. You can have sound files in a directory play one after the other. You can change directories and even delete sound files you dislike after sampling them. Wave After Wave also allows you to create play lists of WAV, MIDI, and audio CD files. With a play list, you play only those sound files you want to hear in the order you want.

- ♪ **Assorted WAV and MIDI files.** Vitesse, Inc. has donated 13 Windows waveform (WAV) files from its two collections. You can then introduce some variety in your Windows environment by replacing the basic four

Windows WAV files with these. For example, you can hear an alien space gun as you start Windows or a scream as you exit. I've also included a few of my favorite MIDI files.

♪ **MIDIKeys.** From Playroom Software, this Windows utility provides a screen representation of a piano keyboard. This keyboard can play individual notes or entire chords. MIDIKeys demonstrates the 128 General MIDI instruments from which a MIDI musician can choose. You can, for example, have the keyboard sound like a trombone or harpsichord. MIDIKeys also allows you to "bend" the note as it is played, sliding the pitch up or down, depending on which side of the key you move your mouse.

Listen Up!

MIDIKeys is very useful for setting up the MIDI Mapper. It lets you audition the sounds on a sound card or MIDI sound module, and it can be fun to just bang out little melodies.

♪ **ListenUp.** From Fred Palmer Software, this DOS program allows you to improve your ability to recognize musical notes. ListenUp combines sound and colors in a graphical user interface to help you improve your sense of pitch. By pairing a color with each note, notes can be recognized quickly and easily. After some practice with ListenUp, you can learn to recognize any note, even when the color pairing is turned off. ListenUp generates notes randomly, so you won't be able to master the drills by rote learning. ListenUp has a choice to use an Ad Lib-compatible sound card.

♪ **TrashMan for Windows.** From CheckBox software, this Windows shareware utility allows you to safely delete files from the File Manager. Once TrashMan is started, you simply drag and drop individual files or entire directories to the trash can in the bottom-right corner of the Windows screen. The files are hidden and stored away until you are sure you wish to remove them. You can change your trash can icon to a different metaphor, such as a toilet. Once you place a file in the toilet, the toilet seat pops open. You can associate WAV sound files to TrashMan events, such as when you place a file in the trash can or empty the trash.

♪ **PC Speaker Driver.** Microsoft provides SPEAKER.DRV to allow non-sound card owners to play with digital sound, such as playing WAV files. The instructions for using this driver are described at the end of Chapter 3. Basically, you will use the Control Panel to install the driver. The complete procedure is provided in Chapter 3.

Bonus Disk Installation

Installing the *Crank It Up!* Disk is easy.

1. Insert the disk in your floppy drive.

2. From the DOS prompt, type:

> **A:** (and press Enter)

in which **A:** is the letter of the floppy drive from which you are installing.

3. Type:

INSTALL (and press Enter)

4. Press the numbers of the software files you wish to install:

```
1 - Install Wave After Wave
        (Windows WAV and MIDI file player)
2 - Install WAV and MIDI sound files
        (16 extra sounds)
3 - Install MIDIKeys
        (Windows piano keyboard)
4 - Install DOS ListenUp
        (DOS ear training exercise)
5 - Install TrashMan for Windows
        (Windows safe file-killing utility)
```

The installation software assumes you have a hard disk (drive C). It will create a directory on your hard disk and copy the files to it. The programs are installed into the following directories:

♪ TrashMan   C:\TRASHMAN

♪ MIDIKeys   C:\MIDIKEYS

♪ Wave After Wave   C:\WAVAWAV

♪ ListenUp   C:\LISTENUP

The WAV and MIDI sound files will be copied to your Windows directory where the default Windows WAV files are kept. Your Windows directory is assumed to be C:\WINDOWS. If not, install these files manually from the A:\WAV directory.

5. Install other choices.

When the installation program is finished, the main menu again appears so you can install other choices.

We hope you enjoy these programs and files. If you intend to use them regularly, please register your product with the shareware author so that product can be improved. Complete documentation and registration information for the programs are found in their respective directories.

Noisy Vendors

Hardware, CD-ROM Drives

The following list of *Crank It Up!* vendors and their products has been checked and double-checked for accuracy. However, because of the nature of sound-card technology, some of the following information may have changed after publication. Prices included here are suggested retail prices.

Intersect MultiSpin 74 ($615)

NEC Technologies, Inc.
1414 Massachusetts Ave.
Boxborough MA 01419-2298
800-632-4636/508-264-8000
FAX: 508-264-8488

Appendix B

T348 MiniSCSI Plus adaptor ($229)

Trantor Systems
5415 Randall Place
Fremont CA 94538-3151
800-872-6867/510-770-1400
FAX: 510-770-9910

Hardware, External Sound Devices

AudioMan ($179)

Logitech, Inc.
6505 Kaiser Dr.
Fremont CA 94555
800-231-7717/510-795-8500
FAX: 510-792-8901

Port Blaster ($199)

Creative Labs, Inc.
1901 McCarthy Blvd.
Milpitas CA 95035
800-998-5227/408-428-6600
FAX: 408-428-6611

Port-Able Sound Plus ($198.95)

Digispeech, Inc.
2464 Embarcadero Way
Palo Alto CA 94303
415-494-8086
FAX: 415-494-8114

Sound Source ($49.95)

Walt Disney Computer Software, Inc.
500 S. Buena Vista St., Burbank Centre, 20th Fl.
Burbank CA 91521-6385
818-973-4015
FAX: 818-846-0454

SoundXchange Model A ($149)
SoundXchange Model B ($289)

Interactive, Inc.
204 North Main
Humboldt SD 57035
FAX: 605-363-5117

Speech Thing ($99.95)

Covox, Inc.
675 Conger St.
Eugene OR 97402
503-342-1271
FAX: 503-342-1283

Hardware, Games

FlightStick ($69.95)
GameCard III Automatic ($49.95)

CH Products
970 Park Center Drive
Vista CA 92083
800-624-5804/619-598-2518
FAX: 619-598-2524

ThrustMaster ($99.95)

ThrustMaster Inc.
10150 SW Nimbus Ave, Ste. E-7
Tigard OR 97223
503-639-3200
FAX: 503-620-8094

Hardware, Midi Equipment

MIDI Kit ($79.95)

Creative Labs, Inc.
1901 McCarthy Blvd.
Milpitas CA 95035
800-998-5227/408-428-6600
FAX: 408-428-6611

MIDI Mate ($69.95)

Media Vision, Inc.
3185 Laurelview Court
Fremont CA 94538
800-845-5870/510-770-8600
FAX: 510-770-9592

Miracle Piano Teaching System ($479.95)

The Software Toolworks
60 Leveroni Court
Novato CA 94949
800-234-3088/415-883-3000
FAX: 415-883-3303

Roland PC-200 MK2 MIDI keyboard ($395)
SCC-1 ($499)

Roland Corp. U.S.
7200 Dominion Circle
Los Angeles CA 90040-3647
213-685-5141
FAX: 213-722-0911

Wave Blaster ($249.95)

Creative Labs, Inc.
1901 McCarthy Blvd.
Milpitas CA 95035
800-998-5227/408-428-6600
408-428-6611

Hardware, Multimedia Upgrade Kits

CDPC XL ($1495)

Media Vision, Inc.
3185 Laurelview Court
Fremont CA 94538
800-845-5870/510-770-8600
FAX: 510-770-9592

Discovery CD Upgrade Kit (16-bit) ($699)
Edutainment CD Upgrade Kit (16-bit) ($799)

Creative Labs, Inc.
1901 McCarthy Blvd.
Milpitas CA 95035
800-998-5227/408-428-6600
FAX: 408-428-6611

Fusion CD 16 ($749)
Pro 16 Multimedia System ($1195)

Media Vision, Inc.
3185 Laurelview Court
Fremont CA 94538
800-845-5870/510-770-8600
FAX: 510-770-9592

Hardware, Multipurpose Sound Cards

Fahrenheit VA ($299)

Orchid Technology, Inc.
45365 Northport Loop West
Fremont CA 94538
800-767-2443/510-683-0300
FAX: 510-490-9312

SOUNDVision ($399)

Cardinal Technologies, Inc.
1827 Freedom Rd.
Lancaster PA 17601
717-293-3000
FAX: 717-293-3055

Thunder & Lightning ($349)

Media Vision, Inc.
3185 Laurelview Court
Fremont CA 94538
800-845-5870/510-770-8600
FAX: 510-770-9592

TyIN 2000 ($279)

> National Semiconductor Corp. (Quadram Products Group)
> PO Box 58090, MS16195
> Santa Clara CA 95052-8090
> 800-538-8510/408-721-5000
> FAX: 408-721-7662

VGAStereo F/X ($129)

> ATI Technologies, Inc.
> 3761 Victoria Park Ave.
> Scarborough ON, CD M1W 3S2
> 416-756-0718
> FAX: 416-756-0720

Hardware, Sound Cards

Gravis UltraSound ($199.95)
Gravis UltraSound 3D ($249.95)

> Advanced Gravis Computer Technology, Ltd.
> 7400 MacPherson Ave., Ste. 111
> Burnaby BC, CD V5J 5B6
> 800-663-8558/604-431-5020
> FAX: 604-431-5155

MultiSound ($599)

> Turtle Beach Systems
> 1600 Pennsylvania Ave., Cyber Center, Unit 33
> York PA 17404
> 717-843-6916
> FAX: 717-854-8319

Pro AudioSpectrum 16 ($299)
Pro AudioStudio 16 ($349)

Media Vision, Inc.
3185 Laurelview Court
Fremont CA 94538
800-845-5870/510-770-8600
FAX: 510-770-9592

Sound Blaster 16 ASP ($349.95)
Sound Blaster Deluxe ($129.95)
Sound Blaster Pro Deluxe ($199.95)

Creative Labs, Inc.
1901 McCarthy Blvd.
Milpitas CA 95035
800-998-5227/408-428-6600
FAX: 408-428-6611

Sound Producer Pro ($199)

Orchid Technology, Inc.
45365 Northport Loop West
Fremont CA 94538
800-767-2443/510-683-0300
FAX: 510-490-9312

SoundMan 16 ($289)

Logitech, Inc.
6505 Kaiser Dr.
Fremont CA 94555
800-231-7717/510-795-8500
FAX: 510-792-8901

SOUNDstudio ($259)

Cardinal Technologies, Inc.
1827 Freedom Rd.
Lancaster PA 17601
717-293-3000
FAX: 717-293-3055

Stereo F/X ($129)

ATI Technologies, Inc.
3761 Victoria Park Ave.
Scarborough ON, CD M1W 3S2
416-756-0718
FAX: 416-756-0720

ThunderBOARD ($129.95)
ThunderBOARD for Windows ($169)

Media Vision, Inc.
3185 Laurelview Court
Fremont CA 94538
800-845-5870/510-770-8600
FAX: 510-770-9592

ViVa Maestro 16 ($349)
ViVa Maestro 16VR ($429)
ViVa Maestro Pro ($229)

Computer Peripherals, Inc.
667 Rancho Conejo Blvd.
Newbury Park CA 91320
800-854-7600/805-499-5751
FAX: 805-499-5742

Appendix B

Windows Sound System ($289)

Microsoft Corp.
One Microsoft Way
Redmond WA 98052
800-426-9400/206-882-8080

Hardware, Speakers and Headphones

Altec Lansing ACS300 ($400)

Altec Lansing Consumer Products
Rt. 6 & 209, P.O. Box 277
Milford PA 18337-0277
800-548-0620/717-296-4434
FAX: 717-296-2213

Bose Roommate Computer Monitor ($339)

Bose Corp.
5 Mountain Road, MS80
Framingham MA 01701
800-444-2673/508-879-7330

HD/1 ($39.99)
HD/2 ($29.99)
HD/4 ($59.99)
HD/6 ($99.99)

Koss Corp.
4129 North Port Washington Avenue
Milwaukee WI 53212
800-USA-KOSS/414-964-5000
FAX: 414-964-8615

Persona PC ($230)
Persona Sub Woofer ($200)

> Persona Technologies
> 274 Wattis Way
> South San Francisco CA 94080-6761
> 415-871-6000

Roland MA-12C Micro Monitor ($145)

> Roland Corp.
> 7200 Dominion Circle
> Los Angeles CA 90040-3647
> 213-685-5141
> FAX: 213-722-0911

Software, Game and Educational

Battle Chess ($79.95)

> Interplay Productions
> 17922 Fitch
> Irvine CA 92714
> 800-969-4263/714-553-6655
> FAX: 714-252-2820

Compton's MultiMedia Encyclopedia for Windows ($695)

> Compton's NewMedia
> 2320 Camino Vida Roble
> Carlsbad CA 92009
> 800-532-3766

F-117A Stealth Fighter ($79.95)

MicroProse Software, Inc.
180 Lakefront Dr.
Hunt Valley MD 21030-2245
800-879-PLAY/410-771-1151
FAX: 410-771-1174

Falcon 3.0 ($39.95)

Spectrum-HoloByte, Inc.
2490 Mariner Square Loop, Ste. 100
Alameda CA 94501
800-695-4263/510-522-3584
FAX: 510-522-3587

Flight Simulator ($59.95)

Microsoft Corp.
One Microsoft Way
Redmond WA 98052
800-426-9400/206-882-8080

LHX Attack Chopper ($24.95)

Electronic Arts
1450 Fashion Island Blvd.
Foster City CA 94404
800-245-4525/415-571-7171
FAX: 415-571-7995

M1 Tank Platoon ($69.95)

MicroProse Software, Inc.
180 Lakefront Dr.
Hunt Valley MD 21030-2245
800-879-PLAY/410-771-1151
FAX: 410-771-1174

Mean Streets ($59.95)

Access Software, Inc.
4910 W. Amelia Earhart Dr.
Salt Lake City UT 84116
800-800-4880/801-359-2900
FAX: 801-359-2968

Microsoft Bookshelf ($195)
Microsoft Golf ($64.95)

Microsoft Corp.
One Microsoft Way
Redmond WA 98052
800-426-9400/206-882-8080

Monkey Island ($59.95)

LucasFilm Games
PO Box 10307
San Rafael CA 94912
800-782-7927/415-721-3300
FAX: 415-721-3344

Multimedia Beethoven: The Ninth Symphony ($79.95)

Microsoft Corp.
One Microsoft Way
Redmond WA 98052
800-426-9400/206-882-8080

Secret Weapons of the Luftwaffe ($99.95)

LucasFilm Games
PO Box 10307
San Rafael CA 94912
800-782-7927/415-721-3300
FAX: 415-721-3344

Sherlock Holmes, The Consulting Detective I and II ($69.95)

ICOM Simulations Inc.
648 S. Wheeling Rd.
Wheeling IL 60090
800-877-4266/708-520-4440
FAX: 708-459-7456

Stellar 7 ($34.95)

Dynamix Inc.
99 West 10th, Ste. 224
Eugene OR 97401
800-326-6654/503-343-0772
FAX: 503-344-1754

Ultima VII: Black Gate ($79.95)
Wing Commander II ($79.95)

Origin Systems, Inc.
12940 Research Blvd.
Austin TX 78750
800-245-4525/512-335-5200

Software, Multimedia

Authorware Professional for Windows ($3000)

Macromedia Inc.
600 Townsend St.
San Francisco CA 94103
800-288-4797/415-252-2000
FAX: 415-626-0554

HSC InterActive Plus ($495)

HSC Software (division of Hayward Systems Corp.)
1661 Lincoln Blvd., Ste. 101
Santa Monica CA 90404
310-392-8441
FAX: 310-392-6015

IconAuthor for Windows ($4995)

AimTech Corp.
20 Trafalgar Square
Nashua NH 03063
800-289-2884/603-883-0220
FAX: 603-883-5582

MacroMind Action! ($495)

Macromedia Inc.
600 Townsend St.
San Francisco CA 94103
800-288-4797/415-252-2000
FAX: 415-626-0554

Make Your Point ($94.95)

Asymetrix Corp.
110 110th Ave. NE Ste. 700
Bellevue WA 98004
800-448-6543/206-462-0501
FAX: 206-455-3071

Appendix B

MediaOrganizer ($795)

Lenel Systems International
19 Tobey Village Office Park
Pittsford NY 14534
716-248-9720

Monologue for Windows/DOS ($149)

First Byte Inc.
19840 Pioneer Avenue
Torrance CA 90503
800-566-6141/310-793-0600

Music Mentor ($149.95)

Midisoft Corp.
PO Box 1000
Bellevue WA 98009
800-776-6434/206-881-7176
FAX: 206-883-1368

Windows 3.1 ($149.95)

Microsoft Corp.
One Microsoft Way
Redmond WA 98052
800-426-9400/206-882-8080

Software, Sound Clips

2001: A Space Odyssey ($69.95)

Sound Source Unlimited Inc.
2985 E. Hillcrest Dr., Suite A
Westlake Village CA 91362
800-877-4778/805-494-9996
FAX: 805-495-0016

Audio Tracks ($49.95)

HSC Software
1661 Lincoln Blvd., Suite 101
Santa Monica CA 90404
310-392-8441
FAX: 310-392-6015

Killer Tracks Multimedia Library ($800)

Killer Tracks
6534 Sunset Blvd.
Hollywood CA 90028
800-877-0078/213-957-4470

Mediasource Library ($395)

Applied Optical Media Corp.
1450 Boot Rd., Bldg. 400
West Chester PA 19380
215-429-3701
FAX: 215-429-3810

Microsoft Soundbits ($39.95)

Microsoft Corp.
One Microsoft Way
Redmond WA 98052
800-426-9400/206-882-8080

Mr. Sound FX ($29.95)
MusicBytes ($100)

Prosonus
11126 Weddington St.
North Hollywood CA 91601
818-766-5221
FAX: 818-766-6098

MusicClips ($70)

Voyetra Technologies Inc.
333 Fifth Ave.
Pelham NY 10803
914-738-4500
FAX: 914-738-4500

Star Trek: The Next Generation ($69.95)
Star Trek: The Original TV Series ($59.95)

Sound Source Unlimited Inc.
2985 E. Hillcrest Dr., Suite A
Westlake Village CA 91362
800-877-4778/805-494-9996
FAX: 805-495-0016

Software, Sound Editing

AudioView ($79.95)

Voyetra Technologies Inc.
333 Fifth Ave.
Pelham NY 10803
914-738-4500
FAX: 914-738-6946

Wave for Windows ($149)

Turtle Beach Systems
1600 Pennsylvania Ave., Cyber Center, Unit 33
York PA 17404
717-843-6916
FAX: 717-854-8319

Software, Screen Savers

After Dark 2.0 ($49.95)

Berkeley Systems Inc.
2095 Rose St.
Berkeley CA 94709
800-344-5541/510-540-5535
FAX: 510-540-5115

Energizer Bunny Screen Saver ($24.95)

PC Dynamics
31332 Via Colinas #102
Westlake Village CA 91362
800-888-1741/818-889-1741
FAX: 818-889-1014

Matinee ($49.95)

Access Softek
2550 9th St. #206
Berkeley CA 94710
510-848-0606
FAX: 510-848-0608

Screen Antics: Johnny Castaway ($34.95)

Dynamix Inc.
99 West 10th, Ste. 224
Eugene OR 97401
800-326-6654/503-343-0772
FAX: 503-344-1754

Soundwav Pro 1 & 2 ($29.95)

Window Ware Inc.
1450 Concordia Ave.
St. Paul MN 55104
800-426-9400/612-544-8581
FAX: 612-644-7410

Star Trek: The Screen Saver ($59.95)

Berkeley Systems Inc.
2095 Rose St.
Berkeley CA 94709
800-344-5541/510-540-5535
FAX: 510-540-5115

Wired for Sound Pro ($79)

Aristosoft Inc.
7041 Koll Center Pkwy. #160
Pleasanton CA 94566
800-338-2629/510-426-5355
FAX: 510-426-6703

Part

SEVEN

GLOSSARY

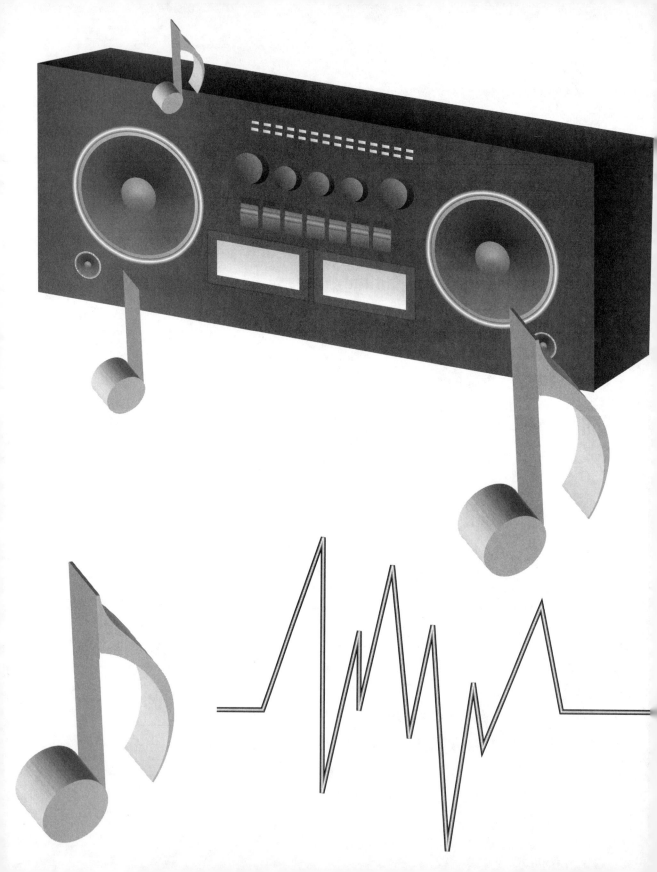

Glossary

8-bit—A popular sampling resolution for digitizing the human voice. 8-bit resolution means a sound can be measured at any of 256 (2 to the 8th power) possible values.

16-bit—A popular sampling resolution for digitizing music. 16-bit resolution means a sound can be measured at any of 65,536 (2 to the 16th power) possible values.

286—Also called the *80286*, the microprocessor found in older computers. A computer with this electronic brain is called an AT, AT-compatible, or IBM AT. The 80386 processor superseded the 286.

386—Also called the *80386*, the microprocessor found in newer PCs. Two types of 386 chips are available: 386DX and 386SX. Sometimes the term *386* refers to an entire family of processors, which includes the 486 processor. All use the same core technology; for example, a 486 processor is basically a 386DX processor with a built-in math chip. See *486*.

486—Also called the *i486* or *80486*, a type of processor from Intel that is a top-of-the-line, en-hanced version of the 386. The 486 comes in two flavors: 486DX and 486SX. The 486DX has a built-in math chip and memory caching for top speed. The 486SX is the same as the 486DX except the math chip is not included. The 25-MHz 486SX is the minimum processor required for a multimedia PC.

accelerator card—Also called an *accelerator board*, small circuit boards that increase the speed of your computer by bypassing or replacing the processor. SX/Now! from Kingston Technology is one example of an accelerator card.

access time—A measurement of the speed of hard disk and CD-ROM drives. Access time (actually, *average* access time) is the time it takes the drive to find the information you've requested. A good access time for a hard disk is under 20 milliseconds (ms). MPC Level 2 specifications require the CD-ROM drive to have an access time under 400 ms.

Ad Lib Music Synthesizer—The first sound card, which sold for $195 in August, 1987. Most sound cards try to be Ad Lib-compatible.

AIF—A file format used for digital audio files created on the Apple personal computer. Such files end with the AIF extension.

amplitude—The intensity, or loudness, of a sound. Amplitude is caused by the strength of the vibrations producing it. Amplitude is measured in decibels, or db.

analog—Representation of an object that resembles, or is analogous to, the original. Sound waves are analog waves because they resemble how and when you speak.

analog-to-digital converter—A small computer chip that turns analog signals (a spoken voice, for example) into digital signals for use on your computer. Also called an ADC.

applet—A software program that is not powerful enough to be considered a software application. Microsoft Windows includes several applets, such as Windows Write or the Sound Recorder.

application—A fancy name for a software program. For example, Microsoft Word for Windows is considered a word processing application, whereas Lotus 1-2-3 is called a spreadsheet application.

ASCII—Shorthand for **A**merican **S**tandard **C**ode for Information Interchange. ASCII is a way for your PC to represent text and numbers. It allows computers to share information. An ASCII, or text, file has no formatting or fonts. (This is why your word processor does not save its work as an ASCII file.) When you save your work as an ASCII file and give it to a friend, your friend doesn't have to retype the words. Some of your PC's start-up files are already in ASCII format, such as AUTOEXEC.BAT, CONFIG.SYS, and WIN.INI. The ASCII standard can represent 128 letters, numbers, symbols, and other characters.

ASP—**A**dvanced **S**ignal **P**rocessors are programmable computer chips found on some sound cards. Sound Blaster 16 ASP, for example, uses an ASP. This chip compresses and decompresses sound files without placing a huge burden on the PC's processor. This makes the card ideal for use with multimedia applications, in which digitized sound is widely used but the computer's brainpower is required to handle other tasks besides decompressing files.

AT—The term for the *IBM Personal Computer AT* introduced in 1985. The phrase *AT* now indicates the set of standards against which other computers must be equal. For example, an AT-compatible computer, such as the 286, 386, or 486, must have a 16-bit bus as did the original IBM Personal Computer AT in order to work. AT also refers to a PC that has a 286 processor. See *286*.

AUTOEXEC.BAT—An important PC file that tells the computer what to do when you start it, such as automatically run Windows or some other software program. If you want to customize your computer, you will have to get comfortable working with this file. Another start-up file is CONFIG.SYS.

Automatic Gain Control (AGC)—A feature found in some microphones and recording software. Automatic gain control dynamically adjusts the recording level of a sound according to how loud it is.

BBS—Stands for **B**ulletin **B**oard **S**ystem. It may also be called an *electronic bulletin board*. Typically, a BBS is composed of a single PC with a modem, bulletin board software, and one or more phone lines. A BBS receives calls from other PCs. Callers can write messages to BBS users, download free software, or read news. (Often, downloading the software is the most popular choice.) The person who operates a BBS is called a *sysop*.

BIOS—Acronym for **B**asic **I**nput/**O**utput **S**ystem. The BIOS is a set of computer instructions that acts as the "boss" of your PC. It tells your software how to work with your PC and ties all the parts (keyboard, monitor, etc.) together. The BIOS is placed inside a computer chip. The BIOS is the first software loaded when your PC starts.

bit—Short for **BI**nary digi**T**s, the very essence of computer information. A bit may be on (1) or off (0). A byte typically contains eight bits.

byte—A common unit of computer storage made up of eight binary digits (bits). A byte holds the equivalent of a single character, such as the letter A, a dollar sign, or decimal point.

CD-quality—High-quality sounds saved to a digital device, such as a computer. CD-quality sound is produced by sampling the analog source at 44.1 KHz (44,100 times per second) and at 16-bit resolution.

CD-ROM—A CD-like disc that provides access to lots of information. An entire encyclopedia (with pictures) can be put on a single CD-ROM disc. A CD-ROM is used in a CD-ROM drive. The CD-ROM drive is an important part of multimedia, which combines sound, text, and pictures into an extensive educational experience.

CD-ROM XA—Abbreviation for **C**ompact **D**isc-**R**ead **O**nly **M**emory e**X**tended **A**rchitecture. CD-ROM XA is a specification created by Sony, Philips, and Microsoft that governs audio compression and allows interleaving, or mixing, of audio and computer data. Not many discs take advantage of XA but the most recent MPC specifications call for a CD-ROM XA-ready drive.

CGA—Short for **C**olor/**G**raphics **A**dapter. CGA was the first color video card. Developed by IBM, this card had a resolution of 320 x 200 pixels and could only display four colors from a palette of 16. One drawback of a CGA video card is that it produces flicker and snow. *Flicker* is the annoying tendency of the text to flash as you move the image up or down. *Snow* is the flurry of bright dots that can appear anywhere on the screen. Good thing this color standard is almost extinct.

channel—The left or right portion of a stereo sound.

client—A Windows application that allows information from another file to be embedded or linked to it. See *OLE.*

clipping—Undesirable distortion caused during digital recording. Clipping occurs when sounds are recorded at too high a level, causing loud segments beyond the tolerances of your equipment. To avoid clipping, reduce your recording levels to withstand the loudest part of your recording.

CMF—Abbreviation for **C**reative **M**usic **F**ormat. CMF is a file format for FM synthesizer music created on a Sound Blaster card. Such files are saved with a CMF extension.

CONFIG.SYS—A special PC file that your computer reads when you first start it. It tells the computer how you want it configured and which *drivers* (small software programs that run special hardware on your PC) to load. If you want to customize your computer, you will have to get comfortable working with this file. Most sound cards load their driver software from CONFIG.SYS. Another start-up file is AUTOEXEC.BAT.

Control Panel—A utility in the Windows Main group that allows you to add drivers for your sound card.

conventional memory—Also known as *low* or *base memory*. Conventional memory is the memory into which you load your programs and work. This memory is your PC's first 1M (1024K) of memory, although only 640K of it is directly available for your work.

CPU—Stands for **C**entral **P**rocessing **U**nit and is the same as the *microprocessor*, or simply processor. In other words, the CPU is your PC's brain, such as a 286, 386, or 486.

daisy chaining—The process of connecting up to seven SCSI devices to one SCSI controller, which may be your sound card. One sound card, for example, may connect to up to seven hard disks, tape drives, CD-ROM drives, or printers.

data transfer rate—A measurement of hard disk or CD-ROM power. The data transfer rate is the amount of data that can be

"shoveled" to your computer from the drive. Data transfer rate is measured in kilobytes per second, or KBps. The recent MPC Level 2 specifications call for a CD-ROM drive to support a data transfer rate of 300 KBps. This figure is often more important than the speed of the drive.

daughterboard—An expansion card that attaches to an existing card to provide additional features or functions. Wave Blaster daughterboard from Creative Labs attaches to the Sound Blaster 16 ASP sound card. Also called a *daughtercard*.

decibel—A measurement of a sound's loudness, abbreviated (db). The rustle of leaves is rated at 10 db, average street noise at 70 db, and nearby thunder at 120 db.

digital-to-analog converter—A small computer chip that turns digital signals stored on your computer into analog signals that can be heard (a spoken voice, for example). Also called a *DAC*.

digitizing—The process of turning an analog signal (such as a spoken voice) into a digital signal of on/off pulses to be used by a computer.

DIP switch—Abbreviation for **D**ual-**I**nline **P**ackage. One way to configure an expansion card. A DIP switch is simply a small bank of toggle switches. How small? The switches are spaced at 10 switches per inch, although many DIP switches only have four switches.

directory—A way of organizing files on your hard or floppy disks. DOS provides these disks with a root (main) directory but allows you to create other directories underneath it. This way, you can organize your work by placing files into easily-recognizable directories. For example, your January letters can be placed in a directory called \JANLET.

disk—A place to store files. The disk may either be a hard disk or a floppy disk.

disk cache—A reserved section of memory created by disk-caching software. Disk-caching software speeds up your computer by reading a part of the hard disk into the computer's faster memory. In a way, disk-caching software tries to anticipate what program and work files you want next from your hard disk. If wrong, it makes the corrections. SMARTdrive from Microsoft is a free disk-caching program included with DOS and Windows.

DMA channel—Abbreviation for **D**irect **M**emory **A**ccess channel. DMA channels are used to speed getting information to and from your PC's memory. They also allow your sound card to play alongside other tasks. Using the DMA controller chips built into your computer, your sound card can bypass the central processor altogether to play a sound.

DOS—Short for **D**isk **O**perating **S**ystem. DOS is the software that organizes how a computer reads, writes, and reacts with its disks, and talks to your PC, including keyboards, screens, serial and parallel ports, printers, modems, and so on. There are few flavors of DOS. The most popular is MS-DOS (pronounced "m-s doss"), which stands for **M**icrosoft **D**isk **O**perating **S**ystem. PC-DOS from IBM stands for **P**ersonal **C**omputer **D**isk **O**perating **S**ystem. (The two versions of DOS are almost the same.)

driver—Also called a *device driver*. A small software program required to add new features to your PC or one of its components. For example, a sound card requires a sound driver. Drivers are loaded from your PC's CONFIG.SYS start-up file.

dynamic bass boost (DBB)—A switch or button found on some amplified speakers that provides a more powerful bass and clearer treble, regardless of the volume setting. The DBB feature only works when your amplified speakers are turned on, not when they are relying on your sound card's direct amplified signal.

EGA—Short for **E**nhanced **G**raphics **A**dapter. Introduced by IBM, this color video card "knocked off" the CGA video card. EGA video cards increased resolution to 640 x 350 pixels. Also, you could show 16 colors at one time from a palette of 64. EGA soon was replaced by VGA which was replaced by super-VGA.

embedding—A method of copying information from one Windows file into another. The embedded object can be edited directly from within the file containing it, although you need the application that created it. To embed, you must be using applications that support OLE (client applications). See *OLE*.

EMS—Short for **E**xpanded **M**emory **S**pecification. EMS is a set of ground rules for turning extended memory into memory that can be used by your software programs. You'll often hear the phrase "Lotus/Intel/Microsoft Expanded Memory Specification (LIM EMS 4.0)." Same thing.

People often use EMS to refer to the memory that has been converted. That's fine. Any software program you own that supports this type of expanded memory can now have access to it. One popular spreadsheet program, Lotus 1-2-3, supports this type of memory.

expanded memory (EMS)—Expanded Memory (EMS) is, for the most part, converted extended memory (XMS). Expanded memory relies on a technical trick known as paging or bank-switching. Paging allows software programs to use large amounts of memory that would otherwise be unavailable. However, the software program must be designed to use the expanded memory. Expanded memory is available to both old (8088) and new (486) PCs. See *extended memory*.

expansion cards—Also called *add-on cards* or *expansion boards*. The circuit boards inserted in your PC that give it new features.

These "plug-and-play" circuit boards are placed in expansion slots and let you add new features to your computer, such as an internal modem or a sound card.

expansion slots—Also called *expansion ports*. The slots inside your PC that allow you to add new features by inserting circuit boards. The original PC had five expansion slots; yours may have three to eight. Circuit boards placed in an expansion slot are called *expansion cards*, *expansion boards*, or *add-on cards*.

extended memory (XMS)—Extended Memory is memory above 1M. This memory is usually not directly available to your computer, except through special programs, such as disk caches. This memory is only available in 286, 386, and higher computers. When the HIMEM.SYS software included with DOS and Windows is used, extended memory can be used by Microsoft Windows.

extension—A period and (usually) a three-letter identifier at the end of a file name. If you have a file name with the extension .TXT, for example, you have an ASCII text file. Extensions help you sort your files when you have a "ton" of them on your disk.

fade in/fade out—Steadily increasing or decreasing volume, respectively. Some sound utilities allow you to create fade-ins and fade-outs.

file—A file is like a piece of paper stored in your PC. It can contain one of two things: a series of instructions (a program file), or words and numbers (a data, or work, file).

floppy disk—A floppy disk is one way to save information permanently. Floppy disks are placed in floppy disk drives so that the information can be recorded to them. Floppy disks come in two sizes: 5 ¼-inch and 3 ½-inch. They also come in several densities. For example, a low-density 5 ¼-inch disk can

hold 360K of information. A high-density 5 ¼-inch disk can hold about four times that—1.2M (1200K).

FM synthesis—The process of imitating a musical instrument when playing music on a sound card. This synthesis is created by several sound cards using an FM synthesizer computer chip. Many cards use the OPL2 (YM3812) or OPL3 (YMF262) chip. Some more expensive cards do not use FM synthesis. Instead, they use the sounds of actual musical instruments recorded on memory chips.

frequency response—The range in which an audio system can record or play at a constant and audible amplitude level. Most sound cards support a range between 30 Hz and 20 KHz.

Game Blaster—First sound card developed by Creative Labs to compete with the Ad Lib Music Synthesizer Card. Game Blaster provides stereo sound but uses AM synthesis, not FM synthesis. Like an AM radio, the sound quality is not very good.

game ports—15-pin D-shaped connectors on the back of your PC or sound card for connecting a joystick.

General MIDI—The name given to the MIDI specifications that assigned specific numbers to musical instruments. This standardization allows a MIDI song to be played back on another MIDI system using the same instruments as the system on which it was created. The General MIDI specs assign unique numbers to 128 instruments.

hard disk—A physical device inside your PC (or connected to it) that can quickly save and retrieve information and software programs. Hard disks are like your PC's file cabinet; they can permanently store much information. The size of a hard disk is measured in megabytes, or M. The speed of a hard disk is measured in milliseconds, or ms. A fast hard disk is typically under 20 ms.

hardware—Any manufactured physical part of your PC, such as the monitor, keyboard, disk drives, printer, and so forth.

hertz—A measurement of frequency, abbreviated Hz. Human hearing is limited to 20 to 20,000 Hz. One thousand Hz is one kilohertz, or KHz.

I/O address—A place assigned in your computer's memory where an expansion card can "talk" to different parts of your computer. Your system's keyboard, for example, has an address. There are also addresses for sound cards. Some I/O addresses are set in stone. For example, a joystick controller (or game card) has a set address of 200-20F.

interrupt (IRQ)—A method used by your computer to give its attention to its expansion cards or other devices. Without interrupts, your computer processor would have to finish whatever work it is doing before letting another part of your computer, such as a sound card, use it.

joystick ports—15-pin D-shaped connectors on the back of your PC or sound card for connecting a joystick.

jumper—A common way to configure an expansion card. A jumper is simply a short piece of wire, encased in plastic, that lets you make an electrical connection between two pins on your card. A jumper is easy to remove and change, but you may want to use needle-nosed pliers to grab it. Also called a *shunt*.

K or KB—Short for kilobyte. One kilobyte equals 1,000 bytes, which may be 1,000 letters or numbers. Your amount of memory or hard disk space is measured in kilobytes.

KHz—Abbreviation for kilohertz, or 1000 hertz (Hz).

linking—The process of creating a reference in one Windows file to an object inserted in another. The linked object can be edited directly from within the file containing it. When the

linked object is edited, the changes are made to the original file. When you double-click on the object, the application that created it is started. You can then edit and update the object.

M or MB—Short for *megabyte* or simply *meg*. A megabyte is about one million bytes or 1024 kilobytes. That's about one million characters, or about 500 pages of text. Hard drives and your PC's memory are measured in megabytes.

mapping—A MIDI term for the process of assigning individual instruments to any of the 16 MIDI channels. General MIDI guidelines assign specific numbers to 128 instruments.

MCI—Abbreviation for **Media Control Interface**. A high-level script language used by Microsoft Windows that plays audio and video sequences without the need for programming. Windows 3.1 Media Player, for example, can play MCI scripts.

memory—Area on your computer where your work and programs are stored as you are using them. This area is called random access memory, or RAM. Your memory may be any of three types: conventional, extended, or expanded.

MHz—Short for *megahertz*. Megahertz is one measurement of how fast your PC is. One megahertz equals one million cycles per second. If one PC has a higher speed than another, it gets the same amount of work done in less time. In other words, the higher the clock speed, the faster your PC.

MID—The file format for MIDI music files. Such files end with the extension MID. See *MIDI*.

MIDI—Short for **Musical Instrument Digital Interface**. Developed in the early 1980s, MIDI essentially is a powerful programming language that lets your computer store and edit or play back music in tandem with a MIDI-compatible electronic musical instrument, typically a keyboard synthesizer.

MIDI Mapper—A Windows utility for customizing MIDI setups, patches, and key maps.

mixer—A mixer allows you to control the volume, gain, and tone of various audio sources. You can, for example, set the recording levels of your microphone and CD player for a voice-over. Sound cards typically include mixer software.

MOD—A file format for playing back sound modules. MOD files use the SOUNDTRACKER format, a format created for the Commodore Amiga computer.

monitor—Also called *screen* or *display*. The monitor looks like a TV set and lets you see your work on your PC. The monitor typically sits atop your computer and provides the visual link between you and your PC. Monitors may support one video standard, such as VGA, or may support several.

motherboard—Your computer's main circuit board. This flat, rectangular board occupies most of the bottom of your computer case and is the foundation of your PC. The motherboard is typically a green or brownish color with copper lines etched into it. All of the parts of your PC either connect to or are a part of the motherboard.

mouse—A palm-sized device that lets you use your software by selecting items on the screen. The mouse is rolled across your desk to move a corresponding mouse cursor on your screen. You press a button on the mouse to make your selections. Mouse software is required to use your mouse with many software programs, although some software programs cannot use a mouse at all.

MPC—Short for Multimedia Personal Computer. To turn your PC into an MPC requires at least the following: 80486SX, 25-MHz computer with 4M of memory, 160M hard disk, super-VGA (800 x 600) monitor with video card, 1.44M 3 ½-inch disk

drive, double-speed CD-ROM drive (300 KBps), 16-bit digital sound card, a pair of speakers, and Windows 3.1.

Who made these requirements? The Multimedia PC Council (MPC), a group of hardware and software manufacturers. Products with the MPC logo on them essentially promise that the product meets minimum MPC standards or works on MPC equipment. These standards are a moving target, however.

MPU-401—The MIDI interface developed by Roland. It was one of the first interfaces designed for the PC. Its design has grown to be regarded as the standard protocol.

MS-DOS—Short for **M**icrosoft **D**isk **O**perating **S**ystem. MS-DOS is one flavor of DOS. It also is the most popular. Several versions of MS-DOS have been introduced. Version 4.0, introduced a few years ago, allowed a drive partition to be larger than 32M. Today, most new hard disk drives are at least 80M. See *DOS*.

multimedia—The capability to merge voice, images, data, and video on a computer at the same time. With so many ways to communicate, this technology is ideal for education. Multimedia applications range from talking encyclopedias to databases of stored video clips. One impetus for the growing number of sound products has been Microsoft Windows 3.1. This version fully supports sound. You can, for example, have Windows play small sound bites, called WAV files, to indicate when you make a mistake or are entering or exiting a program. You can also record sounds, such as adding voice notes to a work file on which you want someone else to work. See *MPC*.

multimedia upgrade kit—A kit that includes almost everything to turn your PC into a multimedia PC. It includes the CD-ROM drive, sound card, software drivers to control everything, cables, and, most importantly, instructions on how to connect everything. You can save several hundred dollars by buying a kit instead of piecing together your own multimedia system.

OLE—Abbreviation for **O**bject **L**inking and **E**mbedding. OLE is a Microsoft Windows feature that lets you transfer and share information between Windows applications. For instance, you can embed verbal instructions in a Windows document. OLE is made possible through clients and servers. The linked or embedded object is created in one application (the *server*) and connected to a second application (the *client*).

on-line service—A large computer system that you can connect to through your PC and modem. The on-line service provides hundreds of services, such as games, free software, discussion areas, news, weather, sports, stock quotes, and more. Examples of popular on-line services include PRODIGY, CompuServe, America Online, and GEnie. These services either charge a flat fee or an hourly fee that often is billed to your credit card. To connect to the service, you either use the on-line service's special software or your regular communications software.

operating system—A special piece of software that brings your PC to life by laying down the law for connecting its many parts. The operating system breaks down complex software instructions into tiny chunks your PC can understand. One popular operating system is DOS. Other systems include UNIX and OS/2.

panning—Process of moving sound from one stereo channel to another, such as left to right.

patch—A MIDI term for a specific instrument, such as a trombone or a flute.

PC—Short for Personal Computer. The PC refers to computers that conform to the PC standard originally developed by IBM Corp. and now loosely held together by Intel Corp., Microsoft Corp., and other major computer companies. The PC is the world's most popular computer; about 80 million PCs are used worldwide. Sometimes, people refer to computers made by Atari,

Commodore, and Apple (Macintosh) as PCs. To prevent confusion, call these "personal computers" or "microcomputers."

PCB—Abbreviation for **P**rinted **C**ircuit **B**oard. A PCB is a flat piece of fiberglass, usually green, that is etched with copper wires and has several electronic components mounted on it. This is why sound cards are also called sound boards.

pitch—The rate at which vibrations are produced and measured in hertz (Hz). The higher the pitch, the higher the frequency.

ports—Ports are where you plug things in your computer. Some popular ports include the *parallel port* (which is used to connect your printer), *serial port* (used for connecting mice and modems), and *video port* (used to attach your monitor).

processor—see *CPU*.

RAM—Short for **R**andom **A**ccess **M**emory. RAM can also be called memory. RAM is basically your computer's primary workspace. Like a desk, RAM is used to place the tools and work you need during a session. Your software program is loaded in memory and then your work, such as a list of numbers or a letter. Before you finish your session, you must save your work in RAM to a disk. RAM loses its information when the computer is turned off.

RAM disk—A temporary disk drive—also called a *virtual disk*—made from memory. The file RAMDRIVE.SYS is a software utility included with Microsoft DOS that temporarily creates this drive. This drive can be created from conventional, extended, or expanded memory. RAM drives are much faster than hard disk drives because your computer can read information much faster from lightning-fast memory than from your PC's hard disk.

resolution—A factor limiting the number of possible digital values at which a sound sample can be measured. Three sound-card resolutions are popular today: 8-bit, 12-bit, and 16-bit. A resolution of 8-bits means a sound can be measured at any of 256 (2 to the 8th power) possible values. A sound measured at 16-bit resolution can be measured at any of 65,536 (2 to the 16th power) values. The more values, the more accurate the recorded sound emulates its original source.

Roland MT-32 Sound Module—One of the first sound cards, which was sold by Roland Corp. for $500. Some games have a sound option for the Roland MT-32.

ROM—Short for **R**ead-**O**nly **M**emory. Unlike RAM chips, a ROM chip is a computer chip that holds its information, even when your PC is turned off. Some sound cards place recorded sounds (such as from musical instruments) onto ROM chips.

sampled audio—See *waveform audio*.

sampling—The process of turning original analog sound waves (such as from speaking or other audio sources) into digital (on/off) signals that can be saved and later replayed. Sampling is like taking snapshots of a balloon as it is blown up. Each snapshot measures the progress of the balloon's size.

sampling rate—The frequency with which an analog sound is sampled, or turned into a digital signal. The higher (or more frequent) this sampling rate, the more accurate the digital sound is to its real-life source. (CD-quality sound is sampled at 44,100 times per second, or 44.1 KHz.) However, the higher the sampling rate, the larger the sound file. A one-minute-long 44.1 KHz-sampled stereo file may require up to 11M of disk space.

SCSI—Short for **S**mall **C**omputer **S**ystems **I**nterface. SCSI is a Cadillac-type of drive controller. It allows you to connect up to seven devices—and not just hard disks—to one SCSI controller.

Often, CD-ROM drives use a SCSI controller. Some sound cards include a SCSI interface so they can operate a CD-ROM drive.

sequencer—A software program or device that records, edits, and plays a MIDI song. Many sequencers allow you to record individual tracks while playing back existing tracks.

server—A Windows application that embeds or links information from itself to another. See *OLE*.

SND—A file format used for digital audio files created on the NeXT personal computer. Such files end with the SND extension.

Sound Blaster—Code-named the "Killer Card," Sound Blaster from Creative Labs was developed to compete with the Ad Lib Music Synthesizer Card. It was introduced in 1990 for $239.95. Several sound cards attempt to be Sound Blaster-compatible.

Sound port—An external sound card, such as the Disney Sound Source or Digispeech Port-Able Sound Plus. These devices provide sound capabilities by attaching to your PC's parallel port.

supersonic—Sound frequencies that are beyond human ability to hear.

SVGA—Short for Super-**VGA**. As its name implies, SVGA is above and beyond VGA. In 1988, nine vendors of graphics products formed the Video Electronics Standards Association, or VESA. This group created the specifications for SVGA. SVGA normally provides a resolution of 800 x 600 pixels and the same colors as VGA. SVGA is required for multimedia.

system unit—The system unit is the largest part of your PC. It is the box that includes the disk drives, memory, processor, and power supply. When people talk about their PC, they're probably talking about the system unit.

text-to-speech—The conversion of text to spoken words. Some sound cards include utilities that can "speak" text you type or highlight. One popular text-to-speech software utility is Monologue from First Byte, Inc.

total harmonic distortion—A measurement of accurate sound production on an audio device. Abbreviated THD, harmonic distortion is measured as a percentage of distortion. The smaller this percentage, the better.

tower—A type of PC case designed to allow the computer to be placed upright. The tower PC is normally next to the user's desk on the floor.

TSR—Short for **T**erminate-and-**S**tay **R**esident. A TSR is a software program that is placed in memory "on top" of your main software program. Normally, you press a key combination like Alt-M to bring a TSR to life. Some TSR programs simply lurk in the background doing other work.

ultrasonic—Sound frequencies that are beyond human ability to hear.

VOC—A Sound Blaster file format for digitized sound. Such files end in a VOC extension. Some sound cards include utilities for converting VOC files to WAV (Windows waveform) files.

voice annotation—The process of adding a recorded message to your Windows documents, spreadsheets, or other files. For example, a business executive could pick up a microphone and embed a message in a contract to give his or her secretary explicit instructions. To leave such messages, your Windows application must support Windows' object linking and embedding (OLE).

voice recognition—The capability of a PC to understand spoken commands. Some sound cards include voice

recognition software for Microsoft Windows. Voice-recognition technology is not totally accurate.

watts—A measure of sound-card or speaker amplification. Usually stated as watts per channel, this is the amount of amplification available to drive the speakers. Many sound cards have built-in amplifiers, providing up to 8 watts per channel. (Most provide 4 watts.) However, the wattage is not enough to provide rich sound. This is why many speakers have built-in amplifiers.

WAV—The extension of digitized sound files that can be played by Microsoft Windows through a sound card and speakers. One WAV file that comes with Windows 3.1 is TADA.WAV. WAV files take up a lot of space. One audio minute may require up to 11M.

waveform audio—Recorded audio sound digitized for use on your computer. The Microsoft Windows waveform file format is called WAV because its three-letter extension is WAV.

Windows—A Macintosh-like face for your PC developed by Microsoft Corp. Microsoft Windows allows you to use a mouse to quickly view and start software programs. Your plain old DOS programs can also be run from within Windows. Windows allows you to organize your software programs and work files into boxes called groups. Learning Windows software programs is easy because the programs have similar commands. Almost all programs, for example, have a File pulldown menu from which you have similar choices, such as "Save" and "Save as." Currently, Windows runs on top of your version of DOS, but eventually Windows NT (New Technology) will combine DOS and Windows into a single, powerful operating system.

Glossary

Windows accelerator card—A special type of video card that contains a graphics coprocessor to relieve your PC's main processor from drawing the elements of a Windows screen. With an accelerator card installed, your computer can concentrate on other work, rather than handling pixels, lines, and other visual data.

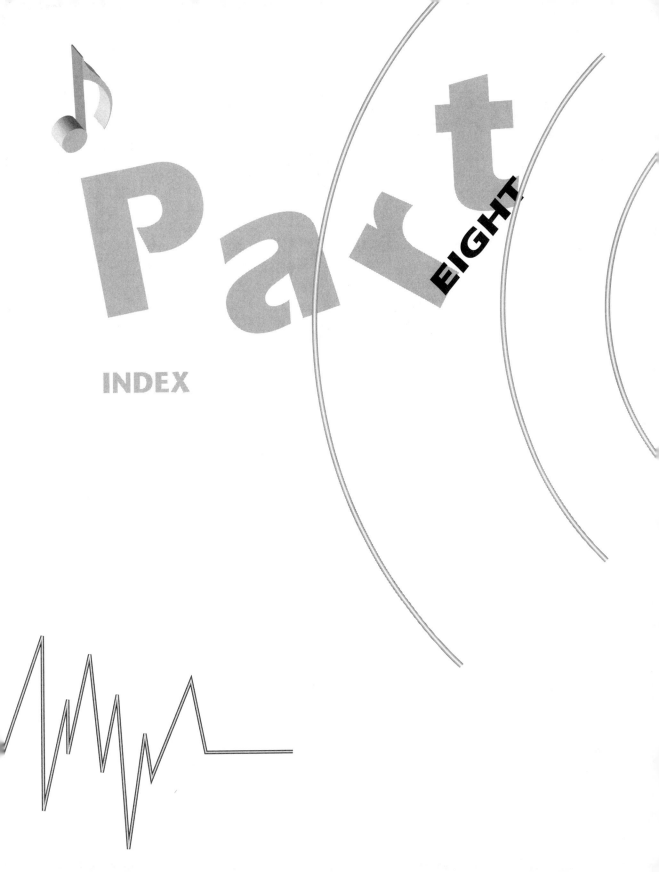

Part EIGHT

INDEX

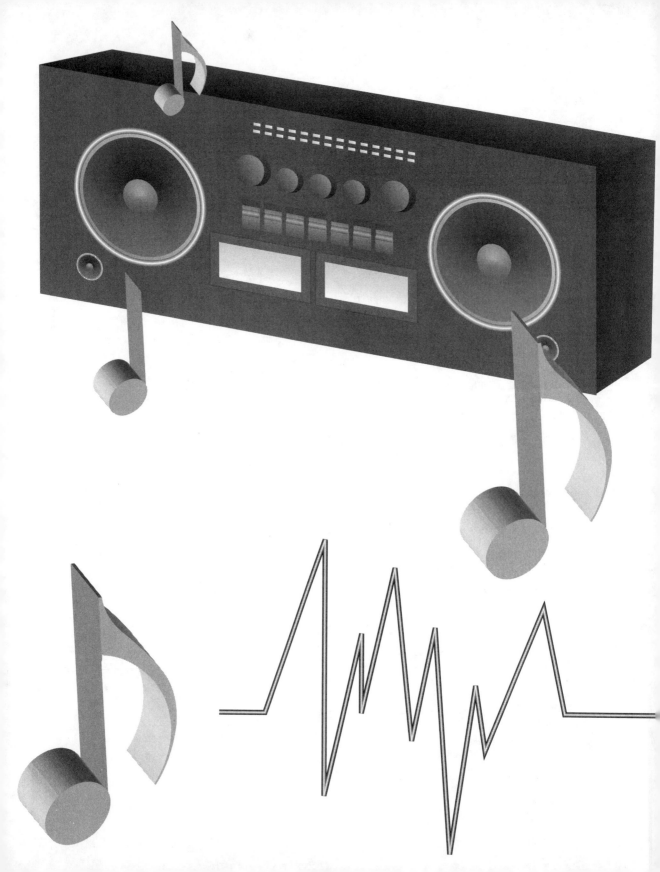

Index

Index

T

U

WANT MORE INFORMATION?

CHECK OUT THESE RELATED TITLES:

Crank It Up!
REGISTRATION CARD

Fill out this card to receive information about other New Riders titles!

Name _____ **Title** _____

Company _____

Address _____

City/State/ZIP _____

I bought this book because _____

_____

I purchased this book from:

☐ A bookstore (Name _____)

☐ A software or electronics store (Name _____)

☐ A mail order (Name of Catalog _____)

I purchase this many computer books each year:

☐ 1–5   ☐ 5 or more

I currently use these applications: _____

_____

_____

_____

I found these chapters to be the most informative: _____

_____

I found these chapters to be the least informative: _____

_____

Additional comments: _____

_____

☐ I would like to see my name in print! You may use my name and quote me in future New Riders products and promotions. My daytime phone number is: _____

New Riders Publishing 11711 North College Avenue • P.O. Box 90 • Carmel, Indiana 46032 USA

Fold Here

PLACE
STAMP
HERE

New Riders Publishing
11711 North College Avenue
P.O. Box 90
Carmel, Indiana 46032
USA

OPERATING SYSTEMS

INSIDE MS-DOS 6

NEW RIDERS PUBLISHING

A complete tutorial and reference!

MS-DOS 6

ISBN: 1-56205-132-6

$39.95 USA

DOS FOR NON-NERDS

MICHAEL GROH

Understanding this popular operating system is easy with this humorous, step-by-step tutorial

Through DOS 6.0

ISBN: 1-56205-151-2

$18.95 USA

INSIDE SCO UNIX

STEVE GLINES, PETER SPICER, BEN HUNSBERGER, & KAREN WHITE

Everything users need to know to use the UNIX operating system for everyday tasks

SCO Xenix 286, SCO Xenix 386, SCO UNIX/System V 386

ISBN: 1-56205-028-1

$29.95 USA

INSIDE SOLARIS SunOS

NEW RIDERS PUBLISHING

Comprehensive tutorial and reference to SunOS!

SunOS, Sun's version of UNIX for the SPARC workstation version 2.0

ISBN: 1-56205-032-X

$29.95 USA

WINDOWS TITLES

GRAPHICS TITLES